LO 118662
XII/90

107 DM

GW01548560

Theories and Applications in the Detection of Deception

Gershon Ben-Shakhar   John J. Furedy

# Theories and Applications in the Detection of Deception

## A Psychophysiological and International Perspective

The order of authorship is alphabetical, connoting equally shared responsibility for our collaborative enterprise.

Springer-Verlag
New York  Berlin  Heidelberg
London  Paris  Tokyo  Hong Kong

Gershon Ben-Shakhar
Department of Psychology
The Hebrew University of Jerusalem
Jerusalem 91905
Israel

John J. Furedy
Department of Psychology
University of Toronto
Toronto, Ontario
Canada M5S 1A1

Library of Congress Cataloging-in-Publication Data
Ben-Shakhar, Gershon.
 Theories and applications in the detection of deception: a psychophysiological and international perspective/Gershon Ben-Shakhar, John J. Furedy.
  p. cm.
 Includes bibliographical references.
 ISBN 0-387-97065-7 (alk. paper)
 1. Lie detectors and detection.  I. Furedy, John J.  II. Title.
HV8078.B46  1990
363.2′54−dc20                                                89-19660

Printed on acid-free paper.

© 1990 by Springer-Verlag New York Inc.
All rights reserved. This work may not be translated or copied in whole or in part without the written permission of the publisher (Springer-Verlag, 175 Fifth Avenue, New York, NY 10010, USA), except for brief excerpts in connection with reviews or scholarly analysis. Use in connection with any form of information storage and retrieval, electronic adaptation, computer software, or by similar or dissimilar methodology now known or hereafter developed is forbidden.
The use of general descriptive names, trade names, trademarks, etc., in this publication, even if the former are not especially identified, is not to be taken as a sign that such names, as understood by the Trade Marks and Merchandise Marks Act, may accordingly be used freely by anyone.

Typeset by Publishers Service, Bozeman, Montana.
Printed and bound by Edwards Brothers, Inc., Ann Arbor, Michigan.
Printed in the United States of America.

9 8 7 6 5 4 3 2 1

ISBN 0-387-97065-7 Springer-Verlag New York Berlin Heidelberg
ISBN 3-540-97065-7 Springer-Verlag Berlin Heidelberg New York

*I would like to dedicate this book to the memory of Israel Lieblich, my long-time teacher, colleague, and friend, who contributed so much in all three ways.*

*GBS*

# Preface

"Polygraphy," "lie detection," and the "detection of deception" are all terms that refer to an application of the science of psychophysiology, which itself employs physiological measures to study and differentiate between psychological processes. The issues raised by polygraphy are controversial. One such issue is whether the polygraph is a genuinely scientifically based application, or merely a purported application, of psychophysiology. Such concerns are of interest not only to polygraph practitioners and to specialists in psychophysiology, but also to such other specialists as those in the legal and forensic professions. Moreover, there are two sorts of nonspecialists who should also be concerned. On the one hand, there are the potential "users" of the polygraph—for example, a manager who employs a polygrapher to check on subordinates; on the other hand, there are those "used by" the polygraph—the employee who is subjected to the polygraphic examination.

To begin with the user of the polygraph, this person should know not only about its overall accuracy, but also about the rationales of the various detection methods and their validity for different purposes in different sorts of situations. This information is important, because even for the potential user there are costs as well as benefits. Aside from the lack of trust generated by the polygraph, there have also been successful suits by employees against employers, so there are traps in polygraph usage that employers (and managers) need to keep in mind.

For the potential examinee, the question of accuracy is again important, though in a different way. The innocent examinee needs to think out the implications of the assertion that "If you are innocent, you need have nothing to worry about"; this commonly made statement implicitly asserts that the polygraph is 100% correct in classifying the innocent. Again, when agreeing to take the polygraph, the examinee needs to understand precisely what is involved in such a "test"—the nature of its underlying rationale and its inference rule for classifying individuals as guilty versus innocent. Even more importantly, the potential examinee should be aware of the risks involved in taking such a "test," and should know whether he or she merely is agreeing to a detection test or whether he or she is implicitly agreeing also to the polygraph's confession-inducing, "psychological-rubber-hose" (Furedy and Liss, 1986) function. Often the conditions under which the individual has to decide whether to be an examinee are highly stressful and not ideal for thoughtful reflection.

Nonpsychophysiological specialists also need to know about the polygraph. Judges may have to make decisions about its scientific status. In addition, in deciding whether a confession following a polygraph was voluntarily obtained, they need to be clear on what, exactly, is entailed for the examinee. Lawyers (for both prosecution and defense) also need to be clear on these issues. Finally, psychologists who have to make decisions concerning the validity of various psychological assessments need to know about this form of psychological assessment. One essential issue is whether the polygraph test is a test in the sense that an IQ test is a test.

Even specialists in psychophysiology itself may be at sea when it comes to the polygraph. As we shall detail below, a number of crucial terms used in polygraphy may be systematically misleading in the sense that the referents of these terms are quite different from what is understood even by the specialist in the science of psychophysiology, who, however, has not made a detailed study of the polygraph. So at least some forms of the polygraph examination are not tests but rather unstandardized interviews. Again, the most modern form of the American polygraph, the control question technique (CQT), does not involve "control" in the normal scientific sense of that term. And the so-called quantified method of chart assessment in the CQT does not conform to normal psychophysiological standards for quantification.

Finally, this book is also directed at the practitioner community, as a source of information and argument from a psychophysiological as well as a cultural perspective. We are aware, of course, that much of what we say may not be received with unalloyed delight by many in that community. Nevertheless, we think that a better understanding of the psychophysiological processes that underlie the different types of polygraph procedures, and of the limitations of those procedures, should, in the long run, be beneficial for the polygraphic profession.

The book begins with a history and description of detection-of-deception procedures that employ psychophysiological measures. The focus is on the procedure that is most widely used in the field: the North American control question test. The rival guilty knowledge test (GKT) is also described. The second chapter presents a systematic comparison of the CQT and GKT in terms of the basic assumptions underlying each procedure. The third chapter discusses the issues of reliability and validity of psychophysiological detection methods. In addition to a general methodological discussion of the difficulties involved in any attempt to validate polygraphy, we present the research data relevant for estimating the validity of both the CQT and GKT. The fourth chapter considers laboratory studies designed to examine the role of various factors in psychophysiological detection, with most emphasis on the more specifiable GKT.

In Chapter 5 we take a fresh look at the problem of the detection of deception, using the psychological process of deception as our starting point and adopting a strictly psychophysiological perspective. From this perspective, we argue for a specific-effects logic of evaluation, according to which the issue is not whether a particular procedure is accurate overall, but whether the additional psychophysiological information provided has a specific, beneficial (i.e., improving) effect on the accuracy of the detection of guilt.

The sixth chapter considers theoretical accounts of the detection of deception, again focusing on the only specifiable procedure: the GKT. The next chapter describes cultural differences in polygraph usage, while Chapter 8 offers some general societal considerations, with utility as the central concept of concern. In this chapter we discuss various applications of polygraphy from a decision-theoretical perspective with a special focus on the legal usage. The final chapter offers some thoughts on future perspectives on science-based technologies in the detection of deception.

The writing of this book has been a thoroughly collaborative enterprise. It began with each of us writing first drafts of five (Chapters 2, 3, 4, 6, and 8 by GBS) or four (Chapters 1, 5, 7, and 9 by JJF) chapters. Then each chapter was reviewed by the other author and was argued over in further drafts. Accordingly, the final version of each chapter represents our joint views, and the alphabetical order of authorship represents our equally shared responsibility for this collaborative book's contents.

The single person who has been most influential in our thinking about psychophysiological detection has been David Lykken. He was the first to stress the weaknesses of the CQT (Lykken, 1974, 1981) and offered the alternative GKT in the late 1950s (Lykken, 1959). We have disagreed about some aspects of the polygraph (e.g., Furedy and Heslegrave, 1989b; Lykken, 1989), but we still consider him an important thinker in the field.

There are three others whose influence on GBS has been considerable. One is Sonny Kugelmass, who initiated the research on psychophysiological detection in Israel in the mid-sixties and who constructed one of the first psychophysiological laboratories focusing on this topic. From the early days of the Israeli research program, Kugelmass has realized the importance of dealing with both theoretical and practical issues. He has established a strong collaboration with the Israeli police—a collaboration that has been fruitful from both scientific and applied perspectives. A second scientist who had influenced GBS was the late Israel Lieblich, who supervised, together with Sonny Kugelmass, his M.A. as well as his Ph.D. theses. Lieblich's clear theoretical conception, coupled with an excellent methodological understanding and critical thinking, had a major influence on GBS's scientific work in general and his psychophysiological research in particular. The current work of GBS in this area is a continuation of the research program set by Kugelmass and Lieblich. Don Campbell, with whom GBS spent a postdoctoral year at Northwestern University, is the third scientist whose influence shaped GBS's scientific thinking. Campbell's contributions to "program evaluation," as well as his critical approach to research methodology in general, have influenced GBS's work in the evaluation of psychophysiological detection.

Of the two individuals who have particularly influenced JJF, one was the University of Sydney philosopher John Anderson, who held the Chair of Philosophy at the university from 1927 to 1958. Anderson's influence on JJF's research has been detailed elsewhere (Furedy, 1989). With regard to the polygraph, the Andersonian insistence on being concerned with "what is the case," together with a concern for adequately defining basic terms, has been especially helpful. The other major source of influence was Emeritus Professor R.A. Champion, who, in the process of supervising JJF's B.A., M.A., and Ph.D. research, failed to *convert* him to his own psychological (S-R) position, but succeeded in *educating* him about how to think about, conduct, and evaluate psychological research.

We would also like to acknowledge as sources of information: Gordon Barland, Wolfram Boucsein, Eitan Elaad, Wayne Evans, Ronald J. Heslegrave, Yo Miyata, Ken White, Rosemary Wolfe, and Roy Wolfe. And we are indebted to the following, who read drafts of some or all of the chapters: Irving Biederman, Jeffrey Biederman, Eitan Elaad, Christine Furedy, Maria Gurevich, Sonny Kugelmass, and Michal Steinberger. But, finally, we have to acknowledge E-mail, without which we could not have carried on our collaboration.

# Contents

Preface     v

Chapter 1.   History and Description     1

Chapter 2.   A Critical Comparison of the Major Methods of Polygraph Interrogation     18

Chapter 3.   Reliability and Validity of Polygraph-Based Classifications     32

Chapter 4.   Laboratory Studies: Factors Affecting Psychophysiological Detection     58

Chapter 5.   The Detection of Deception: A Psychophysiological, Specific-Effects-Oriented Perspective     92

Chapter 6.   Theoretical Issues in Psychophysiological Detection     101

Chapter 7.   International Usage Contrasts: Cultural Factors     115

Chapter 8.   Beyond Validity: Utility and Legal Considerations in the Application of Psychophysiological Detection     125

Chapter 9.   Future Perspectives     137

References     146

Index     157

CHAPTER 1

# History and Description

This chapter will begin by outlining the historical origins of the detection of deception. Next, the development of the so-called control question test (CQT) will be given. As practiced by the American Polygraph Association (APA), the CQT is today's most commonly used method of lie detection. The third section will give a brief account of the guilty knowledge test (GKT); a more detailed consideration of GKT and comparisons with the CQT are left to Chapter 2. In the fourth section of this chapter, a critical analysis of the CQT will be provided, wherein we discuss terminological issues, describe what the CQT really involves, and elaborate on six major problems that arise. Finally, we shall describe several usages of the polygraph. In this description, we shall draw a major distinction between those procedures that focus on a specific event and attempt to clarify whether a given person was involved with that event (i.e., event-related usages), and those that attempt to classify people without relating to a specific event (i.e., event-free usages).

## Origins

Deception is an important survival skill in most animals. It is employed in its nonverbal forms by both hunters (as in the case of the stealthy approach) and the hunted (who strive to hide their presence). Often when engaged in intraspecies conflict, animals will, for instance, give the impression of being larger than they are, which again is a form of deception.

Deception in humans is commonplace, usually in its verbal manifestations. More specifically, deception involves asserting a proposition which the assertor believes to be false, and where there is an *intention* to persuade the audience that the proposition is true. From a scientific perspective that stresses different psychological processes, the central problem is that of *differentiating* deception from other processes. This sort of differentiation, as it employs physiological measures such as changes in skin conductance (GSR), is part of the science of psychophysiology, which studies psychological processes by means of measuring slight changes in physiological functions (Furedy, 1983).

From an applied perspective, however, the main issue is the *detection* of deception in individuals. More specifically, the content of the deception is critical. The lie involved must not be merely a "white" one, but rather must classify the liar as *guilty* of an act that is considered evil by the society in which the individual lives, i.e., a crime. In fact, for applied purposes, the practical aim is not the detection (or differentiation) of deception per se, but rather the detection of individuals who are *guilty*. When physiological changes are employed for this purpose, the technology involved is that of *applied* psychophysiology, and the modern *polygraph* is just such a purported application of psychophysiology.

The psychophysiological detection of guilt holds considerable potential attraction. If successful, it is a way to bypass the deceiver's ability to voluntarily control behavioral manifestations, and to deal instead with physiological changes (usually controlled by the autonomic nervous system) over which self-control is limited. Hence it is not surprising that this sort of applied psychophysiology has a lengthy past. The earliest recorded instance of this sort of polygraphic rationale is from a Hindu medical source dated about 900 B.C., in which persons falsely denying being poisoners were considered to reveal their guilty identity by such physiological changes as blushing (facial vasodilation). Some 600 years then elapsed before an actual polygraphic success was recorded, but this was indeed an impressive case of detection on the part of Eristratus, physician to Alexander the Great. At around the beginning of the third century B.C., the famous anatomist used the "tumultuous rhythm" of the heart (Trovillo, 1939, p. 850) to determine that the crown prince of the Seleucid court in Syria was deceptive about his impious—and hence guilty—love for his newly acquired stepmother. The ground truth, moreover, of Eristratus's heart-rate-basic polygraphic decision was dramatically confirmed by the later birth of a daughter to the accused pair. This sort of strong confirmation of polygraphic decisions seldom occurs in modern times.

One feature that is common between the above sort of applied psychophysiology and the science of psychophysiology is that the observations that form the basis of the decision are *unobtrusive*. Guilt detection, however, also involved more obtrusive methods. In the Middle Ages in Europe, for example, trial by combat, trial by ordeal, and physical torture were all widely used methods of determining guilt. The last of these methods is particularly relevant to modern polygraphy, because torture was designed to detect guilt by eliciting a confession. The most commonly used version in North America of the modern polygraph—the CQT—also has this confession-inducing role, where the pressure exerted is psychological rather than physical. Aside from ethical problems involved in using either physical torture or the more modern "psychological-rubber-hose" (Furedy and Liss, 1986) or "fourth-degree" (Lykken, 1981) procedures, there is also the more factual concern that the confession-inducing function may interfere with the detection function of the procedure. That is, the confession induced by either physical or psychological pressure may be false, being given only to stop the interrogation process. In more general scientific terms, the problem is the usual one of using obtrusive measures. In this case, the obtrusiveness of the interrogation can interfere with the accuracy of measurement of whether or not the individual is guilty.

Part of the basis for modern polygraphy was laid in the late nineteenth century, when technical advances became sufficient for psychophysiological functions to be measured relatively unobtrusively and with some degree of accuracy. Lombroso (1895) reported data where blood pressure and peripheral vasomotor activity were measured as part of the interrogation of criminal suspects. Another boost occurred more than a decade later, when the application of psychophysiological measurement techniques to forensic problems received approval from a well-known psychologist, Hugo Munsterberg (1908). One of Munsterberg's American students, Marston (1917), should probably be credited with beginning the era of modern American polygraphy, when he reported a 96% accuracy rate using blood pressure as the single measure. Slight changes in respiration were also used during this period as a measure for detection, and again there were reports of high accuracy (e.g., Benuossi, 1914). Of course these high-accuracy rates did not go unchallenged in the experimental psychological literature (e.g., Landis and Gullette, 1925), but polygraphic enthusiasts were not deterred.

Part of this enthusiasm rested on the concept of the "specific lie response," which Lykken (1981) attributes to Marston (1938) as the originator. As detailed in the next chapter, the concept, which assumes that lying is *qualitatively* detectable through a uniquely associated physiological pattern of responding, has no supportive evidence in experimental psychology or psychophysiology. However, as with the evidence against high-accuracy claims, many polygraphers were not overly bothered with the lack of experimental evidence for the specific-lie-response concept. Indeed, it will be suggested in the next section that even those polygraphers who moved to a more quantitative approach were, in fact, adopting the specific lie concept, albeit implicitly.

# Development of the CQT by the APA

Given the absence of support for the qualitative, specific-lie-response notion, it became clear that a move toward a more quantitative, *comparison*-based approach was needed. A necessary (though far from sufficient) condition for this approach is that one be able to compare responding to the *relevant* (crime-related) question with responding to some comparison question. From a scientific perspective, the comparison question should serve as a *control* for the relevant (experimental) question, in the sense that the two are equivalent *except for* what is to be detected: guilt. If this equivalence is satisfied, then stronger responding to the relevant, relative to the comparison, question can be interpreted as indicating guilt, as guilt is the only difference between the relevant and comparison questions.

An early and convenient form of the comparison approach that has been used since the 1920s is the relevant/irrelevant technique (RIT; see, e.g., Larson, 1932). In the RIT, responses to crime-relevant questions (e.g., "Did you break into Mr. Jones's apartment last Friday night?") are compared with responses to irrelevant questions that are entirely neutral and refer to everyday factual matters (e.g., "Are you wearing a green shirt?"). The polygraphic rationale with the RIT was that larger responses to relevant (crime-related) questions than to irrelevant questions indicated deception (and hence guilt) regarding the crime.

It is quite obvious that this sort of comparison question cannot conceivably serve as a *control* for the relevant question. Greater responding to the relevant question than to the irrelevant question might well occur, even in the innocent suspect, simply because the relevant question has more emotional content, it is more threatening, or it has more impact than the irrelevant question.

The patent lack of even *face* validity of the RIT has led most current polygraphers with a professional affiliation (i.e., those belonging to the American Polygraph Association) to use the so-called control question method introduced by Reid (1947), and known now as the CQT ("control" question technique, or "test"). The comparison question in the CQT is designed to have greater emotional content than that in the RIT. Continuing our example above, such a comparison question might be, "Did you ever do anything you were ashamed of?" (to which the suspect answers "no"). As shall be argued below, these comparison questions of the CQT are not genuine *controls* in the scientific sense of the term, but they clearly possess more face validity than do the more neutral comparison questions of the RIT. In addition, some face validity is gained through the very use of the term "control," because those who are not intimately familiar with what the CQT actually involves tend to accept the normal scientific meaning of the term at its face value.

The other later development toward quantification was the numerical scoring method, which was proposed originally by Backster (1962). Prior to this method, the assessment of the physiological responses was purely qualitative or global, a procedure which is fully consistent with the specific-lie-response notion. If there is a unique physiological pattern that identifies deception, then no quantified relevant/control comparison procedure is necessary; one simply identifies deception by looking at the physiological pattern of responding to the relevant question alone, or by noting that only the relevant and not the comparison question elicits the "deceptive" physiological pattern of responding.

However, if one adopts only the weaker assumption that certain physiological responses will occur to a larger *extent* to the relevant questions to which the guilty are lying than to comparison ("control") questions, then it is clear that a numerical scoring method is necessary. The method used in CQT polygraphy, which is also commonly referred to as "objective," assigns numbers (1, 2, and 3) to each pair of relevant/control questions for each physiological measure, depending on the relative magnitudes of the responses to each question. If the relevant question yields a greater response, then the algebraic sign of the number is negative; if the reverse is true, then the sign is positive. The algebraic sum of these scores is then calculated, using question pairs (usually three), physiological measures (three or four), and at least three "charts" or "tests" (i.e., occasions on which the questions are put to the examinee). If the *absolute* value of the sum exceeds 5 (or 6, in the more conservative version), then, depending on the algebraic sign, the examinee is classified as deceptive (negative sign) or truthful (positive sign); examinees with scores falling between −5 (or −6) and +5 (or +6) are classified as "inconclusives."

It is important to recognize that this sort of quantification has considerable face validity inasmuch as it significantly increases the perceived scientific status of polygraphy, because it presents a more quantified estimate of "how much" an individual falls into a given category. So, for example, a score of −20 would be palpably more "deceptive" than one of −7. Moreover, the very provision of scores and numbers appears to bring the modern CQT polygraph into the scientific realm of applied psychophysiology, because scientific psychophysiologists also communicate their results in terms of numerical scores.

The last decade has also seen an improvement in the electronic reliability of the instruments available to polygraphers, an increase in the number of practitioners certified by the APA, and an increase in the number of states in the United States in which evidence based on the polygraph is admissible in criminal cases. Finally, Dr. David Raskin and his students at the University of Utah have developed computerized scoring for the CQT (Kircher and Raskin, 1981, 1983, 1988; Raskin, 1982). This adds considerable face validity. As Raskin (1987) has put it, computerization "combines the parameters in a way a human interpreter couldn't do ... to render a decision in probability" and puts the polygraph "more in a scientific category (p. 2)."

As a consequence of these developments, there is a widespread perception at least in North America that the modern event-related CQT is a scientifically accurate (though not infallible) test for the detection of deception. So, for example, an editorial column in a legal publication recommended increased use of "polygraph examinations" on account of "recent scientific advances" (Levy, 1984, p. 1). Again it is quite common to see newspaper headlines in North America indicating that one or other party to a dispute offers to take a "lie detector test" to determine veracity.

## Development of the Guilty Knowledge Test

In North America, the most visible and determined opponent of the polygraph, Lykken (1974), suggested an alternative way of psychophysiologically detecting guilt (Lykken, 1959, 1960). This is the guilty knowledge test (GKT), which has also sometimes been called the concealed information test (e.g., U.S. Congress, 1983). The GKT is based on an entirely different approach and rationale from either the RIT or the CQT. Rather than using direct questions ("Did you do it?"), the GKT employs indirect questions that make use of certain features of the event in question (i.e., the crime) that are assumed to be known only to people familiar with the event. Another distinctive characteristic of the GKT is that it utilizes multiple-choice questions. Thus, a typical question in a GKT might relate to the color of a stolen car, with several colors serving as alternative answers, one of which is the true color of the stolen car. The question could be formulated in the following way: "Was the color of the stolen car red? Was it white?" Etc.

Since it is assumed that the true color is known only to a person involved in the event, this color has a special meaning only for this person. An innocent suspect with no "guilty knowledge" should not respond differently to the different colors. The inference rule of the GKT is based on the comparison of the responses to the relevant item (the true color) with the responses to the irrelevant alternatives (all other colors). A pattern of consistently larger responding to the relevant alternative is taken as an indication that the subject does possess guilty knowledge. Unless a reasonable explanation for this guilty knowledge is provided (e.g., the true color of the stolen car was published in the local newspaper that reported the crime), it is inferred that the subject is guilty.

Naturally, a single presentation of one question with a few alternatives would not be sufficient, because an innocent subject might then show greater responsivity to the correct alternative just by chance (i.e., a false-positive error). The rate of such false-positive errors can be reduced to a (specifiably) low level by using several different questions that focus on different features of the crime (e.g., the kind of weapon used, the amount of money stolen) and by frequently repeating each series of questions. Using different questions should also permit identification of *innocent* crime-related knowledge of specific items, such as the color example given above. That is, an innocent suspect might accidentally acquire one piece of knowledge concerning the car (i.e., its color), but not all the other bits of knowledge (e.g., whether it is a five-speed, four-speed, or automatic; whether it has a radio, a radio with tape deck, a CB, or none of these items).

As detailed in the next chapter, the GKT, unlike the CQT, rests on sound psychophysiological and psychological principles as a standardizable test or detector of guilt (though not of deception per se). Moreover, the GKT's validity as an experimental procedure has been amply supported in the literature (e.g., Balloun and Holmes, 1979; Ben-Shakhar, Lieblich, and Kugelmass, 1970; Davidson, 1968; Lykken, 1959, 1960). However, in regard to real-life *field* development in North America in the hands of professional polygraphers (i.e., members of the APA), the GKT has not gotten off the ground. On the other hand, in Japan the North American version of the CQT is rarely used, and it is the GKT that is the preferred technique. In Chapter 7, we shall present further details of, and possible reasons for, these marked cultural differences in polygraphic field practices between industrialized democratic countries with equivalent levels of technological development.

# Critical Analysis of the CQT

The CQT requires analysis before any criticism, because the basic terminology is misleading, and this in turn means that descriptions of what occurs are not accurate. Accordingly, before considering the problems associated with the CQT, we need to take up terminological issues and then provide a description of the CQT with those terminological issues as background.

## Terminology

It is customary to accept, at face value, the terms used by practitioners to describe their particular technology, but this practice results in misdescriptions when the basic terms involved are used in a misleading way. This is particularly the case with the CQT, where even such strong opponents as Lykken (1981) implicitly accept some of these misdescriptions when they refer to it as a "test" (albeit a poor one), use the term "control" without qualification when referring to the so-called control questions, and use the expressions "polygraph" and "detection of deception" interchangeably [a usage which suggests that the CQT measures (no matter how poorly) deception rather than (at best) guilt]. On the other hand, proponents of the CQT employ additional misleading concepts, which include referring to the procedure as quantified and citing accuracy figures (which suggests that error rates can be specified in a way that is possible only with standardized tests). Finally, the inferences drawn by polygraphers from the CQT results rest on a number of unexamined (and implausible) psychophysiological and physiological assumptions.

One may think that these terminological issues are matters of mere semantics, with little practical impact. For example, it may seem that whether the CQT is or is not a test has limited relevance. However, as we suggested already, an essential factor in the perceived importance of a decision tool like the CQT is its *face* validity. In the next two subsections, a more detailed account is provided of why the a priori, real validity of the CQT is so questionable. The more empirical issue of the CQT's actual predictive validity, in the light of the available evidence, will be considered in Chapter 3.

## Description of the CQT

In the following brief description of the typical CQT procedure, it must be borne in mind that, because the procedure is not standardized, the description is not as specific as would be the case with a standardized genuine test procedure like that of IQ testing. However, just as it is possible to provide a general description of even relatively unstructured interview procedures, it is equally possible to give an outline of the CQT.

The procedure itself is preceded by a variable period of days or weeks during which time the examinee has become a suspect with respect to a particular crime. This prepolygraph period varies not only in duration, but also in the way in which that time is spent. An important component of the prepolygraph period is how the examinee arrives at the "voluntary" decision to take the polygraph examination [how "voluntary" the decision truly is and whether the consent is really an informed one are both moot issues (see, e.g., Furedy and Liss, 1986)].

Usually the examiner receives information about the examinee just before the beginning of the polygraph session. This information (which is another source of variability) is usually quite extensive and includes material that is likely to produce a prepolygraphic opinion in the examiner's mind concerning whether the examinee is truthful or deceptive. This in turn can produce variations in the administration of the polygraphic procedure itself.

The polygraph session proper consists of four phases. The first, "pre-test-interview" phase lasts from about 30 to 60 minutes. During this interview the examiner seeks to convince the examinee that the polygraph is infallible, raises various topics (e.g., mother's death) that may be useful during the "post-test-interview" phase when an attempt is made to induce a confession (e.g., "Your poor dead mother would have wanted you to confess!"), and discusses the formulations of both the relevant and "control" questions with the examinee. The relevant questions are reformulated until the examinee indicates that he or she finds them unambiguous, and can clearly answer "no" to them (i.e., indicating innocence). The "control" questions are reformulated until a version is arrived at for which, in the examiner's view, the examinee's answer ("no") is either totally deceptive or at least not confidently truthful.

In addition, some examiners will ask a number of medically related questions. Because there is no logical relation between the answers to these questions and the scoring of the polygraph chart, it is at least likely that the function of these questions is to increase the perceived professional status of the polygrapher, and perhaps even to institute a doctor-patient relationship which may enhance the examiner's confession-inducing ability during the later post-test-interview phase.

The next phase is the "test" phase, which lasts for about half an hour and is begun by connecting the physiological recording instrument to the examinee. The instrument most commonly used by modern CQT examiners records an electrodermal (GSR) channel, a relative-blood-pressure channel (cardio), and two channels of respiration taken from the chest and stomach. Changes that immediately follow questions are compared with more or less specificity, depending on the measure. In the case of the electrodermal channel, the change can be specified in terms of phasic, unidirectional amplitude (i.e., resistance decrease or conductance increase). In the case of the cardio, decreases or increases in relative blood pressure may be considered and/or such other topographical features as the duration of a particular decrease or increase. In the case of respiration, features that can be looked at include amplitude and frequency changes, as well as more local changes such as an increase in the duration of breath-holding following an inspiration or an expiration.

The test phase proper is often preceded by the card or "stim" test, where the examiner uses the instrument to detect which of a number of cards the examinee is thinking of. This sort of physiological detection is relatively easy to perform, but just in case of error, the stim test is rigged to ensure correct detection. This is because although the stated (to the examinee) purpose is to check that the instrument is working, the actual purpose (as indicated in polygraph administration manuals and courses) is to once again reinforce the infallibility of the polygraph in the examinee's mind. The "test" proper then follows, comprising a set of questions [usually three relevant (e.g., "Did you take the money?"), three control ("Aside from the crime under investigation, did you ever take more than $5 that was not yours?"), three irrelevant (e.g., "Is your name Furedy?"), and an initial buffer question, which is supposed to eliminate initial orienting or novelty effects] which are presented about 30 seconds apart. Each repetition through the list is called a "test," and there are about three to five "tests." After three "tests," the examiner can decide whether or not to give one or two more.

When the examiner has decided to stop giving "tests," the third phase is initiated. During this phase, the examinee is left alone for some 20 minutes, while the examiner leaves to score the physiological records. At the beginning of this third phase, the detection part of the polygraph procedure has been concluded, but clearly the third phase has a role in the confession-inducing function of the polygraph, because during this phase the examinee has little else to do except worry about whether he or she will be judged deceptive by the examiner.

If the examiner decides that the examinee has been deceptive, the examiner tries, upon returning, to induce a confession of guilt during the "post-test interview." This fourth phase can last from 10 minutes to several hours. That is, this last phase is terminated either by a confession or by the examiner's decision that he or she will not be able to get a confession.

## Problems with the CQT as a Scientifically Based Method of Detecting Deception

In the following subsections we discuss six of the most serious problems that arise from considering the CQT polygraph in terms of elementary principles of scientific testing. Each problem by itself, in our view, seriously compromises the scientific status of CQT polygraphy.

### CQT Does Not Detect Deception in the "Deceptive" but Rather in the "Truthful" Examinee

This paradoxical conclusion follows if one grants the assumption, suggested by Podlesny and Raskin (1977) and Raskin and Podlesny (1979), that the control questions do in fact elicit deception, or at least a state of uncertainty about whether the questions have been answered truthfully (the answers, by prior agreement, are "no"; the answers to the relevant questions, of course, are also "no"). In that case, the guilty examinee should not be detectable, since he or she is being deceptive *both* to the relevant questions (being guilty) *and* to the control questions (following carefully prepared examiner instructions). The physiological differentiation of deception should occur only in the innocent, who are (at least to some degree) deceptive *only* to the control questions. So it seems that larger autonomic responses to the control relative to the relevant questions in the innocent subject (classified as "truthful" by the examiner) must be interpreted as the "detection of deception." What this paradoxical conclusion shows, of course, is that the expression "detection of deception" should not be taken at face value when considering what is *actually* involved in the CQT.

### CQT Does Not Involve "Control" in the Normal Scientific Sense of That Term

The normal sense of the term "control" in an experimental/control comparison is that the control condition is equivalent to the experimental condition in all important respects except for what the comparison is intended to measure or differentiate. From the above paradox, it is already clear that if the intended process for differentiation is deception (as is implied by the descriptor "detection of deception"), a control question like "Did you ever do anything you were ashamed of?" cannot possibly be a control for a relevant question like "Did you steal the money?" The two questions are not differentiated in terms of the absence and presence, respectively, of deception, and they are also not equivalent in all important respects except for deception.

However, even if the target for detection is not the process of deception, but the guilt of the examinee, the relevant/control comparison does not involve control in the normal scientific sense of that term, because the two questions differ on a number of dimensions besides that of whether or not the examinee is guilty or innocent. When pressed by opponents in print (e.g., Lykken, 1979), proponents of the CQT admit that the control involved is not of the normal scientific sort, but is rather meant to provide an "emotional standard" (Barland and Raskin, 1973, p. 430). The validity of the rationale behind this sort of "standard" will be considered in Chapter 3, but even if that rationale is sound, it remains the case that no *control* in the normal, scientific sense of that term is involved in the CQT, so that the use of the term in referring to the CQT is misleading.

## *CQT Is Not a "Test" in the Normal Psychological Sense of That Term*

A "psychological test is essentially an objective and standardized measure of a sample of behavior" (Anastasi, 1988, p. 23). The key reason for denying test status for the CQT is the lack of standardiz*ability* of the procedure. It is helpful, in this context, to consider IQ tests, which, though controversial, are genuine tests because they are standardized. That is, the items presented and the results obtained are equivalent between competent operators. In other words, while the *validity* of IQ tests is controversial (because they may be biased by cultural factors, or may not, in fact, measure intelligence at all), the *reliability* is adequate. Similarly (and as argued in more detail in Chapter 2), the GKT is a genuine test, with specifiable items that are relatively constant from one competent operator to another.

In contrast, the CQT procedure (as briefly detailed above) is a complex, dynamic interview with variable pre-interview components (i.e., the information given to the examiner before the interview potentially biases that examiner and therefore has a variable effect on the procedure itself) as well as a variable interrogatory component. Accordingly, the CQT is highly dependent on the operator not only in regard to how the operator interprets the results of the physiological measurements, but also in regard to *what* the control questions will be (which are made up in conjunction with the examinee and are therefore affected by the examiner-examinee *rapport*) and *how* the questions are put to the examinee. As a result, accuracy rates are dependent on specific examiners, examinees, and their interaction. Indeed, even the same examiner gives a *different* "test," or rather provides different experiences, to different examinees.

Moreover, competence in a CQT examiner involves quite different attributes from those required in an IQ (or GKT) tester. The CQT operator needs interrogator skills (to induce confessions), psychodynamic skills (for generating control questions), selling skills (for persuading or deceiving the examinee concerning the false proposition that the polygraph is infallible), and, as we shall see in more detail in the next subsection, interpretative skills (for the scoring of the physiological records). None of these skills is relevant for competent IQ (or GKT) operators. If anything, the skills are probably *negatively* related to competent IQ (or GKT) testing, because their deployment is likely to produce bias or lack of *standardization* in administering IQ (and GKT). Accordingly, even if there are some CQT examiners who are close to 100% accurate (and many examiners do, in fact, believe that they are), their decisions are based not on a test but on an unstandardizable interrogatory-interview procedure. This means that the validity of the procedure in a general sense (i.e., independent of particular operators) will be difficult, if not impossible, to assess even in principle.

## CQT Is Not "Quantified" in the Normal Psychophysiological Sense of That Term

Measurement quantification in psychophysiology means that dependent-variable changes are expressed in units that can be objectively stated, and hence are invariant across competent measurers or operators. Such measurement is objective, even though there may be considerable controversy regarding the *interpretation* of such objectively specified measures. Again, the distinction lies between reliability (which objective measurement provides) and validity (for which it is also necessary that the *interpretation* of the measure be sound). So, for example, psychophysiologists disagree on whether T-wave amplitude (TWA) is an adequate index of sympathetic influences (e.g., Furedy and Heslegrave, 1983) or whether it is a thoroughly misleading index that should be abandoned (e.g., Schwartz and Weiss, 1983), but there is no disagreement on the specification of TWA (in units of micromhos), because it is quantified in the normal psychophysiological sense of that term.

In polygraphic CQT measurement, however, the numerical scores (3, 2, and 1) are assigned on the basis of qualitative, *subjective* considerations of whether the differences are "marked," "clear," or "slight," *according to the operator*. Therefore, descriptors such as "quantified" and "objective" are inappropriate when applied to CQT numerical scoring, even though the method does represent an improvement over earlier global methods. This is true even if it is shown that operator-to-operator reliability with respect to the scoring of charts is quite high (at least under conditions where the examiners know that they themselves are being examined in a research study). Even so, that reliability depends on the ability and willingness[1] of particular operators to be consistent, rather than on the

---

[1]Ability and willingness need to be distinguished. Even if the examiner is trained sufficiently in the principles of testing to score in a standardized way, the examiner may not be *willing* to do so when he or she is convinced, through nonphysiological evidence, that

sort of genuine quantification that is involved in psychophysiological measurement. Accordingly, the apparent similarity between the numerical scores used by psychophysiologists and CQT polygraphers is misleading, because polygraphic scores are not based on genuine quantification.

## *Underlying Psychophysiological Assumptions*

There are a number of assumptions which are necessary for the adequacy of the CQT. The assumptions vary in the degree to which they have been explicitly discussed, but what is common to them all is that they all make stronger claims than is warranted by the weight of evidence.

The first of these is the specific-lie-response (SLR) assumption. As we have indicated, the SLR assumption is clearly required for any purely global, qualitative method of scoring.

Another assumption made by many polygraphers is the lie-guilt-arousal (LGA) link. This assumption underlies polygraphy's original rationale: lying (probably in childhood) is associated with punishment and hence guilt, which in turn increases arousal, which is registered by the measured physiological changes. The strongest version of the LGA assumption asserts that *only* the LGA link is responsible for detection. In that case, psychopaths should be completely undetectable, but this sort of test of the polygraph's rationale is, in practice, difficult to perform, if only because the identification of psychopathy itself is subject to error. However, the weaker and more plausible form of the LGA assumption is that guilt feelings about lying make some contribution to detection, and this generates a more feasible empirical test of the assumption, which is that deception in psychopaths should be harder to detect than that in normals.

This test of the LGA assumption was carried out by Raskin and Hare (1978), and the interpretation of the outcome provides descriptive insight into the status of the underlying assumptions in the polygraphic community. The result of the study was that there were no differences in detectability between psychopaths and normals. It would be normal scientific deductive-testing practice to treat these results as disconfirmatory for the polygraphic LGA assumption. However, the polygraphic interpretation of these results (e.g., Raskin, 1978) was that they were supportive, since they showed that the CQT worked *equally* well for both populations.

It is true, however, that, in contrast to all other polygraphers, Raskin appears to have rejected the basic LGA assumption and favors, instead, a signal value or threat rather than guilt interpretation (see, e.g., Raskin, 1979). This lie-threat-arousal (LTA) position assumes that "concern about deception" produces threat (because of consequent punishment, rather than past-established guilt about lying), and that the innocent can be differentiated from the guilty through their

---

the examinee is deceptive. In such cases, the examiner is really using the polygraphic procedure to confirm a preconceived notion rather than testing, in an unbiased manner, whether the examinee is truthful or deceptive.

greater responding to the so-called control questions as compared with responding to the relevant questions (see also Raskin and Kircher, 1989, p. 5). However, the LTA position rests on a very strong, and almost certainly false, psychophysiological assumption that it is possible, through physiological measures, to separate concern about possible deception from concern about the *content* of the question. Consider, for example, an actual child sex abuse case where the relevant question was, "Did you lick X's vagina?", where X was a 4-year-old and the examinee was a 74-year-old crossing guard who had had neither a previous record nor a reputation for child molestation and who was likely to have been aroused by the *content* of the question (as would anyone) even if he was innocent. No psychophysiological evidence exists that would support the notion that measuring, say, the GSR to this question would allow the examiner to separate the concern about deception from that of the question's content.

A final assumption that is necessary for the CQT polygraph is that the measured physiological responses are not manipulable by the examinee either by physical or by psychological means. The evidence relevant to this assumption (which is usually referred to as the countermeasures problem) will be dealt with in Chapter 4. Here we want only to indicate the scope and strength of the assumption, especially as it relates to psychological (e.g., thinking of specific events) rather than physical (e.g., nail in shoe) manipulations. In this regard, it must be noted that while *inhibitory* psychological manipulations (e.g., relaxing thoughts) may not be effective, *excitatory* ones are probably more so, because increases in blood pressure and heart rate can be more readily produced through thinking of emotive events.

## *Underlying Psychological Assumptions*

Polygraphers make a number of psychological assumptions that derive not from psychological principles, but from the problems inherent in the basic control/relevant comparison, which, as indicated above, bears only a superficial resemblance to the normal, scientific control/experimental comparison. These assumptions all assert extraordinary powers in the examiner to manipulate *and* calibrate psychological influences. These powers are necessary because the CQT procedure itself is not a standardized test with properly controlled manipulations in terms of either independent- or dependent-variable considerations.

One such psychological assumption is revealed by the claim that the "differential arousal value of test questions is established during a pretest review of the questions with the subject" (Raskin and Kircher, 1989, pp. 4–5). This claim implies the assumption that each polygraph CQT examiner can *measure* the psychological arousal value of questions during what is an unstandardized, dynamic interview. It bears emphasis that the above claim was not an oral one made to a group of people who are unfamiliar with principles of introductory psychology. Rather, the claim is a written assertion in the course of debate by specialists in psychology and psychophysiology.

Another equally unlikely assumption is that each polygraph CQT examiner can manipulate the arousal value of the control question in the innocent in such a way that its arousal value will exceed that of the relevant question in the innocent. One problem with accepting this assumption is that such a manipulative skill is likely to vary from examiner to examiner, as well as being a function of examiner-examinee *rapport* (the better that rapport, the more arousing the control question the examiner can develop). Accordingly, we are again faced with the fact that the CQT is completely operator-dependent for its accuracy, in contrast to a standardized test. The other problem is that it is not likely that even the most skillful examiner enjoying the maximal rapport with the examinee is able to reduce, in the innocent, the arousal value of relevant questions related to sex abuse in children. Moreover, as with the first assumption, this assumption has also been defended in print by polygraphers. For example, a paper coauthored by a polygrapher and a sociologist claimed that when asked the question, "After you had sex with your daughter, did you wipe yourself off with....?", an "innocent person should feel *comfortable* [our emphasis] with this type of test" (Desroches and Thomas, 1985, p. 60). It is a tribute to the face validity of the polygraph that this statement was published in a refereed journal.

Finally, there are a set of metaphorical psychological assumptions which are stated only orally, and usually before audience members who do not specialize in psychology. So, for example, a polygrapher will testify in court about the "test" he or she has performed, and will refer to having been involved in "bleeding dry a thought process" (testimony from the Royal Commission, 1988). Nonpsychological, legal specialists do not usually question such formulations, and these formulations may be persuasive at a pop-psychology level, although, of course, they have no support in the psychological literature.

## Usages of the Polygraph

In the previous section, we described the different methods of polygraph interrogation without relating them to the objective for which these methods are used. In this section, we shall focus on several usages of polygraphy. Distinguishing between the different usages is as important as distinguishing between the methods. Just as the accuracy and validity of the test may depend upon the specific method being used, it may also depend upon the specific goal and application it is used for. A polygraph procedure can be relatively valid and accurate for one purpose and totally inaccurate for another.

The major applications of polygraphy to date are in the criminal and the industrial contexts. In the criminal context, polygraphs are used by the police, together with other techniques, to help connect suspects to a specific crime. The industrial application refers to the screening of employees or prospective employees by their current or prospective employers. At one time, this industrial application formed the main staple of American polygraphic activity and also was quite common in Canada.[2]

---

[2]In Toronto, in the late seventies, fast-food firms employing student casual labor routinely required prospective employees to "take a polygraph," and in those days of relatively high unemployment, most applicants complied.

## Event-Related Versus Event-Free Usages of the Polygraph

On closer examination, the distinction between criminal and industrial applications is not clear, because sometimes a criminal act is the basis for screening employees in the industrial setting, and because often in the industrial application the test focuses on deception and on the possibility that a job applicant has been involved in illegal acts in the past (e.g., drug abuse, theft from a previous employer). Therefore, a different, although usually equivalent, distinction between usages of the polygraph is used in this chapter. One class of polygraph usages concerns a specific event (e.g., a crime), and the purpose of the procedure is to determine whether a given individual was involved in that event (e.g., committed the crime, knew about the crime). The expression "event-related application" is used to describe this class. The other type of polygraph usage is event-free, in the sense that the procedure does not focus on a particular known event, but rather attempts to determine more general behavioral characteristics or tendencies of a given individual as reflected in that individual's past behavior (e.g., honesty as reflected by past employment record).

The criminal application is usually an event-related usage of the polygraph in that the procedure is usually conducted because a certain crime has been committed. The industrial application, however, is most often of the event-free type, since its usual aim is determining whether a candidate is suited for a certain job, with no specific event being used as the basis of the test. Thus in the job-screening case, for example, the polygrapher might utilize relevant questions pertaining to hypothetical crimes (e.g., "Did you ever steal anything from your previous employer?"). This differentiation of the event-relatedness of the criminal and industrial applications is important because it can shed some light on the nature of these different applications, and it can reveal some reasons for possible differences in the accuracy and validity of the polygraph in its different applications.

Two important features of the event-related vs. event-free distinction of polygraph usage are relevant to the present discussion: ($a$) the type of inferences being drawn from the inference rules and ($b$) the test methods being used. In the event-related usage the inferences made on the basis of the test's results relate to the single situation at hand, and no attempt is made to generalize across situations. In addition, it is typically used for providing information only about the past. The event-free usage, on the other hand, is typically specifically aimed at generalizing across situations and at making predictions regarding the future behavior of the individual. Thus, in the event-related case, there is a single source of error — weaknesses and inaccuracies in the design of the inference rule or in its application. In the event-free usage, two sources of error can play a role: ($a$) error in the inferences drawn from the physiological responding (e.g., in deciding whether the subject lied when he denied stealing from past employers) and ($b$) error in generalizing from past behavior to future behavior. Typically, the polygraph's aim is to predict future on-the-job behavior, but even a person who admits having stolen in the past, for example, will not necessarily steal again. In other words, the event-free usage of the polygraph depends not only on the inference rule of the particular polygraphic procedure used, but also on the controversial assumption of cross-situational consistency of human behavior (e.g., Epstein, 1979, 1986; Mischel, 1968; Mischel and Peake, 1982; Rushton and Erdle, 1987).

Sackett and Decker (1979) made a distinction between identification and prediction. In the event-related application, the goal of the polygraph is to identify the individual(s) involved in the event. In preemployment screening, on the other hand, the goal is to predict whether a candidate will be engaged in any misconduct (steal from the organization, use drugs, be frequently absent, etc.). According to Sackett and Decker (1979), "The generalization of an accuracy figure from a criminal investigation to a pre-employment context assumes that past behavior is a perfectly valid predictor of future on-the-job behavior. The accuracy figure for identification should be multiplied by the best estimate one has of the strength of the past behavior–future behavior relationship to obtain a more realistic picture of the value of the polygraph in pre-employment screening" (p. 497).

As for the choice of testing procedures, only in an event-related application is it possible to make use of the known features of the event to construct a GKT procedure and to establish a sound inference rule on the basis of the test's results. Only a known event can provide specific features that will be relevant only for persons familiar with that event. The event-free application, on the other hand, must rely upon general relevant questions that are likely to be threatening to any individual taking the test. Thus, it is very difficult to construct proper control questions for this type of polygraph test, control questions that would be as arousing and threatening as the relevant questions to all truth-telling subjects.

In the event-free application, not only can the GKT not be utilized, but even the more controversial method of the CQT cannot be applied in a straightforward way. In the CQT, the relevant questions pertain to a specific event (crime), while the control questions relate to general misdeeds. In order to use it for detecting hypothetical crimes, general misdeed questions (which play the role of control questions) must play the role of the relevant questions, with nothing left to serve as controls. In other words, enhanced physiological reactions to the CQT-type control questions (e.g., "Did you ever steal from your employer?") are now taken as an indication of deception, and a consistently high level of responding to those questions might mean that an applicant for a certain job would be rejected on the grounds of failing the polygraph test. But in order to make such inferences one must compare the responses to those critical items with responses to equivalent items. However, it is difficult to construct such items, because equivalent items must relate to other hypothetical crimes of similar importance, and naturally a consistent responding to those items is not going to make a job applicant more attractive as a future employee.

In practice, the common usage of the polygraph for screening job candidates is done by RIT, the relevant/irrelevant technique (U.S. Congress, 1983), which is based on comparing the responses to relevant items with the responses to completely neutral items. Clearly, such a procedure poses even greater concerns about the logic of the inference rules for deriving conclusions from the polygraph, and in particular it means that the risks of false-positive results are extremely high.

Another polygraph procedure, which is often used for preemployment screening, is based on comparisons between responses to different relevant questions, with an attempt to detect sensitive issues in the job applicant (e.g., theft, drug or alcohol abuse). This method of using the polygraph for screening purposes is also problematic, because it rests on the assumption that all the relevant questions, which can cover areas ranging from theft to issues of sexual behavior, are equally threatening for the innocent truth-telling applicant. For a further discussion of this method, see Lykken (1981), who labeled it the "relevant/control test" because the relevant questions serve as controls for each other.

By the time this book is published, the event-free use of the polygraph in industry will probably have disappeared in the United States. The main reason for this prediction is that a 1988 act of Congress outlawed the polygraph's "industrial" use. However, that act allowed the event-related, "specific-issue" use, which, in the United States at least, effectively means the use of the CQT polygraph. The main focus of this book, therefore, will be on event-related versions of polygraphy.

CHAPTER 2

# A Critical Comparison of the Major Methods of Polygraph Interrogation

The previous chapter described the development of psychophysiological techniques for detecting deception. Three methods of polygraph-assisted interrogation were mentioned—the RIT, the CQT, and the GKT—with an emphasis on the most commonly used method, the CQT. In this chapter we shall critically compare the three methods with respect to their inference rules, their underlying rationales and assumptions, and their potential for becoming a scientifically based tool in the true sense of the term.

Gustafson and Orne (1964) have divided polygraph usages into "guilty information" (GI) and "guilty person" (GP) techniques. The GI usage is aimed at procuring specific information from a given person (i.e., detecting which of several items has relevance for the person). The GP technique is used when the purpose is to classify the individuals themselves (e.g., as guilty vs. innocent; deceptive vs. truth-telling; possessing particular information vs. ignorant of the particular information).

In practice, both usages of the polygraph utilize similar procedures in which several questions or items are presented to the subject, and several physiological measures are taken at each presentation. Then, either the subject or the items are classified, as per the above categories, on the basis of those physiological reactions. In general, a decision rule is defined for the physiological measures, so that every value (or combination of values) of these measures is associated with a specific classification of the item or the person under investigation. The term "inference rule" will be used throughout this chapter to describe those relationships between the physiological measures and the conclusions derived therefrom. The inference rules are the backbone of the entire polygraph interrogation, and the accuracy and validity of such an interrogation depend on the rationale and validity of its inference rule.

Since there is no absolute meaning to a given size or pattern of a physiological reaction, and given the magnitude of individual differences in those measures (e.g., Lacey and Lacey, 1958), the inference rule must be based upon a relative interpretation of the physiological measures. In other words, in order to evaluate whether a response of a given individual to a given item is large or small, this response must be compared with other responses from the same individual on the same physiological measure. Thus, all methods of polygraphy must use some type of control questions to allow for proper comparisons of the responses and to establish relativistic evaluation of the physiological measures. Indeed, all methods of polygraph interrogation have realized this necessity, and all of them include the use of control questions. In their choice of control questions, however, the different methods differ drastically. Furthermore, it will be shown that the problem of choosing proper control questions is the kernel of the polygraph controversy.

## The Choice of Control Questions

In both the RIT and the CQT, there is a fundamental difference between the relevant and the control questions. While the relevant questions are directly crime-relevant questions of the "Did you do it?" type (e.g., "Did you break into Mr. Jones's apartment last Friday night?"), the control questions either are entirely neutral, as in the RIT method, or focus on general sins (e.g., "Did you ever take something that did not belong to you?"), as in the CQT. Because of these obvious differences, we argued in Chapter 1 that the term "control" is misleading in this context. The problem is perhaps best demonstrated by the fact that anyone can immediately perceive these differences and can classify any question as relevant or control.

In the GKT, on the other hand, the control questions are formulated exactly like the relevant ones (e.g., "Was the color of the stolen car red?" "Was it white?"). The only difference between the two types of questions is that only the relevant questions refer to features of the event in question (the guilty knowledge), and therefore only people possessing the guilty knowledge are capable of distinguishing relevant from control questions.

In other words, in the CQT all questions (relevant and control) are threatening, but to different (and unknown) degrees. In the GKT all questions are a priori neutral, and only guilty subjects can discriminate between the different questions, and, therefore, only those subjects are expected to show differential response patterns to the relevant questions.

## The Inference Rules

Generally, the inference rules used by the different methods of polygraph interrogation are similar: A pattern of consistently larger responses to the relevant than to the control questions is taken as an indication that the subject is guilty (the typical CQT examiner will label such a subject as deceptive; whereas the inference drawn when a GKT procedure is applied would be that the suspect possesses guilty knowledge).

Clearly, many different decision rules and cutoff points may be defined for each method (an example of such a cutoff point was mentioned in Chapter 1, when the Backster quantification technique was described). However, these variations are not essential parts of the methods. (We shall elaborate on how an optimal cutoff point should be determined in Chapter 8.) In spite of this rather superficial similarity between the different methods, the validities of the inference rules may differ significantly from one method to the other. The validity of an inference rule based on a comparison between responses to relevant and control questions depends primarily on the choice and rationale of the control questions. Because the control questions used by the different methods differ so drastically, the rationale and face validity of the inference rules must be carefully examined.

## The Rationale and Assumptions Underlying the Three Methods of Psychophysiological Detection

In the next three sections we shall examine more closely the rationales and assumptions underlying the inference rule for each method of polygraph interrogation, and subsequently these rationales will be compared.

### The Rationale of the RIT Method

Clearly, the two classes of questions—relevant and irrelevant—are very different in their nature and content and in terms of their posing a threat to the subject. While it may be sensible to assume that guilty persons will show a greater response to the relevant questions than to the irrelevant ones, it makes little sense to assume that innocent suspects will show the opposite pattern of physiological responsivity. The idea that entirely neutral questions such as "Are you sitting down?" can serve as controls for the relevant questions that focus on real crimes must rest upon a set of rather strong assumptions. It depends on the notion that the physiological responses extracted during the polygraph interrogation reflect deception and only deception, and that where there is no deception there will be no variation in the responses. Therefore an innocent suspect giving truthful answers to all questions will respond similarly to all questions, regardless of their obvious differences. In other words, the basic assumption underlying the RIT method is that there is a specific "lie response," or that deception is a necessary and a sufficient condition for a certain pattern of physiological responding. The necessity component of that assumption is crucial because it means that the specific pattern of physiological responding cannot occur unless the subject gives a deceptive answer to the question. Indeed, under this assumption, we can expect that nondeceptive subjects would give similar responses to the relevant and the irrelevant questions.

However, as was indicated in the previous chapter, the science of psychophysiology does not provide any empirical support for this assumption. On the contrary, it seems that the very same physiological measures used in polygraph interrogations are associated with a large number of different psychological states and processes. Psychologists and psychophysiologists have been intrigued by the possibility of differentiating between emotions through the use of bodily reactions. This is a very attractive idea because it would suggest objective and quantitative measures of human emotions. Unfortunately, most attempts to verify this possibility have not been very successful (see, for example, Schachter and Singer, 1962). Even phenomenologically distinct emotions such as fear and anger are characterized to a large extent by a similarly high level of autonomic activation. Furthermore, it seems that the individual differences in the patterns of physiological responsivity exceed the effects caused by psychological states. Lacey and Lacey (1958) have formulated the principle of relative response specificity, meaning that "For a given set of autonomic functions (hence the term *relative*) subjects tend to respond with an idiosyncratic pattern of autonomic activation in which maximal activation is shown by the same physiological function whatever the stress" (p. 50). By this principle, the same stimulus may result in a great variety of physiological reactions in different persons, and different stimuli may be accompanied by similar physiological reactions in a given individual. For example, the physiological measures standardly used by polygraphers may be sensitive to strong emotions such as anger or fear, but they are also sensitive to much weaker psychological states such as surprise caused by a change in stimulation. The work of Pavlov (1927), and later on of Sokolov (1963), on orienting responses (OR) suggests that any stimulus change may be reflected by physiological reactions of a similar nature to those used for the detection of deception.

In conclusion, while deception may be accompanied by a set of physiological changes, there is no basis to assume that these changes distinctly characterize deception. On the contrary, they may occur as a result of different psychological states created by a great variety of stimuli. Consequently, the assumption of a specific lie response is unreasonable, and therefore the inference rule underlying the RIT method should yield a large proportion of false-positive classifications (i.e., innocent suspects classified as guilty as a result of displaying larger reactions to the relevant questions than to the irrelevant ones).

There is a weaker assumption that might be used to argue for the validity of the RIT inference rule. Provided that all subjects have an absolute faith in the accuracy of the polygraph test, innocent suspects should feel confident of passing the test and therefore should feel no special concern over the relevant questions. The RIT method takes this absolute faith as a reliable fact and considers it sufficient to prevent false-positive results.

There are two problems with this assumption. The first is that it is impossible to guarantee that a subject has acquired the necessary absolute faith in the test. Polygraphers make specific efforts to increase the faith of their subjects in the polygraph. They typically do this by conducting a rigged card test, or a "stimulation test" as it is sometimes called by polygraphers. In this card test the subject is asked to choose a card from a deck. The examiner then asks a series of questions in the form: "Did you choose card X?" to which the subject is requested to give a negative answer. The deck of cards, however, is prearranged so that the examiner knows exactly which card has been picked by the subject.[1] Eventually the chosen card is detected, presumably by the machine (for further discussions of stimulation tests see Lykken, 1981, and Reid and Inbau, 1977). Such a demonstration may be quite powerful in convincing subjects of the polygraph's accuracy, but it is questionable whether it is powerful enough to completely eliminate all doubts. It is particularly doubtful if we remember that people taking polygraph tests have access to the literature and may have read any of the books or articles, like this one, in which polygraph procedures including rigged card tests are described.

The second problem with relying on absolute faith to eliminate false-positive results is that there are reasons, other than concern at being found guilty, which could cause innocent subjects to show larger physiological reactions to the more loaded relevant questions than to the irrelevant ones. We have already cited the studies demonstrating that anger and even surprise can evoke responses similar to fear. Additionally, it has been well demonstrated that emotionally laden words evoke larger physiological responses than neutral words in laboratory conditions (e.g., Lazarus and McCleary, 1951).

## The Rationale of the CQT

The control questions used in the CQT can be assumed to be more arousing and threatening than the irrelevant questions used as controls in the RIT method. On the other hand, they are not completely equivalent to the relevant questions. This is particularly evident if we consider the typical polygraph subject in the criminal interrogation context. For a suspect in a specific crime, the polygraph test is just one part of a broader investigation process in which the relevant questions (of the "Did you do it?" type) play a major role. Therefore, it is unlikely that specific relevant questions will be equivalent to more general control questions from the point of view of a suspect, whether innocent or guilty.

This inherent difficulty is recognized by polygraphers, who have developed their technique to overcome it. The pre-test interview is used, as described in Chapter 1, to produce a concerned answer from the suspect. Raskin (1979) describes how this is accomplished, with an example of a hypothetical theft of a ring. The subject is presented with one of the control questions in the following manner:

"Because this is a matter of a theft, I need to ask you some general questions about yourself with regard to stealing and your basic honesty in order to establish what type of a person you are with regard to stealing and whether or not you are the type of person who might have stolen the ring. Therefore, if I asked you, 'During the first 18 years of your life, did

---

[1] In their description of polygraph test procedures, Reid and Inbau (1977) emphasize the importance of administering the card test immediately after the first sequence of questions. Reid and Inbau (1977) state that "the cards are arranged and shown to the subject in such a way that the examiner will immediately know which card has been picked by the subject" (p. 42).

you ever take something that did not belong to you?' how would you answer?" The manner in which the question is posed to the subject and the behavior of the examiner are designed to intimidate or embarrass the subject into answering: "No." If the subject answers "Yes" and makes admissions, the question is reworded slightly so that the subject will answer "No" (Raskin, 1979, p. 590).

It is assumed that this manner of presenting the control questions to the subject creates conditions where the subject is either deceptive in answering the control questions or at least unsure of being truthful (who can be completely sure of never having taken anything belonging to someone else?). At the very least, the subject is assumed to be very concerned about the control questions (e.g., Podlesny and Raskin, 1977). This is a critical assumption underlying the inference rule of the CQT. However, even a guarantee that all subjects are very concerned about the control questions is not yet a sufficient basis for the CQT because the inference rule is based on the notion that guilty subjects must be more responsive to the relevant questions than to the control questions, whereas the innocent will respond more to the controls. In order to justify this inference rule, we must justify these two additional assumptions: (a) that the concern created in innocent subjects over the control questions will be greater than their concern over the relevant questions and (b) that for guilty subjects the situation will be reversed. The first assumption rests on the more basic assumption discussed earlier in relation to the RIT method—that the subject has complete faith in the accuracy of the polygraph.[2] Only with such faith could the relevant questions be less threatening than the controls. Faith in the polygraph's accuracy makes the relevant questions nonthreatening for an innocent suspect, because he or she believes that the physiological reactions measured by the polygraph will reflect truthfulness. The difficulties involved with the complete-faith assumption have been discussed earlier in relation to the RIT method. The second assumption is particularly nontrivial. If the efforts of the polygrapher during the pre-test interview are successful, then all subjects are concerned about the control questions. Why should a guilty suspect be less concerned with the control questions, given that this suspect is under the impression that a deception to those questions might be harmful to his or her case? Raskin (1979) states that "a guilty subject who is deceptive to the relevant questions should perceive the control questions as less significant..." (p. 591), giving no explanation as if this were obvious.

---

[2]Eitan Elaad, an experienced polygraph examiner with the Israeli Police Force, claimed (personal communication, 1988) that experience has taught him that too much faith in the polygraph may create a state of indifference on the part of the subject, which may interfere with detection. On the other hand, Elaad admits that some level of faith in the polygraph is necessary for detection. According to this view, the polygraph examiner must assess in each case the desired level of faith required for achieving optimal detection conditions. Furthermore, he or she should be able to create in the subject precisely that level of faith. Clearly, this assumes a very precise calibration ability on the part of the polygraph examiner. It is doubtful whether even the most experienced and knowledgeable polygraph examiner can achieve such an ability.

There are several difficulties with this set of assumptions, among them the previously described difficulty of guaranteeing that the subject has complete faith in the polygraph, but the major problem stems from the fact that all subjects can easily perceive the difference between the relevant and control questions. It is extremely doubtful whether manipulations and stimulations introduced by the examiner during the pre-test interview could rectify this situation. No matter how skillful the polygraph examiner may be, and no matter how effective the pre-test interview is, unless the examiner knows in advance whether the suspect is guilty or not, there is no reason for the examiner's manipulations to create different attitudes in guilty and innocent subjects. It is probable that those manipulations make the control questions more threatening than they would be without the examiner's efforts, but it is much less clear why it would do so only for innocent subjects.

Clearly, a set of such strong assumptions must be carefully examined and subjected to a great deal of research before a method based so heavily upon them is implemented. Unfortunately, direct evidence for the plausibility of the assumptions underlying the CQT is unavailable. For the meantime, then, it might seem that it should be possible to resolve the issue by an empirical examination of the validity and accuracy of the CQT. We shall discuss these issues in Chapter 3 and see why it is not simple to resolve them empirically.

The conceptual and logical difficulties of the assumptions underlying the CQT are very well demonstrated by an alternative type of control question that could in principle answer those difficulties. Some versions of the CQT include an alternative type of control question called "the guilt-complex question" (e.g., Lykken, 1981; Reid and Inbau, 1977). This question is related to a fictitious crime of the same type as the crime under investigation. Since the crime is fictitious, the subject's answer to the guilt-complex questions is known to be true. This is why Lykken (1981) calls this procedure a truth control test. On the other hand, the question is formulated exactly like the relevant question, and therefore it is as threatening to the innocent suspect as the relevant question. Only guilty subjects differentiate between the relevant questions (to which they answer deceptively) and the guilt-complex ones (to which they give truthful answers). Therefore, an inference rule based on a comparison of the responses to the relevant and the guilt-complex questions would make a lot of sense. The guilt-complex questions, unlike the regular control questions, constitute a real control in the scientific and logical sense of the term. The problem with this procedure is practical rather than theoretical or logical. In order for the procedure to be effective, the subject must believe that he or she is actually a suspect (and to the same degree) in the two crimes. In order to achieve this, the whole interrogation process from its outset must focus on both the real case and the fictitious one. It is perhaps this practical difficulty that accounts for the infrequent use of guilt-complex questions instead of "control" questions.

## The Rationale of the GKT

The rationale of the GKT, as in all other polygraph techniques, attempts to justify both aspects of the inference rule: that innocent subjects must show similar responsivity to the relevant and the irrelevant alternatives and that guilty subjects must show larger responses to the relevant items.

The first part of the inference rule is justified relatively easily. It depends on a single assumption: that the correct answers to the test questions are unknown to all but guilty individuals. In other words, polygraphers must be careful not to use items that were made public, and more importantly, they must be careful while interrogating the suspects not to disclose any of the items to be used in the GKT.

Several laboratory studies have attempted to examine the robustness of the GKT against possible disclosures of the guilty information to innocent subjects. Giesen and Rollison (1980) designed a mock crime experiment of the GKT, in which all subjects were exposed to the critical items—one group by acting out a mock crime and the other group in an innocent context. The results indicated that while there was a general tendency to produce larger skin resistance responses to the relevant compared with the neutral items, the two groups were clearly differentiated and all 20 innocent informed subjects were classified correctly. Stern, Breen, Watanabe, and Perry (1981) conducted a similar study and obtained similar results—23 out of their 26 innocent subjects who were exposed to the crime-relevant information were correctly classified. More recently, Bradley and Warfield (1984) extended the previous studies and designed an experiment in which three out of four groups of subjects simulating the innocent condition were exposed to the crime-relevant information. They either witnessed the crime, were told the crime details, or carried out innocent activities involving crime-relevant information. As in the previous studies, there were clear differences in differential electrodermal responsivity between the "guilty" subjects and all three informed innocent groups. However, the pooled data of all three informed innocent groups indicated that the detection scores in those groups were significantly larger than chance. Furthermore, the decision rule used by Bradley and Warfield (1984) for classifying subjects into guilty and innocent categories produced no false-negative errors, and no false-positive errors among the uninformed innocents, although 10 of the 24 informed innocents were classified as guilty. These studies taken together suggest that although the GKT seems to be quite robust against disclosure of guilty information to innocent subjects, great precaution is advisable because Bradley and Warfield's results suggest that such disclosure seems to increase the false-positive rates. If disclosure can be avoided, it logically follows that a pattern of similar responses to all the items can be expected from an innocent subject, because, just as in the guilt-complex procedure, the relevant and control items are undifferentiated.

It also should be emphasized that some precaution must be exercised while constructing the questions and choosing the items for a GKT procedure. For example, it is advisable to test whether all the alternative items of a given GKT question are a priori equivalent in terms of their arousal value. Lykken (1981, Chap. 21) has clearly demonstrated how this can be achieved, by a pedagogical detective story. In this story the detective constructs an ideal type of GKT procedure including an a priori examination of the items' equivalence.

The second part of the inference rule may be somewhat more difficult to justify. First, it must be assumed that the guilty person is aware of the true alternatives. Therefore, for the GKT to be effective, only salient features of the event can be chosen. However, it is not always clear that a given feature was indeed perceived by the guilty person or that it was correctly remembered at the time of the test. In spite of this obvious weakness in rationale, some positive evidence was recently provided by a set of experiments which showed that differential responding to the relevant items is robust to some distortions. Ben-Shakhar and Gati (1987) demonstrated, for example, that a relevant face produces larger electrodermal responses than an irrelevant face, even when one or two features of the relevant face (e.g., hat, glasses) were either omitted or replaced.

A second assumption required is that recognizing the true alternatives will lead to an enhanced physiological response to them. This assumption is supported by many experimental demonstrations (e.g., Ben-Shakhar, Leiblich, and Kugelmass, 1970; Davidson, 1968; Gustafson and Orne, 1963, 1965b; Lieblich, Ben-Shakhar and Kugelmass, 1976; Lykken, 1959, 1960) as well as by psychophysiological theory relating differential responsivity in the GKT to mechanisms of orientation (e.g., Ben-Shakhar, 1977; Lykken, 1974; Raskin, 1979).

# A Critical Comparison of the Three Methods for Psychophysiological Detection

So far we have described the possible interrogation methods used for psychophysiological detection. We have laid out the rationale and the basic assumptions underlying each method. Clearly, a great many differences between the methods emerge. The main difference relates to the choice of control questions, but each type of control question is justified by a different set of assumptions, and it results in a different inference rule. In this section, the detection methods will be compared with respect to several important factors.

## A Comparison of the Three Methods with Respect to Their Rationales and Assumptions

It is clear from the previous sections that the three methods of polygraph interrogation differ drastically with respect to their rationales and underlying assumptions. These differences follow directly from the differences in the choice of control questions and more specifically from the fact that the control questions used in the RIT and CQT methods clearly differ from the relevant questions (and, hence, are not really controls at all), whereas these obvious differences do not exist in the GKT.

Only when the GKT is the method being used is it possible to guarantee that innocent subjects will not be able to discriminate between relevant and control items. Under such circumstances the probability of a false-positive classification (classifying an innocent suspect as guilty) can be controlled by the examiner. For example, if the decision to classify a subject as guilty is based upon the observation that the largest response was evoked by the relevant item, then the probability of a false-positive classification is exactly $1/k$ when a single question with $k$ alternative answers is presented to the subject just once. When two such questions are used, the above-mentioned decision rule would yield $1/k^2$ probability of false-positive decisions. However, it must be remembered that this reduction in the false-positive rate, which can be quite easily achieved, involves usually an increase in the false-negative rate. The desired exchange rate between the two types of errors depends on the purpose of the test and on the social context in which polygraph-based interrogations are used. These issues will be further discussed and elaborated upon in Chapter 8. At this stage we wish to emphasize the fact that only under the GKT can the false-positive rates be controlled. In the other methods these rates (i.e., the probability that an innocent subject will show more responsivity to the relevant than to the control questions) are unknown, because the two types of questions are not equivalent and some innocent subjects might be aware of the special nature of the relevant questions. It is difficult to estimate the proportion of those innocent suspects, partly because little good appropriate research is available and partly because the test is unstandardized and the exact nature of the questions is dependent on a specific case and on a specific examiner.

With regard to guilty subjects, the differences between the methods are less clear. One can argue that in all three methods guilty subjects are expected to show consistently larger reactions to the relevant questions. In the GKT this will occur if the relevant item relates to a salient feature of the event—a feature that was perceived and remembered by the subject. In the RIT this pattern of responding is expected because of the obvious and very clear differences between relevant and irrelevant questions. Unfortunately, this characteristic responding is of little use because not only guilty subjects, but any subject, should display this pattern of physiological responsivity. Similarly, in the CQT, guilty subjects will typically perceive that it is the relevant questions that are really important and, therefore, will be more concerned about them (however, so will the typical innocent subject). Nevertheless, since the construction of control questions is not standardized, but rather depends largely on the particular examiner, there might be cases where emotionally loaded control questions would be constructed--questions that might elicit large responsivity even from guilty subjects. In this case, rather than the innocent subjects being classified as guilty, the guilty subjects could be classified as innocent.

## A Comparison of the Methods with Respect to Standardization

As was detailed in Chapter 1, the CQT procedure lacks standardization, as the formulation of the questions depends on the individual examiners and on their interaction with the subjects. Thus, a given subject undergoing two CQT polygraph interrogations by two independent examiners could be presented with two different sets of questions preceded by two different pre-test interviews. This feature of the CQT method characterizes the RIT as well. From this viewpoint both techniques do not deserve the term "test" as usually defined, although they are so called by many writers. In most texts dealing with tests and measurement, psychological tests are defined as standard and objective. For example, according to Anastasi (1988), "A psychological test is essentially an objective and standardized measure of a sample of behavior" (p. 23).

In the GKT, on the other hand, the questions are determined by the features of the event under investigation, and they do not depend upon the examiner-examinee interaction. Since the set of all features of a given event may be fairly large, different examiners may construct different questions for a GKT procedure. However, because the set of questions chosen by a GKT examiner is sampled from the features of the event, two GKT procedures may be viewed as two equivalent forms of a vocabulary test, each containing different items sampled from the same set of words. In addition, the specific content of a GKT question is not important as long as just one alternative answer is a salient feature of the event that can be assumed to be known to a person familiar with that event. The set of questions to be used in a GKT procedure can be prepared in advance, on the basis of a thorough examination of the event. This can be done without any interaction with the suspect, and in fact before a suspect has even appeared on the scene.[3] Such a procedure is standard and objective, and as such, approximates the concept of a psychological test much better than either the CQT or the RIT.

## A Comparison of the Methods with Respect to Contamination

Both the RIT and the CQT are contaminated in the sense that the polygraph examiner knows much more than revealed by the psychophysiological information proper. This is so because the pre-test interview is an essential part of these procedures and a great deal of information can be extracted from the suspect in the course of this interview. The GKT, on the other hand, does not depend upon a pre-test interview and can be conducted without relying upon such an interview. This follows directly from the discussion in the previous section in which we argued that the construction of GKT questions depends only on the event. Thus, the GKT examiner does not need to know anything about the suspect, and the test could be administered in a blind fashion similar to the way psychological experiments are administered. In fact, the GKT questions might be prerecorded by someone who has never seen the suspect. In this way an identical set of questions presented in an identical manner could be used for all suspects tested with the GKT in a given case.

It can be argued that there is nothing wrong with the fact that polygraph examiners have access to many sources of information. However, contaminated polygraph interrogations may have several important implications:

---

[3]Clearly, before administering the GKT questions, it should be clarified whether the subject has some knowledge of the critical items. A positive answer makes the question inappropriate for a GKT test.

1. It is difficult to separate the different sources of information. Thus, the reasons for a given conclusion drawn by a CQT polygraph examiner are unclear. The examiner may have reached the conclusion, whether correct or erroneous, from an inspection and analysis of the physiological responses, but he or she may have reached the same conclusion from the behavior of the suspect during the pre-test interview, or from something he or she knew about the suspect before the administration of the polygraph examination. Ben-Shakhar, Bar-Hillel, and Lieblich (1986) discussed the legal implications of contaminated polygraph examinations and argued that the contamination issue in itself is sufficient to prohibit the use of polygraph examiners as expert witnesses in a court of law and to avoid granting the polygraph-based evidence a status of admissible evidence. These issues will be further discussed in Chapter 8.

2. The nonphysiological information may influence the polygraph examiner when analyzing and interpreting the polygraph charts. This is particularly possible when the interpretation of the physiological charts is impressionistic and subjective. When no clear a priori rules of chart interpretation exist, the interpretation depends upon the judgment of the examiner, who cannot ignore the prior information that was provided.[4] As was argued in the previous chapter, the common practice of CQT chart interpretation is subjective and impressionistic. Even the so-called objective scoring method suggested by Backster (1962) is basically subjective because no exact rules were set for assigning numerical values to a given pattern of physiological responses.

The close relationship between the polygrapher's prior knowledge and the conclusion the polygrapher draws after the polygraph interrogation, was demonstrated by Barland (1975). He reported a high rate of agreement between polygraph examiners' final evaluations and those solicited just before the actual polygraph interrogation. Although it might be difficult to generalize from Barland's study because he asked the examiners to make a commitment before conducting the actual polygraph examination, the possibility of contamination must be kept in mind whenever interpreting the results of a polygraph validation study, since it implies that the observed validity may not be due exclusively to the physiological data.

3. The nonphysiological information may influence the manner in which the polygraph interrogation is conducted. Given that the polygraph examiner knows a great deal about the suspect and the case even before the suspect is examined, the examiner's notions may affect the way the interrogation is conducted. It can be hypothesized that in the course of the pre-test interview the examiner forms an opinion regarding the suspect. Specifically, the examiner may form a hypothesis about whether the suspect is innocent or guilty. It is possible that this hypothe-

---

[4]It should be noted that some polygraph agencies (e.g., the polygraph unit of the Israeli Police Force) routinely use, in addition to the polygraph examiner, another polygraph expert, who was not involved in the interrogation, to analyze the chart. Such a procedure may considerably reduce the risks of this source of contamination.

sis will affect the manner in which the questions are presented to the suspect during the polygraph interrogation phase. The implications of this possibility and of the whole contamination issue will be discussed at length later. At this stage, it suffices to mention the extensive research body dealing with the "experimenter expectancy effect" (e.g., Rosenthal and Rubin, 1978). This literature demonstrates that expectations formed by an experimenter may influence the behavior of subjects. Furthermore, this effect extends beyond the experimental laboratory and holds true for many real-life situations (e.g., the expectations of a schoolteacher affecting the performance of students, Rosenthal and Jacobson, 1968).

If the experimenter expectancy effect applies to the polygraph interrogation situation, then it would mean that the polygraphers' prior knowledge affects not only the chart interpretation but also the pattern and magnitude of the physiological responses to the different questions. Therefore, it would be impossible to overcome this problem just by using blind chart interpreters as was done in several studies (e.g., Podlesny and Raskin, 1978).

While contamination is inherent to the methods of RIT and CQT because those methods include the pre-test interview as an essential part of the procedure, the GKT could easily be decontaminated by avoiding the pre-test interview altogether and by using blind interrogation procedures or even prerecorded questions.

## Summary and Conclusions

In this chapter, we compared three approaches to designing a polygraph test. We focused on how each approach deals with the problems of choosing control questions and setting sound inference rules. We have not yet dealt with the empirical status of the different methods of polygraph interrogation, so that at this stage the methods have been compared only with respect to their a priori rationales without referring to their accuracy and validity. From our description of the methods and the assumptions underlying them, it is clear that both the RIT approach and the CQT suffer from a fundamental problem: the control questions used by those methods are not equivalent to the relevant questions and, hence, are not genuine controls. Thus, the validity of inference rules based on a comparison of the responses to these two types of questions is shaky. Only under a set of rather strong assumptions can the inference rules of the RIT and the CQT be justified. We examined these assumptions and concluded that thus far there is neither a psychological theory nor empirical evidence that can provide a sound base for those assumptions. Furthermore, the inference rule for the CQT is based to a large extent on the skills of the polygraph examiner in conducting a proper pre-test interview and in presenting the control questions to the suspect in a certain manner. In fact, in order for the CQT to be effective, the suspect must be tricked into believing that the control questions play a different role than they actually do. This has two major implications. First, the CQT is not a standard-

## Summary and Conclusions

ized, objective test in the psychometric sense, because it depends to a great extent on the examiner and on his or her interaction with the suspect. Thus, a single suspect can undergo very different tests when interrogated by several independent polygraph examiners on the same event. Second, the fact that the CQT is based in part on misleading the suspects implies that its use is rather limited. The true nature of the control questions could very easily become known to many suspects, thus jeopardizing the very logic of the CQT's inference rule because innocent suspects familiar with the CQT would not be concerned with the control questions, but only with the relevant ones.

The third approach—the GKT—also stands on certain assumptions, but we have shown that those assumptions are plausible, compatible with psychological theory, and supported by extensive research. Furthermore, the GKT can be designed very much like a standardized and objective test, without a need for special examiner-suspect interactions or complex pre-test interviews.

CHAPTER 3

# Reliability and Validity of Polygraph-Based Classification

In the previous chapters we described various methods of psychophysiological detection and discussed their rationales. The discussion was based on logical and theoretical considerations, and it led us to conclude that only one method, the GKT, is based on a sound rationale, whereas all the other methods suffer from serious logical and theoretical flaws. The proponents of CQT polygraphy, in defending their practice, usually turn to an empirical approach, arguing that since the CQT has proved to be an efficient tool for detecting guilt or deception, the logical arguments raised against it are not relevant. In this chapter we shall closely examine the empirical approach as applied to psychophysiological detection, and in particular, we will try to clarify whether there is indeed any substantial evidence supporting the validity of the CQT.

First, we shall briefly explain the basic concepts involved in any attempt to evaluate empirically the various detection methods. We shall formulate several necessary conditions which any study attempting to assess psychophysiological detection must fulfill. Then, we will review the polygraph validity studies conducted thus far in light of these principles. We shall argue that this set of studies does not meet the necessary requirements and, therefore, does not permit generalization to realistic settings in which the various detection methods are typically used. Nevertheless, we shall present a summary of the research results, differentiating between several classes of studies: those that focus on the CQT vs. those that attempt to evaluate the GKT; and those that use data from real polygraph interrogations vs. experimental studies that have utilized a simulated design. We shall argue that the results of the available research do not provide sufficient evidence for the validity of any psychophysiologically based method for detecting guilt in realistic settings.

## Methodological Considerations

In order to grasp the complexity involved in an empirical attempt to assess psychophysiological detection, it is necessary to understand some of the critical methodological considerations. In many discussions of polygraphy the issues are presented as if there were a simple answer (sometimes expressed as a single number) to the question of how accurate the polygraph is. From Chapters 1 and 2 it is already clear that the accuracy question cannot be presented without specifying the method of polygraphy that is being evaluated and the specific application for which it is being used. However, even for a given method and application, validation is not a simple matter of data collection. If the accuracy question has not been resolved yet, and if different experts have extremely different estimates of the polygraph's validity, it is not only because research has not been extensive enough in this area. Rather, it is also because the question is actually quite complex and because the various experts differ in their methodological approach to the validity issue. To understand the issue, then, we will present a relatively extensive account of the methodological aspects relevant to the evaluation of polygraphy.

## The Concepts of Reliability and Validity

For the purposes of this discussion we shall use the standard terminology of the psychometric and testing literature. Two basic criteria have been standardly applied to the evaluation of psychological and educational tests: reliability and validity. Reliability refers to the consistency (or reproducibility) of the test scores. A test is considered reliable if its results tend to be replicated when the same individuals are tested several times under similar circumstances. In classical reliability theory, reliability is estimated by a correlation between two sets of equivalent measurements, such as administering the same test twice to the same group of subjects or administering two equivalent forms of the same test. In some circumstances reliability is estimated by correlating two sets of scores obtained from two independent observers (or judges) evaluating the performance of a given group in a specified condition. The different types of reliability estimates focus on different sources of inconsistencies, or measurement errors, and the choice of an appropriate reliability coefficient depends on the purposes of the specific measurement and on the desired range of generalizability. Sometimes more than one type of reliability estimate will be required.

In the case of the polygraph the "test scores" are either numerical values that reflect the differences in magnitude of physiological responding to the relevant and control questions (e.g., the "quantified" method suggested by Backster, 1963, or the more objective quantification used more recently by Kircher and Raskin, 1988) or a qualitative classification of the subjects into specified categories (e.g., guilty, innocent, and inconclusive). Reliability of polygraph-based scores, whether expressed by numbers or by qualitative categories, refers to the degree to which these scores tend to be stable across measurement situations. Stability could be estimated by using one of two approaches: (*a*) testing the same individual twice on the same issue, using the same polygraphic method, but having two independent examiners administer the tests; or (*b*) testing the subject just once, but letting two independent experts score the charts. Clearly, the second method yields reliability estimates of very limited use for evaluating psychophysiological detection because two independent examiners could, in principle, reach complete agreement (especially if they were trained by the same polygraph school and if they used a quantified scoring method) despite a very low test-retest consistency. In other words, the second approach relates to just one source of measurement error—errors in chart scoring and interpretation. But the crucial question here is not whether two polygraph examiners could be trained to read a given polygraph chart consistently, but whether the procedure as a whole (including the most critical stage—constructing proper relevant and control questions) is reliable. In order to obtain proper estimates of the polygraph's reliability (i.e., estimates of measurement errors that are related to the test as a whole), one must use the first approach and administer the whole polygraph-based interrogation twice, using two independent examiners.

Unfortunately, reliability studies of polygraph-based classifications are scarce, and, incredibly enough, those that have been conducted have used only the between-examiners agreement approach (e.g., Barland, 1975; Horvath and Reid, 1971). Thus, it is impossible to conclude from the available data whether, or to what extent, a given subject interrogated twice by independent examiners will be similarly classified.

Reliability refers to precision in measurement without specifying the goals of the measurement procedure or the concept being measured. Thus, some tests can produce scores that are very precise and reliable but have no relation to the concept being measured. This is why reliability alone is insufficient for evaluating tests or measurement procedures, and additional criteria must be defined. The most important criterion for evaluating measurement procedures is validity, which refers to the degree to which inferences made on the basis of the test scores are true. In order to assess the validity of inferences made on the basis of a polygraph interrogation, one must have access to the "true state of the world" (i.e., whether the subjects interrogated using a polygraphic procedure are in fact guilty regarding the specific case under investigation). In psychological testing terminology, the true state of the world is labeled the "criterion," and validity is measured by correlating the test scores (in our case judgments made on the basis of the polygraph examination) with the criterion.

Because reliability is only a necessary, but not a sufficient, condition for validity, and because proper reliability estimates of polygraph-based scores or classifications are unavailable, this chapter will focus exclusively on the issue of validity, beginning with what we consider the necessary requirements for a proper study of the validity of psychophysiological detection procedures.

## Necessary Requirements for an Empirical Assessment of Polygraphy

In order to estimate the validity of inferences made on the basis of polygraph-based interrogations, one has to design a scientifically valid study in which those inferences are compared with a criterion. A proper validity study must fulfill certain requirements, especially if the goal is to estimate validity under realistic circumstances. In our discussion of those requirements we will be assuming that the focus of interest is the physiological responses to the questions, rather than other information that might be available to the polygraph examiner. Additionally, we are assuming that the ultimate goal is to generalize the validity results to real-life situations where polygraphs might be used.

## Sound Criteria

A necessary requirement of any validity study is the availability of a good measure of the criterion. It is difficult to fulfill this requirement in many testing situations, but it is particularly difficult in the case of the polygraph. In the large majority of cases the truth—whether the suspect is in fact guilty or innocent—is unknown and cannot be determined with sufficient certitude. In many criminal investigations all of the suspects are dismissed because the evidence is insufficient. Clearly this does not mean that they are all innocent. In other cases even after charges are made and some suspects are brought to trial, the court dismisses the charges because of insufficient evidence. And even when the court renders a verdict, there is no assurance that it matches the truth. This concern is of special weight in societies whose legal procedures are based on an adversary system. Court decisions in such societies may reflect the ability and experience of legal attorneys rather than the absolute truth. Later, we shall present and discuss several solutions that were suggested for the criterion problem, but all of them include some flaws and none is completely satisfactory.

## Noncontaminated Polygraph Results

If the goal of a validity study is to evaluate specifically the psychophysiological component of the polygraph-based interrogation procedure, then it must be guaranteed that the inferences made on the basis of the interrogation are not affected by any other factor than the subject's physiological responses to the questions. As is clear from our description of polygraph interrogation procedures, particularly the CQT, there is usually much more information available to the polygraph examiner than just the pure psychophysiological information—for example, the background of the suspect, information available to the police about the suspect, impressions of other examiners, and impressions formed by the polygraph examiner during the pre-test interview and during the test itself on the basis of the suspect's behavior. It is impossible to differentiate between the effect of the large amount of prior information and that of the specifically psychophysiological information on the inferences made, for which reason these are called contaminated procedures. Whether the inferences are true or false, the basis for them could be attributed to the nonphysiological as well as the physiological information. A proper validity study must take this factor into account and must use a design that guarantees a noncontaminated procedure. We shall elaborate on this issue in our discussion of the "specific-effects approach" in Chapter 5.

## Independence Between Test and Criterion

The measurement of the validation criteria must be completely independent of the test results, as any degree of dependence between the two might bias the validity estimates. Such a dependence could exist either if the measurement of the criterion were directly affected by the test scores or if the two variables were jointly affected by other factors. For example, if court decisions are used as a criterion for validating polygraphy, it must be guaranteed that the court is not exposed to the results of the polygraph interrogation or to the conclusions made by the polygraph examiner before making its decision. Furthermore, it must be guaranteed that the polygraph examiner is not exposed to any of the information available to the court before interrogating the subject and scoring the polygraph charts. As we shall see later, many polygraph validity studies have not been able to establish complete independence between the outcome of the polygraph interrogation and the criterion of guilt vs. innocence.

## External Validity

External validity is a term used to describe the degree to which the results of a given study can be generalized across conditions and across subjects (see, for example, Cook and Campbell, 1979). Generalization (in particular across conditions) is crucial for a polygraph validity study, because the conditions that characterize most experiments in this area are very different from the conditions of the typical criminal interrogation situation. For example, many of the validity studies utilized the "mock crime" design (e.g., Podlesny and Raskin, 1978) in which volunteering subjects are requested by the experimenter to "steal" something from an office and then to deny this "theft" in a subsequent polygraph interrogation. Clearly, this situation differs from the realistic criminal interrogation situation in many ways. Two important distinctions between the two are the nature of the deception (voluntary in the realistic setting vs. induced by an experimenter in the simulated situation) and the potential consequences of the polygraph interrogation for the subject. In the mock crime situation the subject will be released and thanked as soon as the experiment is over, irrespective of the outcome of the polygraph interrogation (in some experiments the subjects will receive a few dollars bonus if found innocent by the examiner); whereas in a criminal interrogation the suspect (whether guilty or innocent) might suffer severe consequences if the outcome of the polygraph-based interrogation is unfavorable. Because of these crucial differences, the external validity of the mock crime procedure is highly questionable (see, for example, Lykken, 1978a, 1979). In the following subsections we shall discuss some critical features that might increase the external validity of a polygraphic validity study.

### Realistic Consequences for the Subject

The mock crime example mentioned above demonstrates the importance of the perceived consequences of the interrogation. The critical question is, of course, whether those differences in the perceived consequences will affect the results of the validity study, and in what direction (e.g., whether the results of a mock crime study might produce inflated or deflated validity estimates). Unfortunately, it is impossible to give a conclusive answer to this question, mainly because empirical evidence is largely unavailable. Nevertheless, we shall try to analyze the problem using common logic. First, it would seem advisable to discuss the issue separately for the GKT and the CQT. In the GKT all items are a priori equivalent and undifferentiated for the innocent subject. Therefore, even if the overall level of concern and anxiety might be affected by the perceived consequences of the test, the relative response to the relevant alternative need not be affected by this factor. In particular, the relative responses of an innocent suspect to the critical item could not be affected by the suspect's level of anxiety as long as he or she does not possess the guilty information.

The situation is, however, entirely different when the CQT is the interrogation method used. The whole logic of this method depends on the ability of the examiner to make the control questions look more threatening for innocent suspects and to make the relevant questions look more threatening for the guilty. This logic was severely criticized in the literature, and critics of CQT polygraphy (e.g., Lykken, 1981) questioned the ability of polygraph examiners to create such a differential concern about the different types of questions for the different kinds of subjects. However, in our mock crime example there is very little threat involved in the relevant questions. Thus, one can argue that in this situation it might be relatively easy to formulate control questions (which, unlike the relevant ones, relate to real events from the subject's life history) that would be more threatening for an innocent suspect than the relevant questions that are related to a simulated event which is of absolutely no concern to an innocent subject. Thus, mock crime experiments are likely to yield considerably underestimated rates of false-positive errors as compared with the more realistic situation in which real suspects are interrogated about real crimes. By the same token it could be argued that the guilty subject in a simulated situation might show less relative responsivity to the relevant questions than an actual guilty individual in a real criminal interrogation. This argument can be made because the control questions are of a similar nature in both the simulated and the real situation, and the difference between the two situations lies only in the nature of the relevant questions. On the other hand, the subjects simulating the guilty are to some extent involved in a crime, though simulated, and their "criminal" act might give some meaning and significance to the relevant questions. Therefore, the overestimation of false-negative errors should be less serious than the underestimation of false-positive errors in simulated validity studies. Clearly, the extent of bias in estimating the error rates in mock crime studies is unknown, but it is important to realize that such a bias is very likely to occur and that it might artificially decrease the false-positive rate and increase the false negatives.

## Voluntary Perpetration of the Crime

A second factor that might be important for maintaining external validity is the nature of the crime. There is a very significant difference between an illegal act, or a deception, performed because the subject chose to do it and an act performed in an experimental context because an experimenter told the subject to do it. In fact, it could be argued that when a subject in an experiment, in following the instructions of the experimenter, does not tell the truth, that subject is not really deceiving. In the typical mock crime situation, subjects are just following instructions, and none of their acts are performed out of their own choice. It is very doubtful whether they perceive themselves as deceptive in this artificial situation. Therefore a proper validity study of polygraphy should include the crucial element of a voluntary deception or illegal action.

Subjects Should Be Unaware of the Experimental Nature of the Situation

In an experimental situation it is usually clear that the "truth" is known to the experimenter (e.g., the card chosen by the subject in a card test design), and therefore the subject knows that ultimately the "deception" will be revealed. This is clearly not the case in a real polygraph interrogation, and this distinction between the simulated and the real situation is an additional factor that might interfere with external validity.

## Solutions Provided by Current Research

In the previous section we laid out several methodological problems that might interfere with any empirical attempt to estimate the accuracy of polygraph-based interrogations. In this section we wish to discuss various solutions that have been offered to those problems by researchers attempting to validate psychophysiological detection methods. These solutions can be classified into two general classes: (*a*) studies conducted under controlled laboratory conditions which usually provide high levels of internal validity but pay a heavy price in terms of external validity and (*b*) studies which use data from real polygraph investigations, thereby achieving satisfactory levels of external validity, but which are questionable with respect to all other methodological problems, especially the verification of the criterion and its independence of the outcomes of the polygraph interrogation.

### *Experimental Attempts to Validate Psychophysiological Detection*

Experiments designed to examine the validity of polygraphic methods have typically used the mock crime procedure mentioned in the previous section. This procedure was employed mostly by Raskin and his colleagues at the University of Utah (e.g., Barland and Raskin, 1975a; Kircher and Raskin, 1988; Podlesny and Raskin, 1978; Raskin and Hare, 1978), and to a smaller extent by other researchers (e.g., Dawson, 1980). Mock crime experiments utilize true experimental designs in that they allocate the subjects randomly into "guilty" and "innocent" conditions. The typical mock crime procedure involves a simulated event in which subjects in one group, simulating the "guilty" condition, are instructed by the experimenter to perform some act (e.g., to enter an office after the secretary has left it and take an envelope containing a $10 bill from a desk in the office). Subjects simulating the "innocent" condition do not perform that act and are not involved with it. In the second stage, all subjects, both "innocent" and "guilty," are interrogated by a "blind" polygraph examiner. This design answers many of the methodological concerns raised. Regarding the former sorts of concerns, there is complete assurance about who is guilty and who is innocent. Also, the random assignment of subjects into conditions and the double-blind procedure guarantee an independence between the criterion and the physiological data. As for the concern that the physiological data themselves are contaminated, this problem is not solved by using "blind" examiners to score the physiological charts, because the examiner's prior expectations could affect the physiological responses to the questions.

The methodological concern that this experimental approach to the problem of validating polygraphy completely fails to satisfy is that of external validity. None of the conditions necessary for maintaining external validity are satisfied by the mock crime design. The subjects participating in these experiments are always aware of the simulated nature of their task, they know that no harm will be inflicted upon them irrespective of the outcome of the polygraph's interrogation, and they are not really deceiving because they are acting in accordance with the experimenter's demands. Therefore, despite the above-mentioned advantages of the mock crime design, it is nevertheless impossible to make any generalizations from the results of simulated validity studies to the real situation where real suspects are interrogated regarding real crimes.

## *Field Studies Designed to Validate Polygraphy*

An alternative to the experimental approach for validating polygraphy, and one that has been used by many researchers, is to take polygraph charts from actual interrogations and match them with some criterion. Two types of criteria have been used in the various field studies: (*a*) judgments made by a panel of legal experts who are privy to all the information gathered about the case, except for the polygraph results, and (*b*) the use of a restricted sample of cases for whom guilt or innocence can be determined through there having been a confession of guilt by one of the suspects (such a confession virtually makes the confessed individual a "verified" guilty suspect, while all the other suspects in the same crime become the "verified" innocent suspects). The first approach was used in just a few studies (e.g., Barland and Raskin, 1976; Bersh, 1969), while the confession criterion has been used quite frequently (e.g., Horvath, 1977; Hunter and Ash, 1973; Kleinmuntz and Szucko, 1984b; Slowick and Buckley, 1975).

Both of these approaches suffer from serious methodological flaws related to their choice of criteria. The panel criterion is problematic because (*a*) it is based on judgments which might be wrong and (*b*) the judgments made by the panel are not really independent of the judgments made by polygraphers. Although the legal experts do not have access to the actual polygraph results, dependency might be introduced because the panelists and the polygraph examiner might have been exposed to the same information, and as was argued before, the conclusions drawn by the polygraph examiner may reflect the examiner's prior knowledge rather than the objective physiological responses of the examinee.

The use of confessions as criterion might be even more problematic than the use of legal experts. Unfortunately, it is impossible to assume that confessions are independent of the outcomes of the polygraph interrogation. Polygraph-based interrogations are not designed just to discover the truth, but they typically have a confession-inducing function as well (see, for example, Furedy and Liss, 1986). Polygraphers are more likely to try to induce a confession from a suspect whose chart shows clear signs of deception than from a suspect whose chart does not have such signs. Thus, a guilty suspect who showed larger responses to the control questions than to the relevant ones, and therefore was classified as innocent by the polygraph examiner, is less likely to be included in the confession-criterion studies. In other words, the sample in the typical confession-criterion validity study will be biased, inasmuch as it includes an underrepresentative proportion of false-negative errors (guilty subjects classified as innocent by the polygrapher). Recently, Iacono (1989) argued and demonstrated how a polygraph examiner functioning at an overall chance-level accuracy rate might accumulate a sample of polygraph records from confessed suspects with a near perfect accuracy level.

## *An Alternative Methodology for the Validation of Polygraphy*

A unique attempt to study polygraphy in a realistic situation, and at the same time maintain complete control over the criterion, was made by Ginton, Daie, Elaad, and Ben-Shakhar (1982). This study was designed to meet all the necessary requirements discussed in the previous sections. The subjects in the Ginton et al. experiment were 21 Israeli policemen participating in a police course. They were given a paper-and-pencil test that was presented as a requirement of the course. Beneath the answer sheet there was a hidden chemical page that received an impression of what was written on the answer sheet. After completion of the test, the answer sheet was separated from the rest of the pages and handed back to the subjects. The correct answer keys were then handed out and the subjects were asked to score their own tests, which gave them an opportunity to cheat by revising their initial answers. However, it was possible to know exactly whether and how each subject had tampered with his answer sheet by comparing it with the chemical copy with the original answers. It turned out that seven of the subjects cheated while scoring their tests. Later, subjects were told that they were suspected of cheating, were offered an opportunity to take a polygraph examination, and were told that their future careers in the police force might depend on the outcome of this examination.

Under this design the deception is authentic, both guilty and innocent subjects are truly concerned with the outcome of the interrogation, and yet there is no question about the validity of the criterion. Unfortunately, this study demonstrates, more than any of the other validity studies, how difficult the mission of validating polygraphy really is. Although initially all 21 subjects agreed to be polygraphed, at a later stage one guilty subject did not show up for the examination, and two subjects (one guilty and one innocent) refused to take it. Three other guilty subjects confessed just before the polygraph interrogation, so the final sample included only two guilty and thirteen innocent subjects. This rendered the drawing of conclusions very difficult.

# Review of the Various Attempts to Estimate the Validity of Psychophysiological Detection

Systematic attempts to validate the different methods of psychophysiological detection began in the early sixties, but it took about two decades for data to accumulate. At present there are a few dozen published reports that focus on the validity issue, and several reviews and summaries of these studies have been published (e.g., Ben-Shakhar, Lieblich, and Bar-Hillel, 1982; Kircher, Horowitz, and Raskin, 1988; Saxe, Dougherty, and Cross, 1985). The studies can be classified into four categories, using the following two-by-two classification: studies attempting to validate the CQT vs. studies focusing on the GKT; and studies that use a simulated design vs. those that use data from real polygraph interrogations. Actually, only three of the four possible categories will be reviewed, because all the GKT studies used experimental designs and were conducted in controlled laboratory conditions, so that field studies validating the GKT are unavailable.

## Experimental Attempts to Validate the CQT

This category consists of simulated mock crime studies. We use the term "experimental" in the sense that those studies are based on an experimental design insofar as the subjects are randomly allocated to treatments (in our case "guilty" and "innocent"), where only the "guilty" subjects commit the mock crime at the request of the experimenter. Typically, the guilty and innocent groups are of equal size, and the subjects are either university students or individuals recruited from the community through classified newspaper advertisements. The experiment is conducted in two stages: in the first, "guilty" subjects are instructed to commit the mock crime (e.g., to steal a ring from a secretary's desk), while subjects simulating the innocent condition are engaged in some neutral activity. In the second stage all subjects undergo a standard CQT polygraph interrogation by an examiner who is unaware of their particular experimental condition. The charts are then evaluated either by the original examiner or by another examiner who does not know anything about the subject, or, in some studies, by both. The evaluation of the charts has been done by the global subjective method, by the semiobjective, semiquantified method originally suggested by Backster (1963), or by both methods. Usually, subjects in both conditions receive a bonus if found innocent by the polygraph examiner.

The first systematic attempt to apply the mock crime paradigm to estimate the validity of the CQT was carried out by Barland and Raskin (1975a). Their sample consisted of 72 students who volunteered to participate in the experiment. Half the subjects committed the mock crime, and all subjects were interrogated using the standard CQT procedure, including the pre-test interview. The subjects were promised a $10 bonus if found innocent by the examiner. The polygraph charts were evaluated by the original examiner using a version of the numerical scoring technique suggested by Backster (1963). The subjects were further divided into three feedback conditions (feedback was provided on the basis of a card test). In the positive-feedback condition subjects were led to believe that the polygraph was effective; in the negative-feedback condition they were led to believe that the machine was not working properly; in the third condition no feedback was provided to the subjects. The results across feedback conditions indicated that 63.9% of the subjects simulating the guilty condition were correctly detected, 8.3% were classified as innocent (false-negative errors), and 27.8% of them were inconclusives. The rate of correct detection in the innocent condition was 41.7%, with 16.7% false-positive and 41.7% inconclusive.

In a subsequent study Podlesny and Raskin (1978) extended the previous experiment and included two versions of the CQT as well as the GKT. Subjects were recruited from the local community, were allocated to the guilty and innocent conditions, and were offered a $10 bonus for appearing truthful on the lie detector test. Twenty subjects in each condition were interrogated using the CQT. Charts were scored using the numerical scoring technique by an independent blind evaluator who had no contact with the subjects. The combined results of both CQT versions indicated 15% false-negative and 5% false-positive errors. The inconclusive rate was 10%.

In an additional study that used the mock crime design, Raskin and Hare (1978) examined a sample of 48 prisoner inmates, half of which were selected for high levels of psychopathy (by a clinical assessment) and half for low levels. The prisoners volunteered for the experiment and were offered a $20 bonus for producing truthful polygraph charts. The evaluation of the polygraph charts was done by the original examiner using the numerical method. Among the 24 subjects simulating the guilty condition, 87.5% were correctly detected, with 12.5% inconclusives and no false negatives. In the innocent condition 75% were correctly classified, with 4.2% false-positive errors and 20.8% inconclusive decisions.

Recently, Patrick and Iacono (1989) conducted a constructive replication of the Raskin and Hare study with the following modifications: (a) Instead of offering the subjects a monetary reward for producing favorable polygraph results, Patrick and Iacono used a group contingency threat procedure. The subjects (who were prisoner inmates) were led to believe that their personal performance on the polygraph test could decide benefits and penalties for the whole group. (b) Patrick and Iacono (1989) used a blind scoring procedure in addition to the original examiner's evaluations of the polygraph charts. Based on the blind scoring they obtained 83.3% correct classifications among the 24 subjects simulating the guilty condition, with 12.5% false negative outcomes and 4.2% inconclusive decisions. On the other hand, only 41.7% of the 24 subjects simulating the innocent condition were correctly classified, with 33.3% false positives and 25% inconclusive decisions.

Another study conducted by Raskin and his colleagues (Honts, Hodes, and Raskin, 1985) focused on the effects of countermeasures on the accuracy of the CQT. The countermeasures issue will be discussed at length in Chapter 4, but in this chapter we shall report the results of the Honts et al. (1985) study based on the conditions which did not include the countermeasure instructions. Two experiments were conducted by Honts et al. using samples of students and the standard mock crime procedure. The polygraph charts were numerically evaluated by both the original and an independent examiner using two versions of the numerical scoring method. Only the results of the independent evaluator using the Utah version of the numerical scoring technique (which according to Honts et al. removes biases against the innocent subjects that exist in the original Backster method) will be reported here. The combined results of the two experiments, based on the innocent condition and on the control guilty condition (where no countermeasure instructions were given), indicate that 77.4% of the 31 subjects simulating the guilty condition were correctly detected; 3.2% of those subjects were misclassified (false negatives) and 19.4% of the decisions were inconclusives. Among the 31 subjects simulating the innocents, 45.2% were correctly identified, with 19.4% false positives and 35.5% inconclusive decisions.

In a more recent study by the University of Utah group, Kircher and Raskin (1988) tried to computerize the various physiological measures for detection. They generated a discriminant function based on a sample of 100 subjects recruited from the local community, and then used an additional sample of 48 subjects to cross-validate the obtained discriminant function. Both samples were equally divided between the guilty and innocent conditions, and the procedure was similar to the one used in the other mock crime experiments. In addition to the computerized data analyses, the charts were evaluated by an examiner who had no contact with the subjects, using a numerical scoring method similar to those used in the other mock crime studies. Because there were no significant differences between the computerized and the human evaluations, only the latter will be reported in order to permit comparisons to the other mock crime studies. The results based on a combination of the two samples indicate that among the 74 subjects in the guilty condition, 87.8% were correctly detected, with 4.1% false negatives and 8.1% inconclusive decisions. In the innocent condition, 85.1% of the subjects were correctly classified, with 6.8% false positives and 8.1% inconclusives.

Very few mock crime studies have been conducted by researchers not associated with Raskin and his group. One such study was reported by Dawson (1980), who used a sample of 24 actors trained in the Stanislavsky acting method. The subjects were randomly allocated to the guilty and innocent conditions, and all of them were instructed to use their acting method to appear innocent on the polygraph test. In addition to the standard CQT method, another method was used in which subjects were asked to delay their answers to the questions. Only the results based on the more common immediate answer test will be reported here. The polygraph charts were evaluated by the original examiner using a numerical scoring technique similar to the one used in the previously mentioned mock crime studies. The results revealed a 91.7% correct detection rate among the 12 guilty subjects, with 8.3% inconclusive decisions and no false-negative errors. In the innocent condition, on the other hand, there were 58.3% correct decisions, with 25% false-positive errors and 16.7% inconclusive decisions.

Szucko and Kleinmuntz (1981) conducted a mock crime study attempting to compare the ability of polygraph examiners to classify subjects into guilty and innocent groups to a computer-generated statistical model. They used a sample of 30 students, who were randomly assigned to guilty and innocent conditions. The subjects were interrogated by four examiner trainees who used the CQT, and the charts were evaluated by an independent group of six experienced polygraph interpreters. The evaluations of the charts were rated on a scale of 1 to 8, where 1 represented a "definitely truthful" judgment and 8 represented a "definitely untruthful" judgment. A cutoff point was set at 5, such that a score equal to or greater than 5 yielded a classification of the subject as guilty and a score of less than 5 resulted in a classification of the subject as innocent. The average rates of correct and incorrect classifications based on this decision rule revealed that 70.7% of the 15 guilty subjects were correctly identified, with a 29.3% false-negative rate. The average correct detection rate among innocent subjects was, however, only 51.3%, with a 48.7% false-positive rate.

The last study we shall review in this category is the Ginton et al. (1982) experiment which was described earlier. Actually, this is not a mock crime study, because the act of deception was undertaken voluntarily by the subjects rather than at the request of the experimenter. In addition, the subjects were not aware of the experimental nature of their polygraph interrogation. Nevertheless, we have decided to include it in the experimental category because, unlike all field studies, the criterion was completely verifiable. The results, based on numerical scoring of the polygraph charts conducted by an examiner who had no contact with the subjects, revealed that one of the two guilty subjects was correctly detected, while the other was classified as inconclusive. Among the 13 innocent subjects, 38.5% were correctly identified, with 7.7% false positives and 53.8% inconclusives.

The studies included in our review are described in Table 3.1. The table includes a summary of the results of each study, as well as the weighted averages of the accuracy rates across studies.

The overall results of the mock crime studies provide a relatively favorable picture for the CQT—80% of the guilty subjects and 63% of the innocents were correctly classified (against a chance expectancy of 50%). However, one must keep in mind the severe limitations of these studies and in particular their weak external validity. Thus, it is impossible to make any generalizations from these results to real-life conditions where CQT polygraphy is actually used. Furthermore, as our methodological discussion indicates, there are compelling reasons for believing that the false-positive rates obtained in the mock crime experiments are biased and that they underestimate the false positives that might be obtained in real setups. It is therefore interesting to note that in eight out of the nine studies reviewed, the false-positive rates exceeded the rates of false-negative errors,

TABLE 3.1. Summary of the results of mock crime studies attempting to validate the CQT.

| Study | Sample | Method of chart interpretation | Guilty condition | | | | Innocent condition | | | |
|---|---|---|---|---|---|---|---|---|---|---|
| | | | N | Percent of correct decisions | Percent of false-negative errors | Percent of inconclusive decisions | N | Percent of correct decisions | Percent of false-positive errors | Percent of inconclusive decisions |
| Barland and Raskin (1975a) | 72 students | Numerical evaluations by original examiner | 36 | 63.9 | 8.3 | 27.8 | 36 | 41.7 | 16.7 | 41.7 |
| Dawson (1980) | 24 actors | Numerical evaluations by original examiner | 12 | 91.7 | 0.0 | 8.3 | 12 | 58.3 | 25.0 | 16.7 |
| Ginton et al. (1982) | 15 policemen | Numerical evaluations by blind interpreter | 2 | 50.0 | 0.0 | 50.0 | 13 | 38.5 | 7.7 | 53.8 |
| Honts* et al. (1985) | 62 students | Numerical evaluations by blind interpreter | 31 | 77.4 | 3.2 | 19.4 | 31 | 45.2 | 19.4 | 35.5 |
| Kircher and Raskin (1988) | 148 adult males from the local community | Numerical evaluations by blind interpreter | 74 | 87.8 | 4.1 | 8.1 | 74 | 85.1 | 6.8 | 8.1 |
| Patrick and Iacono (1989) | 48 prisoners | Numerical evaluations by blind interpreter | 24 | 83.3 | 12.5 | 4.2 | 24 | 41.7 | 33.3 | 25.0 |
| Podlesny and Raskin (1978) | 40 adult males, recruited from the local community | Numerical evaluations by blind interpreter | 20 | 75.0 | 15.0 | 10.0 | 20 | 85.0 | 5.0 | 10.0 |

TABLE 3.1. *Continued.*

| Study | Sample | Method of chart interpretation | Guilty condition | | | | Innocent condition | | | |
|---|---|---|---|---|---|---|---|---|---|---|
| | | | N | Percent of correct decisions | Percent of false-negative errors | Percent of inconclusive decisions | N | Percent of correct decisions | Percent of false-positive errors | Percent of inconclusive decisions |
| Raskin and Hare (1978) | 48 prisoners | Numerical evaluations by original examiner | 24 | 87.5 | 0.0 | 12.5 | 24 | 75.0 | 4.2 | 20.8 |
| Szuco and Kleinmuntz (1981) | 30 students | Evaluations by independent judges | 15 | 70.7 | 29.3 | + | 15 | 51.3 | 48.7 | + |
| Weighted averages | | | 238 | 80.1 | 7.3 | 12.6 | 249 | 62.9 | 15.4 | 21.7 |

*Data from two experiments excluding the countermeasure conditions.
+ The decision rule did not allow for an inconclusive category.

sometimes by quite a large margin. For example, Dawson (1980) reported 25% false positives and no false negatives; Szucko and Kleinmuntz (1981) obtained a false-positive rate of 49% vs. 29% false negatives, and Patrick and Iacono (1989) reported 33.3% and 12.5% false positives and false negatives, respectively. Across studies the false-positive rate is twice as high as the false-negative rate. Our comparison of the mock crime and the real interrogative situations leads to the conclusion that in real setups the ratio of the false-positive rate to the false-negative rate might be much larger than 2:1. We shall elaborate on the implications of this issue in Chapter 8.

Other reviews of the mock crime literature (e.g., Kircher et al. 1988; U.S. Congress, 1983) include a somewhat different list of studies. For example, the study of Bradley and Janisse (1981a) is included in previous reviews but not in ours, because it reported accuracy rates based on single physiological measures rather than the overall results. The Bradley and Ainsworth (1984) study is included in the Kircher et al. review, but since most subjects either committed the mock crime or were interrogated in a state of intoxication, we chose not to include it in our report. Both of those studies will be discussed in the next chapter. The studies by Rovner, Raskin, and Kircher (1979) and by Kircher and Raskin (1982) were not mentioned because their data were used by Kircher and Raskin (1988) and were included in our review under the Kircher and Raskin (1988) label.

In addition, it should be noted that some of the entries in Table 3.1 differ slightly from the equivalent entries reported in earlier reviews. For example, Kircher et al. (1988) cite the results of the Dawson (1980) study as though all the guilty subjects and 75% of the innocents were correctly identified on the basis of the immediate answer test alone. As can be seen in Table 1 of Dawson (1980, p. 11), these rates are not the ones reported in the original study. Kircher and Raskin tend to inflate the accuracy rates of the Ginton et al. (1982) study as well. They report 100% correct detections for the guilty subjects and 85% for the innocents. These figures represent the rates achieved by the original examiners using global evaluations. In all the other cases Kircher and Raskin prefer (for good reasons) the numerical scoring techniques and the blind chart evaluation procedures. As can be seen in Ginton et al. (1982, p. 134), the results based on those preferred procedures are much inferior. We note this point because it demonstrates the dangers involved in reviews and meta-analytic treatments of complex studies. Typically, polygraph validity studies include a large variety of results based on various techniques, measures, etc. Therefore, it is always necessary to make some selection in the results that are reported in a given review. However, one has to be extremely cautious when making such selections, in order to avoid a biased presentation of the results.

## Field Studies Attempting to Assess the Validity of the CQT

The validity studies we shall review in this section studied the CQT using data gathered from actual polygraph interrogations. They enjoy much greater external validity than the studies reviewed in the preceding section, but they suffer from other serious methodological weaknesses, such as unclear criteria and selection biases (in particular, in the selection of subjects for the guilty condition). The majority of field studies used confessions as the basis for their criteria, and for those studies, therefore, only subsamples of confessed suspects were used. Few studies utilized a panel of experts to assess the guilt or innocence of the subjects. Both types of studies are described in Table 3.2, which was constructed following the example set by Ben-Shakhar, Lieblich, and Bar-Hillel (1982), with few additional studies included. We shall not describe each individual study, but present the main results of each study, as well as the weighted averages of the different outcomes. Finally we shall discuss the results and their implications.

The validity studies included in our review differ from each other in many respects. The selection of cases differs from one study to another, and in many studies the selection process is not even specified. Some critiques have raised the possibility that it is biased in favor of the polygraph (see, for example, Ben-Shakhar, Lieblich, and Bar-Hillel, 1982). The scoring of the charts is also not uniform. In most studies the charts were globally evaluated, with no attempt to assign numerical values to the various comparisons of relevant and control questions. In some studies the charts were evaluated by the original examiner (thus increasing the amount of possible contamination), while in others an independent (blind) judge who had no contact with the suspects made the evaluations. In some cases the scoring procedure did not allow for the inconclusive category, thus inflating both the rates of correct classifications and the error rates relative to studies which allowed for inconclusives. The definition of the criterion in the panel-criterion studies was based on a majority decision of the panel. In some cases, however, the panel could not even reach a majority decision. Those cases were excluded from the statistical analysis, but they appear in Table 3.2 under the label "inconclusive by the criterion." In many studies the charts were evaluated by several interpreters. In these cases the statistics in Table 3.2 represent averages across the different judges.

The overall results of Table 3.2 indicate that both rates of correct detections are better than a chance expectancy level (50%). A comparison between the results displayed in Table 3.2 and those described in the previous section reveals that in both cases the rate of false positives is much larger than the false-negative rate. However, the results of the field studies are less stable than those obtained under the mock crime situation. For example, the false-positive rate in the field studies ranges between 5% and 50%. The reasons for these rather large variations are unclear. One cannot argue that the large error rates were obtained as a result of using improper polygraph procedures because the two studies in which the largest rates of false positives were obtained were conducted by very experienced polygraphers (Barland, 1975; Horvath, 1977). It is interesting to note that those two studies were conducted under careful academic supervision, as they were the basis for Ph.D. dissertations. On the other hand, most of the studies in which small error rates were obtained were conducted by polygraph examiners working in a private polygraph firm (John Reid and Associates). This fact together with all

TABLE 3.2. Results of field studies attempting to assess the validity of the CQT.

| Study | Method of chart interpretation | Number of independent evaluations | Total sample size | Guilty suspects ||||| Innocent suspects ||||| Type of criterion |
|---|---|---|---|---|---|---|---|---|---|---|---|---|---|---|
| | | | | N | Percent of correct decisions | Percent of false negatives | Percent of inconclusive decisions | | N | Percent of correct decisions | Percent of false positives | Percent of inconclusive decisions | | |
| Barland* (1975) | Numerical scoring by original examiner | 1 | 64 | 35 | 94.3 | 0.0 | 5.7 | | 20 | 20.0 | 50.0 | 30.0 | | Panel of experts |
| Barland and Raskin+ (1976) | Numerical evaluation by a blind interpreter | 1 | 92 | 47 | 83.0 | 2.1 | 14.9 | | 17 | 29.4 | 35.3 | 35.3 | | Panel of experts |
| Bersh‡ (1969) | Global evaluation by the original examiner | 1 | 243 | 104 | 85.6 | 14.4 | — | | 112 | 89.3 | 10.7 | — | | Panel of experts |
| Horvath (1977) | Global evaluation by a blind interpreter | 10 | 56 | 28 | 77.1 | 22.9 | — | | 28 | 51.1 | 48.9 | — | | Confession |
| Horvath and Reid (1971) | Global evaluation by a blind interpreter | 10 | 40 | 20 | 85.0 | 15.0 | — | | 20 | 90.5 | 9.5 | — | | Confession |
| Hunter and Ash§ (1973) | Global evaluation by a blind interpreter | 7 | 20 | 10 | 87.1 | 10.0 | 2.9 | | 10 | 85.7 | 14.3 | — | | Confession |
| Kleinmuntz and Szucko (1982) | Global evaluation by a blind interpreter using a 1–8 scale | 6 | 100 | 50 | 76.0 | 24.0 | — | | 50 | 62.7 | 37.3 | — | | Confession |
| Slowick and Buckley (1975) | Global evaluation by a blind interpreter | 7 | 30 | 15 | 83.8 | 15.2 | 1.0 | | 15 | 90.5 | 6.7 | 2.9 | | Confession |
| Wicklander and Hunter (1975) | Global evaluation by a blind interpreter | 6 | 20 | 10 | 90.0 | 8.3 | 1.7 | | 10 | 86.7 | 5.0 | 8.3 | | Confession |
| Weighted averages | | | 665 | 319 | 84.0 | 13.0 | 3.0 | | 282 | 72.2 | 23.1 | 4.7 | | |

*In nine cases the panel was unable to reach a decision.
+In 28 cases the panel was unable to reach a decision.
‡An additional 80 cases were excluded from the study by Bersh because their files contained insufficient information, and in 27 cases the panel was unable to reach a decision.
§Only the first analysis of the charts is reported.

the methodological concerns raised earlier (e.g., contaminated polygraph interrogations, contaminated criteria, biased samples) leads us to treat the results of the field studies with great caution; at best they should be regarded as providing upper limits to the accuracy rates achievable by polygraphers using the CQT in the field.

Note that the rates of both types of errors were larger in the field than in the simulation condition. This is not surprising with regard to the false-positive errors, because, as was noted earlier, the mock crime procedure is likely to produce underestimated values for this type of error. On the other hand, the sample selection in the confession-criterion studies is likely to bias the false-negative errors and to produce underestimated rates for them. Therefore it is quite surprising that the false-negative rate in the field studies (13%) is almost twice as high as the rate obtained in the simulated studies (6.7%). This observation demonstrates once again the weaknesses of the mock crime procedure and the dangers involved in any attempt to generalize from the results of studies based on such a design. The rate of 13% false negative should certainly be taken as a lower bound for the true rate that might be obtained in real CQT polygraph interrogations.

The fact that the false-positive rates exceed the rates of false negatives may be interpreted in two ways. First, these results may simply reflect the inherent weakness of the CQT rationale and the lack of equivalence between the control and the relevant questions. As was pointed out by Lykken (e.g., 1974, 1981), it is naive to assume that the innocent will be little concerned with the relevant questions in a real-life situation. Consequently, it is not surprising that the innocent suspect often shows larger levels of physiological responding to the relevant questions than to the control ones. On the other hand, it should be recalled that the decision rules that guide polygraph examiners are completely arbitrary. In fact, polygraphers are free to choose decision rules and cutoff points as they please, and, in particular, they can use nonsymmetrical rules (e.g., using the field numerical scoring technique, they could classify suspects as guilty on the basis of scores of $-10$ or less, and they could make an innocence classification of any suspect showing a score greater than $-5$). Thus, the relatively high false-positive rates may reflect the polygraphers value system which is biased in favor of correctly identifying guilty suspects, even at the price of increasing the rates of false-positive errors. This interpretation sharply contrasts with the claims often made by proponents of CQT polygraphy: that the procedure protects the innocent.

## Experiments Designed to Assess the Validity of the GKT

A large number of studies have used one or another version of the GKT. Most were conducted as experiments designed to examine the effects of certain manipulations, such as level of motivation or type of verbal response on psychophysiological differentiation. These experiments will be described in the next chapter. In this section we will focus exclusively on the validity issue, and therefore only a subset of GKT studies will be reviewed: these used the guilty person version of the GKT (i.e., where the goal is to classify subjects into guilty vs. innocent categories rather than to detect relevant information within each subject). Studies that used simply a card test and studies that did not include a control group of subjects simulating the innocent (subjects with no guilty knowledge) were excluded. Most studies used the mock crime design and several GKT questions pertaining to various aspects of the mock crime (e.g., the amount of money that was stolen, the location of the weapon that was used). In some studies the guilty subjects were instructed to learn several code words (e.g., Waid, Orne, Cook, and Orne, 1978). Some studies were excluded because the GKT questions were always presented following the administration of a CQT procedure (e.g., Bradley and Janisse, 1981a; Waid, Orne, and Wilson, 1979a).

Most studies designed to examine the validity of the GKT conformed to Lykken's pioneering attempt to study the GKT by incorporating his procedures and scoring methods. Lykken (1959) constructed six GKT questions, each with four or five alternative answers, one of which represented the guilty knowledge. All the alternatives were ranked, within each question, according to the GSR amplitude elicited by them (only the electrodermal measure was used in this as well as in most subsequent studies). Each question was assigned a score of 2 if the largest response was elicited by the relevant alternative and a score of 1 if the second largest amplitude occurred to that alternative. In all other cases the question was assigned a score of 0. These scores were summed across the six questions for each subject, thus forming a scale ranging from 0 to 12. A value of 0 on this scale would mean a perfect innocence score, while a maximal value of 12 would mean a perfect guilty score. Lykken constructed a decision rule on the basis of this scale, such that all subjects scoring greater than 6 would be classified as guilty, while subjects whose scores were less than or equal to 6 would be labeled innocents. Most researchers that followed Lykken adopted both his scoring method and his decision rule. Usually when a different number of questions was used, the cutoff point was set at a value of $x$, where $x$ stood for the number of GKT questions (thus, a guilty classification could not be reached unless the subject gave a maximal response to the relevant alternative in at least one question).

Ten studies were selected, and their summarized results are displayed in Table 3.3. The table contains some basic information about the sample, as well as the number of GKT questions used in each study. This, we believe, is essential information because clearly a single question is insufficient and might yield large false-positive rates. In addition, increasing the number of questions might be associated with an increased detection efficiency (for example, Lieblich, Naftali, Shmueli, and Kugelmass, 1974, demonstrated an increase in detection rate from 55% to 60% in a single card-test-type question to 93%–96% on the basis of ten questions). The number of alternative answers per question varied in the nine studies between four and six. All nine studies used the electrodermal measure, most of them as the sole measure. Therefore, the results reported in Table 3.3 are based only on this measure. We shall discuss the issue of comparing the various measures in the next chapter.

TABLE 3.3. Results of experimental attempts to assess the validity of the GKT.

| Study | Sample | Number of GKT questions | Guilty condition ||| Innocent condition |||
|---|---|---|---|---|---|---|---|---|
| | | | N | Percent of correct decisions | Percent of false-negative errors | N | Percent of correct decisions | Percent of false-positive errors |
| Balloun and Holmes (1979) | 34 male students selected using the Pd scale of the MMPI | 5 | 18 | 61.1 | 38.9 | 16 | 87.5 | 12.5 |
| Bradley and Ainsworth (1984) | 40 male students | 9 | 8 | 100.0 | 0.0 | 4 | 100.0 | 0.0 |
| Bradley and Warfield (1984) | 40 university students | 10 | 8 | 100.0 | 0.0 | 8 | 100.0 | 0.0 |
| Davidson (1968) | 48 volunteer college students | 6 | 12 | 91.7 | 8.3 | 36 | 100.0 | 0.0 |
| Giesen and Rollison (1980) | 40 female students | 6 | 20 | 95.0 | 5.0 | 20 | 100.0 | 0.0 |
| Lykken (1959) | 49 male students | 6 | 37 | 86.5 | 13.5 | 12 | 100.0 | 0.0 |
| Podlesney and Raskin (1978) | 20 males recruited from the local community | 5 | 10 | 90.0 | 10.0 | 10 | 100.0 | 0.0 |
| Steller et al. (1987) | 87 police investigators | 6 | 47 | 85.1 | 14.9 | 40 | 100.0 | 0.0 |
| Stern et al. (1981) | 52 students | 6 | 26 | 96.2 | 3.8 | 26 | 88.5 | 11.5 |
| Waid et al. (1978) | 98 male college students | 6 | 62 | 72.6 | 27.4 | 36 | 80.6 | 19.4 |
| Weighted averages | | | 248 | 83.9 | 16.1 | 208 | 94.2 | 5.8 |

The table includes only a few essential features of each study, and it should be recalled that the studies differed in many other respects, such as their manipulations and samples. We shall not describe the studies in detail, but will mention some of their unique characteristics that might be relevant for evaluating and interpreting the results.

Balloun and Holmes (1979) used a unique design which is probably the best approximation to the real-life interrogation situation. Their subjects took a written intelligence test on which they were urged to cheat by confederates posing as other subjects. About half of the subjects actually cheated, and all subjects took a GKT test designed to detect whether they cheated or not. This design (like the design used by Ginton et al., 1982) increases the external validity of the study, but on the other hand it should be noted that a nonrandom sample was used in this study. Subjects were selected from a class of 300 male undergraduate students according to their scores on the "psychopathic deviate" (Pd) scale of the MMPI. Eighteen subjects were selected because they scored high on that scale, and sixteen were low-Pd scorers.

Only the results of the first test are reported in Table 3.3. The detection rates in a second test were much lower, perhaps as a result of habituation effects. In addition to the electrodermal measure, Balloun and Holmes used some cardiovascular measures. However, they did not report the detection rates based on these additional measures, but only indicated that these measures were ineffective for the detection of guilt.

Bradley and Ainsworth (1984) focused on the effects of alcohol intoxication on the efficiency of the GKT. Because a state of intoxication may be atypical and unrepresentative of the regular interrogation setup, we decided to include only the data from the control groups used in that study (i.e., subjects who committed the mock crime while being sober, and then were tested in a sober condition). In contrast to all the other studies, Bradley and Ainsworth (1984) chose the cutoff point for determining guilt in a post hoc manner, rather than predetermining it. Any procedure that utilizes cutoff points which, in a given sample, are optimal might produce inflated estimates for the rates of correct detection in the general population. In addition to the electrodermal measure, Bradley and Ainsworth measured respiration and heart rate. The results reported in Table 3.3 are based on the electrodermal measure, but identical detection rates were obtained in this study when the decisions were based on a combination of all three measures.

In the Bradley and Warfield (1984) study, some of the subjects simulating the innocent condition were informed about the relevant details of the mock crime. We therefore decided to include only the control group of uninformed innocent subjects.

Davidson (1968) used 36 subjects to simulate the innocent condition. These subjects were in fact allocated into three groups: in one, the subjects tried to commit the mock crime but failed; in the second, the subjects were motivated to commit the crime but did not get the opportunity; and in the third, the subjects had no knowledge of the crime. As can be seen in the table, this manipulation had no effect on the accuracy of the GKT—perfect detection rates were obtained in all three groups. In addition, Davidson manipulated motivation to deceive by promising different amounts of money as an incentive to different groups of subjects. However, this manipulation also did not affect the outcomes, so we have reported the results based on Davidson's entire sample.

Giesen and Rollison (1980) were interested in the relationship between trait anxiety and GKT detection efficiency. They selected their sample according to the subject's response to a questionnaire item on "palmer sweating." Only those who responded positively to this item were selected for the experiment. Because electrodermal activity is related to sweating, subjects in the Giesen and Rollison experiment might be characterized by a higher level of electrodermal responsivity than the general population. The subjects simulating the innocent condition were exposed to the guilty-knowledge items, but in an innocent context. As can be seen from Table 3.3, this manipulation had no effect on the outcome of the GKT test, because all innocent subjects were correctly classified.

In Lykken's original GKT experiment (1959), the subjects simulating the guilty condition were allocated into three groups, such that in the first group the mock crime was theft, in the second group it was murder, and in the third group subjects simulated both types of crimes. Six GKT questions were constructed for each crime, and the results reflect the rate of correctly classifying each subject into the right group. In order to increase motivation, the subjects in Lykken's experiment were told that they would be given an electric shock if their responses indicated guilt. In fact, they received a shock after every question.

The study by Podlesny and Raskin (1978) examined both the GKT and the CQT. Only the results related to the GKT are displayed in Table 3.3 (the CQT results were presented in Table 3.1). In this study, respiration and cardiovascular measures were used in addition to the electrodermal measure. However, the GKT results expressed as rates of correct and incorrect classifications, are reported only for the electrodermal measure.

Steller, Haenert, and Eiselt (1987) focused on the possible correlation between the Extraversion/Introversion personality dimension and psychophysiological detection using the GKT paradigm. Table 3.3 contains the overall results of the Steller et al. study, while the relationship between extraversion and detection will be discussed in the next chapter.

Stern, Breen, Watanabe, and Perry (1981) focused on the effects of feedback on the efficiency of the GKT. They conducted two experiments, but the first used the guilty information rather than the guilty person design, so only the results of the second experiment are presented in Table 3.3. Like the Giesen and Rollison (1980) study, the innocent subjects were exposed to the guilty information. Because none of the manipulations used seemed to affect detection efficiency, we reported the results from all experimental conditions.

Finally, we included three experiments reported by Waid, Orne, Cook, and Orne (1978). Those three experiments were closely related, and, therefore, we decided to report their pooled results in Table 3.3.

In spite of the many differences among the studies included in our review, their results seem relatively uniform and much less variable as compared with the CQT studies reviewed in the previous sections. The rate of correct detections among the guilty subjects ranges from 61% to 100%, but in only two out of the ten studies was the rate less than 85%. In the innocent condition there is even less variability among the studies, and the correct detection rate ranges between 81% and 100%, with seven of the ten studies reaching the 100% mark. In contrast to the CQT studies, it seems that the GKT can indeed protect the innocent, since the false-positive rate is clearly less than the false-negative rate (5.8% vs. 16.1% on the average). The only study in which the reverse pattern was observed is the one conducted by Stern et al. (1981), but in this study the innocent subjects had access to the guilty information, and even though this information was provided to them in an innocent context, it could have created larger physiological responsivity to the relevant items than would otherwise be observed. The number of studies is not large enough to permit a meta analysis of the results. In particular, it would be difficult to analyze the sources of the between-studies differences. Nevertheless, we might speculate that the number of questions presented to the subjects could be an important factor. In the two studies that used more than the usual number of questions (Bradley and Ainsworth, 1984, and Bradley and Warfield, 1984, used nine and ten questions, respectively), perfect detection rates were obtained in both the guilty and the innocent conditions.

As was noted earlier in this chapter, the mock crime paradigm is weak with respect to external validity. Unfortunately, GKT studies conducted in real-life settings are unavailable, and the differences between the simulated and the realistic condition are too great to permit generalizations. We tend to believe that this problem is somewhat less acute with the GKT than with the CQT, at least with respect to correctly detecting the innocent suspect. As long as this suspect does not recognize the relevant items, there is no reason why he or she would show greater responsivity to those items than to other, completely equivalent, items, regardless of the fear and anxiety caused by the interrogation. Indeed, there is some evidence that the level of stress involved does not affect the efficiency of the GKT (e.g., Bradley and Janisse, 1981a; Kugelmass and Lieblich, 1966). We shall discuss this issue in the next chapter.

There are, however, other factors differentiating the simulated from the realistic situation which might affect the outcomes of the GKT. The GKT is based on cognitive rather than on emotional factors. It is the knowledge of the relevant information that leads to enhanced responding to guilty knowledge items, and not the deception or the emotions associated with the criminal act. Factors affecting cognition should therefore be taken into account when the GKT is concerned. In particular, factors affecting perception and memory might be crucial for the efficiency of the GKT, because this method depends on the assumption that the relevant items were perceived by the guilty person and that this individual remembers them at the time of the test. Unfortunately, all GKT studies used a very simple task in which the experimenters guaranteed that all subjects learned all the relevant items (e.g., six code words were overlearned by the subjects). Furthermore, the subjects are typically tested immediately after being exposed to the guilty information, thus memory does not play an important role in the experimental situation. In real life, things might be entirely different. The guilty subject is faced with a complex scene, and it might be much more difficult to assume that all details were indeed noticed, processed, and stored in memory. Criminal suspects are very rarely tested immediately after committing the criminal act. Typically, they may be tested days, weeks, and sometimes months after the crime was committed. On the other hand, it could be argued that crime-related information is very likely to be perceived and remembered because of its great relevance to the perpetrator of the crime. It is of course unknown whether and to what extent these factors might affect the GKT efficiency, and future research should address these questions.

## Summary and Conclusions

In this chapter we dealt with the fundamental issue of the reliability and validity of classifications based on psychophysiological detection procedures. We began with an extensive discussion of several methodological considerations, the goal of which was to explain why the issues of validity and reliability have not yet been resolved, in spite of extensive research that has been conducted over the past two decades. The reason for this negative conclusion is that the validity studies conducted thus far were unable to maintain both internal and external validity. Experimental attempts to assess the validity of the polygraph achieved good control over the criterion, but suffered from weak external validity so that their results cannot be generalized to real polygraph interrogations. Field studies, on the other hand, used questionable criteria for guilt and biased samples.

Even the relatively simple issue of polygraph reliability cannot be estimated on the basis of current research. Only one aspect of reliability has been studied so far—the interjudge reliability. We argued that this is the least interesting and the least relevant aspect of polygraph reliability, because the critical generalizations are not across polygraph chart interpreters, but across different examinations of the same individual. In particular, crucial sources of possible error of measurement in CQT polygraphy lie in the choice of proper control questions and in the administration of the questions to the subjects. We argued that both simulated and field studies are bound to yield results that are biased in favor of the polygraph. Simulated studies of the CQT will typically yield an underestimation of the false-positive errors, whereas the rate of false negatives will be underestimated in field studies.

In spite of the methodological difficulties, we reviewed the research dealing with the validity of the various methods of polygraph-based interrogations, separating CQT studies from those focusing on the GKT, and separating between the simulated experiments and the field studies. Better-than-chance accuracy rates were found for the CQT. Across studies, averages of correct classification of guilty subjects were 80% and 84% in simulated and field studies, respectively. The correct classifications among innocent subjects were, on the average, 63% and 72%. In light of the methodological considerations it should be clear that these rates should be regarded, at best, as upper limits of the CQT accuracy in real interrogative situations. We discussed the asymmetry of the two types of errors, stressing that the evidence does not support the claims made by CQT proponents that the method protects the innocent.

The review of the GKT validity studies focused exclusively on simulated experiments, as field studies of this method are unavailable. The average accuracy rates across ten studies were 84% for guilty subjects and 94% among those simulating the innocent. We argued that in contrast to the CQT, this method can indeed protect the innocent. It should be pointed out that in addition to the relatively low average rate of false positives, in seven out of the ten studies *no* false positives were observed. It seems that the decrease in the rate of false positives and the general increase in the GKT validity are associated with an increase in the number of GKT questions. Thus, with a sufficiently large number of GKT questions the method can be used quite efficiently. This conclusion must, however, be drawn with great caution because several crucial factors distinguish the experimental setup from real interrogations and make it difficult to generalize from it. At the end of the chapter we discussed some of those factors and suggested further research to examine their role.

CHAPTER 4

# Laboratory Studies: Factors Affecting Psychophysiological Detection

In the past three decades a relatively large body of research data relevant to psychophysiological detection has accumulated. Most of the experimental efforts have been carried out by psychophysiologists and applied psychologists, and most studies have utilized the GKT. The frequent use of the GKT in this type of research is not surprising in light of our description and comparison of the different methods (see Chapters 1 and 2). The GKT is the only standardized method for psychophysiological detection, and the only one which makes use of proper control questions. Therefore only the GKT can permit sound inferences from a given pattern of physiological responding. The fact that most research in this area is based on the GKT, whereas most applications are based on the CQT, is one example of the paradoxical state which characterizes lie detection.

Research on psychophysiological detection and related phenomena can be loosely divided into two categories: (*a*) studies attempting to assess the different methods and applications of polygraphy and (*b*) studies attempting to identify variables that might be associated with psychophysiological detection. In the first case, the studies have usually been concerned with the issues of the reliability, validity, and accuracy of classifications based on the various methods of psychophysiological detection. This research was reviewed and discussed in Chapter 3. In the second case, identification of relevant variables has theoretical as well as practical importance. From a scientific perspective, it is impossible to understand the mechanisms underlying psychophysiological detection without being able to predict which factors will have an effect upon detection efficiency. From an applied perspective, understanding the factors that determine and influence detection could enable practitioners to create the optimal conditions for psychophysiological detection and therefore achieve the best results.

The purpose of this chapter is to outline several factors that were identified by researchers as determinants of psychophysiological detection and to discuss the relevant research. The chapter will focus upon the applied perspective, while theoretical implications and theoretically based research will be discussed in Chapter 6. The various factors to be discussed in this chapter can be divided into two categories: (*a*) situational factors—those that can be manipulated and studied by controlled experiments (e.g., instructions given to the subjects before the administration of the test) and (*b*) subjects factors—those that are subject-dependent (e.g., the educational and cultural background of the subjects taking the test). In addition, a third section will be devoted to a comparison of the utility of various physiological measures in psychophysiological detection.

## Situational Factors

Several factors related to various features of the test's setup will be reviewed. The factors range from those related to the amount and type of stress involved, to procedural aspects such as the relative frequency of the relevant items or the number of repetitions of GKT questions. Some of the factors are interrelated, and it is difficult to separate them and to attribute the effects to a particular factor.

### Similarity of the Test's Setup to Realistic Field Conditions

One of the earliest questions posed by investigators in this area was the question of external validity—the extent to which experimental results in this area can be generalized to real-world situations. Clearly, a negative answer would mean that from a practical point of view, at least, there is not much sense in conducting laboratory experiments to investigate the different aspects of psychophysiological detection. One of the most salient features distinguishing the so-called real-world situation and the typical psychophysiological laboratory is the degree and the type of stress and anxiety to which subjects are exposed. While in real polygraph interrogations both guilty and innocent suspects typically experience severe stress and anxiety, the laboratory situation is innocuous and mild. Subjects usually volunteer to participate in such experiments, and they know very well that no harm will be inflicted on them.

A most crucial question, therefore, is whether the degree of stress affects the outcome of the polygraph test. This was studied by Kugelmass and Leiblich (1966), who experimentally manipulated the level of stress. The subjects in this experiment were police trainees who were instructed to report to the laboratory to take a test that was presented as part of the selection procedure to the police force. The subjects were unaware of the true nature of the experiment, and the word "experiment" was never mentioned to them. All subjects took the standard card test under one of three different conditions: (*a*) subjects in one group were told that they would undergo a test designed just to examine whether the apparatus was functioning properly. (*b*) Subjects in a second group were told that the test was designed to examine whether they belonged to the group of people whose responses could be detected by the machine. (*c*) In a third group, subjects were given the following instructions:

One trait that characterizes a successful policeman, with good chances of promotion, is the ability to control his emotions. A policeman not able to control his emotions has not much chance of promotion, and may not be suitable for service in the Israeli Police Force. We will now see what your chances are for promotion in the future and even whether you will be able to continue your service with the police.... (Kugelmass and Lieblich, 1966, p. 212)

The results revealed that the number of chosen cards correctly identified through inspection of changes in skin resistance was similar in the three stress conditions. The authors concluded that "within a considerable range of stress no necessary decrease in the detection efficiency of the GSR channel need be expected" (Kugelmass and Lieblich, 1966, p. 215). In other words, they concluded that the GKT is externally valid when decisions are based on the electrodermal measure. It should be pointed out, in addition, that inspection of the baseline levels of autonomic reactivity did not reveal differences between the three conditions of this experiment; both basic skin conductance and average pulse rate, taken just before each card test, were very similar in the three conditions. In particular, the baseline autonomic reactivity across the three conditions was higher than reactivity levels during police medical examinations, but lower than levels obtained during criminal lie detection interrogation. Thus it can be argued that the stress level even in condition (c) did not quite reach the level that characterizes the real polygraph test situation.

More recent studies conducted by Bradley and Janisse (1981a,b) support the conclusions drawn by Kugelmass and Lieblich (1966). They threatened half of their subjects with an electric shock if classified guilty by the polygraph. This manipulation did not affect detection efficiency through electrodermal, cardiovascular, and pupillary measures, neither in a GKT procedure nor under the CQT.

## Level of Motivation

Another feature that might distinguish the field from the laboratory situation is the level of motivation. It might be expected that in the field situation guilty individuals are strongly motivated to avoid detection and to appear as though they were not involved in the event under interrogation. It is difficult to create that kind of motivation in the artificial laboratory situation, but several researchers tried to manipulate the motivation factor through instructions.

Most of the studies that have dealt with the factor of "motivation to avoid detection" have followed the lead of the original study by Gustafson and Orne (1963). Gustafson and Orne utilized a card test procedure and manipulated motivation by telling one group of subjects that the goal of the experiment was to examine how well they could keep information away from the experimenter and that this goal could be achieved only by highly intelligent individuals with superior emotional control. The test was thus made ego-relevant with implications for self-esteem and self-perception. In addition, subjects in the high-motivation condition were promised extra money for successfully avoiding detection. The control (low-motivation) condition was created by telling the subjects that the goal of the experiment was to find out how normal people respond physiologically to a series of numbers and letters.

Since then, several studies have investigated the role of motivational instructions on psychophysiological detection, but not all of them obtained clear effects for the motivation factor. While Gustafson and Orne (1963) and more recently Elaad (1987) did obtain significantly larger differential responsivity to the relevant stimuli in the high-motivation condition than they did in the low-motivation condition, Davidson (1968) and Lieblich, Naftali, Shmueli, and Kugelmass (1974) did not. Horvath (1978, 1979) reported on two studies that focused on the motivational factor. In these studies, three groups of 32 subjects each were studied using a GKT procedure. The first group of subjects was motivated to avoid detection, the second group was motivated to be detected, and the third was given no motivational instructions at all. Significant differences in detection rates based on the electrodermal measure were obtained between the three groups, with a lower hit rate for the avoid-detection condition than for the other two groups. Only 13 subjects were correctly detected in the avoid-detection condition as compared with 21 and 23 in the no-motivation and the achieve-detection conditions, respectively. In all three groups the observed rates of detection exceeded the rates expected by chance. These results are inconsistent with the original findings of Gustafson and Orne (1963). It is difficult to ascertain whether the differences between all these experiments stem from differences in the procedures, in the stimuli, or in the subjects or whether they reflect only sampling errors. Since the results of Elaad's (1987) study are based on four independent experiments conducted in different settings, using different stimulus material and different subject populations, and since all four experiments revealed clear effects for the motivational factor (the subjects motivated to avoid detection displayed greater physiological differentiation between relevant and neutral stimuli than those subjects who did not receive any motivational instructions), we tend to believe that this factor does indeed contribute to psychophysiological differentiation between relevant and neutral stimuli, although such differentiation may be possible under low levels of motivation as well.

## Verbal Response

Another factor that received some attention from experimental psychologists interested in psychophysiological detection was the verbal responses given to the questions in the polygraph test. Typically, in a GKT procedure subjects are required to answer "no" to all the items presented to them. Such a procedure guarantees that "guilty" subjects lie when presented with the relevant items and tell the truth when presented with the neutral items; "innocent" subjects give truthful answers to all items. However, it is not clear whether deception is really necessary in order to produce psychophysiological differentiation between relevant and neutral stimuli. Furthermore, it is not clear whether verbal responding to the questions is needed in the first place. Several studies focused on these questions, but their results were not uniform. Gustafson and Orne (1965b) manipulated the verbal responses required in a card test procedure, using three experimental conditions: The subjects in the first group were asked to respond "no" to each and every question presented to them (the "no" condition); the subjects in the second group were requested to give the first word that came to mind (the free-association condition); and the subjects in the third group were required to remain silent as they heard the questions read (the silent condition). The results indicated that the number of successful detections based on changes in skin resistance depended on the verbal-response condition. The "no" condition produced the largest detection rate, and the free-association condition produced the lowest. In both the "no" and the silent conditions, detection rates were significantly greater than those expected by chance. It ought to be emphasized that the effect reported by Gustafson and Orne (1965b) was due, to a great extent, to the very poor detection rates observed under the bizarre free-association condition.

The role of verbal responses was further studied by Kugelmass, Lieblich, and Bergman (1967), who compared the "no" condition with a "yes" condition (i.e., the subjects were instructed to respond "yes" to each and every question). In this experiment no differences were obtained between the two verbal conditions—in both of them the relevant information was detected using changes in skin resistance at better than chance rates. This finding was not replicated in two recent studies (Elaad and Ben-Shakhar, 1989; Horneman and O'Gorman, 1985). In both of these studies the "no" condition was associated with better detection efficiencies than either the "yes" condition or the silent condition.

Elaad and Ben-Shakhar (1989) included an additional condition in which the subjects were requested to repeat each item as it was presented. The "no" condition turned out to be the most efficient for psychophysiological detection, but all modes of verbal responding, including the silent condition, produced detection efficiencies exceeding chance.

Horneman and O'Gorman (1985) tried to explain the differences between their own results and those obtained by Kugelmass et al. (1967) in terms of differences in the motivational levels of the subjects in the two experiments: they suggested that their subjects might have been insufficiently concerned about the outcome of the test. However, the Elaad and Ben-Shakhar (1989) experiments demonstrate that this explanation is unlikely, because no interaction was obtained between the level of motivation and the type of verbal response. The superiority of the "no" condition over all other verbal response conditions was demonstrated by Elaad and Ben-Shakhar under both high and low levels of motivation.

## The Effects of Accuracy Demonstrations and Feedback on Psychophysiological Detection

As was detailed in Chapter 2, one of the critical conditions for a successful application of polygraph methods, such as the RIT and the CQT, is that the subjects have complete faith in the accuracy of the polygraph (see, however, footnote 2, Chapter 2). Indeed, polygraph examiners make efforts to increase the belief of their subjects in the accuracy of the polygraph. One way of doing it is through demonstrations, such as simulation tests or rigged card tests (Lykken, 1981; Reid and Inbau, 1977). It is therefore interesting to examine whether such procedures are effective (i.e., whether they enhance the psychophysiological differentiation between relevant and neutral stimuli, and increase the likelihood of correct detections). A more general formulation of the question is whether feedback information based on the results of the polygraph in one occasion affects the polygraph's results on subsequent occasions, and in what direction.

Gustafson and Orne (1965a) were the first investigators who addressed this question through a systematic experiment. Their result indicated that feedback from an initial card test did interact with motivational instructions to affect the outcomes of a subsequent card test. Whenever the feedback (which was arbitrarily determined by the experimenter) contradicted the subject's motivation, detection rates based on the electrodermal measure were high. Thus, for example, 15 out of the 16 subjects who were motivated to avoid detection and were given feedback to the effect that their chosen card was correctly detected in the first card test were correctly detected in the second card test. On the other hand, only 4 of the 16 subjects who were motivated to be detected and who were provided with a positive feedback were correctly detected in the second test. This finding was viewed as supporting the motivational account for psychophysiological detection. According to Gustafson and Orne, motivation is determined by the perceived success in the initial detection task (where success is a function of the detection situation and could be manipulated by instructions): a failure in the initial task induces an increased motivation in the second, whereas a successful performance on the first card test decreases motivation and accounts for the poor rates of detection in the second card test.

Elaad (1981) also examined effects of accuracy demonstrations using the GKT procedure. In her experiment all 48 subjects were motivated to avoid detection. False feedback was provided to the subjects on the basis of four GKT questions, and its effects were examined using four additional questions. The subjects were assigned to three conditions: (*a*) positive feedback (subjects were led to believe that the relevant information was correctly detected for each question), (*b*) negative feedback (subjects were led to believe that the relevant alternative was never detected), and (*c*) control condition with no feedback. The maximal detection efficiency was obtained under the positive feedback, and the efficiency was poorest under the negative-feedback condition (e.g., detection rates based on the electrodermal measure were 64%, 58%, and 48% in the positive-feedback, control, and negative-feedback conditions, respectively). These results provide partial support for the notion that, in practice, faith in the polygraph's accuracy may increase its efficiency. It is a reasonable assumption that in a real-life situation, guilty suspects are motivated to avoid detection. Positive feedback should thus increase their detection rate. However, the results of Gustafson and Orne (1965a) and Elaad (1981) are based on a card test procedure and are therefore relevant only for the GKT, whereas the assumption that faith in the polygraph's accuracy is a crucial factor was made with regard to the RIT and the CQT (see Chapter 2).

Different results were obtained by Bradley and Janisse (1979, 1981a). They based the accuracy demonstrations on three initial card test questions and manipulated the feedback in four groups such that the different groups were given positive feedback on 0, 1, 2, or 3 trials. In their 1979 experiment they examined the feedback effect using a fourth card test trial and the pupillary measure. They obtained an inverted U-shaped function indicating that both the 0% and the 100% feedback conditions were more difficult to detect than the other two groups. The interpretation given of this result was that uncertainty regarding the polygraph was associated with increased attention, whereas subjects certain about the polygraph's accuracy (in either direction) would pay little attention to the subsequent test. In their 1981 study, Bradley and Janisse extended their initial experiment and used the mock crime procedure and the CQT method, as well as the GKT, and also used additional physiological measures. A clear effect for the feedback manipulation was obtained only for the electrodermal measure and only under the CQT method—the more effective the apparatus appeared to be, the better the discrimination between guilty and innocent subjects that was obtained. It is curious why neither the results of Bradley and Janisse (1979) nor the results of Elaad (1981) were replicated in this later study.

Another study in which feedback manipulations did not affect psychophysiological detection under a GKT interrogation method was reported by Timm (1982). In this study the subjects' attitudes and expectations toward the polygraph were manipulated using two methods: (*a*) false feedback (positive, negative, and no-feedback control conditions were used) and (*b*) placebo manipulation—subjects were given a pill and were told either that it would make it more difficult for them to "beat" the lie detector or that it would make it easier for them to "beat" the lie detector. An additional control group was used in which no placebo was given to the subjects. Neither the feedback nor the placebo manipulation had an effect on detection measures based on electrodermal and respiratory responses, although the feedback manipulation influenced the subjects' expectations about the test's outcome.

Several studies used a different approach to study feedback effects on psychophysiological detection. Instead of providing subjects with false feedback (negative or positive), accurate psychophysiological feedback was used. Stern et al. (1981) used four series of GKT-type questions and the electrodermal measure. In their first experiment, one-third of the subjects were provided with continuous auditory and visual feedback based on their electrodermal responses, one-third of the subjects were given similar feedback on the basis of changes in their heart rate activity, and an additional group was provided with no feedback. The results showed that the feedback manipulation was effective, and both feedback groups displayed an increased differentiation between relevant and neutral stimuli. The electrodermal feedback tended to be somewhat more effective than the heart rate feedback.

In their second experiment, Stern et al. (1981) used the mock crime procedure with six GKT questions. Half the subjects were given an electrodermal feedback, and the other half served as a no-feedback control group. No clear effects for the feedback manipulation were observed in this study. Both subjects simulating the guilty conditions and those simulating the innocent condition (who were exposed to the relevant information in an innocent context) tended to respond more strongly to the relevant items under the feedback condition. This lack of feedback effect may be attributed to a ceiling effect—detection efficiency was very high in all conditions of this experiment (all 13 guilty subjects were correctly detected under the feedback condition, while 12 out of 13 guilty subjects were correctly detected with no feedback. Similarly, 12 and 11 out of 13 innocent subjects were correctly detected under the feedback and control conditions, respectively).

More recently, Timm (1987) used a similar procedure to the one used by Stern et al. (1981). An auditory continuous electrodermal feedback manipulation enhanced detection efficiency with a respiration measure, but it did not affect the electrodermal measure. It is rather difficult to draw conclusions from this set of studies because the results are not uniform. In some studies, feedback was demonstrated to be quite effective (e.g., Gustafson and Orne, 1965a; Elaad, 1981), while in others it had no effects whatsoever (e.g., Timm, 1982). In some studies, only the electrodermal measure was affected by feedback (Bradley and Janisse, 1981a), in another study the pupillary measure showed an effect (Bradley and Janisse, 1979), and yet in a third study the effect was demonstrated with respiration but not with skin conductance (Timm, 1987). Nevertheless, we tend to conclude that feedback has some effect on physiological detection such that positive feedback facilitates detection. The effect is, however, small, and that is perhaps the reason why it was observed only in some studies and only for some physiological measures.

## Effects of Type and Content of the Relevant Information on Psychophysiological Detection

We have reviewed many studies which focused on different aspects of psychophysiological detection and examined the effects of several variables on the validity of the GKT. The different studies used a great variety of procedures and utilized different versions of the GKT. Some studies used a simple card test procedure (e.g., Gustafson and Orne, 1963; Kugelmass et al. 1967), while others used a mock crime design (e.g., Lykken, 1959; Podlesny and Raskin, 1978). In some studies, subjects were required to steal an envelope containing money (e.g., Bradley and Janisse, 1981a; Forman and McCauley, 1986); in others they were asked to learn a list of code words (e.g., Waid and Orne, 1980; Waid, Orne, and Wilson, 1979a,b) or to watch a videotaped "crime" (Iacono, Boisvenu, and Fleming, 1984).

It is interesting to examine whether those differences affect the outcomes of the GKT. Unfortunately it is impossible to compare different studies because there are too many differences between them (e.g., motivational instructions, verbal responses, physiological measures used), and it would be difficult to attribute different outcomes to one particular variable. Only few studies attempted to compare the type of stimuli used in a systematic way.

Thackray and Orne (1968a) compared the impact of two types of information upon psychophysiological detection: (*a*) personal items (e.g., the subject's first name) that are inherently relevant for the subject and (*b*) neutral items made relevant to the subjects in the experimental context (code words the subject was instructed to memorize). Three GKT-type questions were used for each type of information, and the electrodermal measure was used for differentiating between the relevant and neutral items within each question. The results indicated that personal items were easier to detect, although both types of items were detected at levels exceeding chance expectation. In an additional report, Thackray and Orne (1968b) compared eight physiological measures for their detection efficiency using both personal and neutral items. A significant advantage for the personal items was obtained only for the electrodermal measure.

In a constructive replication of that study, Cutrow, Parks, Lucas, and Thomas (1972) compared nine indices for psychophysiological detection, using either personal items (e.g., subject's name), words memorized by the subject (e.g., names of birds, flowers, and trees), or items involving money taken by the subject. Just as in the Thackray and Orne (1968b) study, a significant effect for the type of material used was obtained only when the electrodermal measure (palmer galvanic skin response) was used. Detection of personal stimuli was significantly more successful than detection of involvement or neutral stimuli. None of the other eight measures used in this study revealed significant differences in detection as a function of the stimulus material.

Stern et al. (1981) also manipulated the personal involvement of the stimulus material. They compared detection of a geometric figure, chosen by the subject among a set of geometric figures, and detection of the subject's social security number. Again detection efficiency based on an electrodermal measure was greater for the personal material than for the neutral figures made relevant in the experimental context.

Lieblich (1969) manipulated the content of both the relevant items and the neutral control items, and predicted successfully the order of detection efficiencies in six GKT questions. For example, the efficiency of detecting the subject's first name using an electrodermal measure decreased dramatically when the control items were changed from common names, known not to be related to the subjects, to names from the immediate family circle of the subject (e.g., father, brother). A further decrease in detection efficiency was obtained when the critical item was changed from the subject's first name to a fictitious name given to the subject.

The degree of involvement with the relevant information was also manipulated in several other studies, which used a somewhat different method (Bradley and Warfield, 1984; Giesen and Rollison, 1980; Stern et al., 1981). In those studies the same relevant information was presented to all the subjects, but some subjects received it in the context of a crime (i.e., the relevant information was related to details of the hypothetical crime, such as the amount of money that was demanded in a blackmail scheme); while others were presented with the very same information, but in an innocent context (e.g., the same amount of money was referred to as a special award received for an outstanding performance by a secret agent working for the federal government). Thus the critical items used in the GKT had a special meaning to all subjects. Nevertheless, the results of all three studies indicated that the crime-related items produced stronger differential responsivity than the same items in an innocent context.

The conclusion that can be drawn from the studies reviewed in this section is that personal involvement with the information is another factor contributing to psychophysiological differentiation between relevant and neutral items. Nevertheless, it seems that psychophysiological detection is possible even without personal involvement. Even neutral information such as arbitrarily chosen numbers, letters, or geometric figures were capable of evoking differential physiological responsivity when the experimental procedure singled them out from a set of similar items (e.g., by instructing subjects to choose one object from a set).

## The Effects of Some Procedural Variables on Psychophysiological Detection

There is an extensive literature and a heated debate on the issues of the validity and accuracy of the CQT (e.g., Ben-Shakhar, Lieblich, and Bar-Hillel, 1982; Kleinmuntz and Szucko, 1984a; Lykken, 1978a, 1979; Podlesny and Raskin, 1977; Saxe, Dougherty, and Cross, 1985). Much less attention has been given to certain procedures that may influence the accuracy of the polygraph test. Some of these procedures are very simple and easy to implement, and at the same time may significantly affect the test's outcomes. In this section we shall describe procedural factors that have been shown to affect the accuracy of the GKT.

### The Relative Frequency of Relevant Items

Lieblich, Kugelmass, and Ben-Shakhar (1970) manipulated the number of neutral control items that were used together with a single relevant item in a card test experiment. The results of this experiment indicated that the larger the set of control stimuli used, the higher the card detection efficiency when based on the skin conductance measure. This result was later replicated and generalized in a series of additional experiments (e.g., Ben-Shakhar 1977, 1980; Ben-Shakhar, Lieblich, and Kugelmass, 1975, 1982). The conclusion that can be drawn from those experiments is that detection efficiency is negatively related to the relative frequency of the relevant question—the less frequently this question is presented, the better is the obtained detection efficiency when detection is based on the skin conductance response. The theoretical implications of these findings will be discussed in Chapter 6, but the practical implications for the application of the GKT are quite clear. They depend on taking the findings obtained in laboratory conditions using the card test procedure and generalizing them to a real-life application of the GKT. Another point that should be kept in mind is that the above-mentioned experiments manipulated the relative frequency of the relevant stimulus only within a limited range. The lowest level used was one relevant stimulus to seven neutral control stimuli. Thus, it is not clear whether the relationship between detection efficiency and relevant stimulus frequency extends beyond the range used in the research.

## The Serial Position of the Relevant Items

Another factor that might be associated with detection efficiency is the serial position of the relevant alternative. In a typical GKT procedure one relevant item is presented among a series of neutral control items. Ben-Shakhar and Lieblich (1982) manipulated the serial position of a single relevant item in a sequence of eight items. Four groups of subjects were presented with the relevant item in serial positions 2, 4, 6, or 8. The results of this experiment revealed a clear advantage for early presentation. The differentiation between the electrodermal responses to relevant and neutral items was much stronger when the relevant stimulus was presented in trials 2 or 4 than when it appeared in trials 6 or 8. However, this result was not replicated by Ben-Shakhar, Asher, Poznansky-Levy, Asherowitz, and Lieblich (1989), who obtained almost identical detection efficiencies for early and late presentations of the relevant stimulus. The theoretical implications of these findings will also be discussed in Chapter 6, but from a practical perspective it may be concluded that there is no advantage for presenting the relevant item late in the stimulus sequence.

## The Number of GKT Questions Used

A third factor that might be important for creating optimal conditions for the application of the GKT is the number of questions used. Clearly, a single question is insufficient because enhanced responses to the relevant item of a single question could occur just by chance. For example, if five alternative items of a single question, such as possible colors of a stolen car, are used, the probability that the correct item will produce the largest response from an innocent subject is 20%. To overcome this difficulty, a GKT procedure might be based on several questions pertaining to different features of the event. Alternatively, if there is only one salient feature of the event, the single question could be repeated several times. Even without an empirical examination of this factor, it follows from psychometric considerations that increasing the number of questions is associated with an increased reliability of the total score based on an aggregation of the data from all the questions (e.g., Lord and Novick, 1968). However, this general rule might not be applicable to polygraph test procedures because the different questions, or the various repetitions of a single question, might not constitute parallel measurements as required by classical reliability theory. Specifically, the physiological measures used for the polygraph test are subject to a process of habituation—a gradual decrease in response magnitude with repeated presentations of the questions. In principle, the responses to all questions, relevant as well as neutral, habituate, but without specific parametric investigation it is not clear whether *differential* responsivity (the response magnitude to the relevant stimuli relative to the response magnitude to the neutral ones) decreases across repetitions and at what rate. Nevertheless, even if relative responsivity to the relevant stimuli does decrease over repetitions, it is still possible that aggregating data of several repetitions increases the overall reliability and accuracy of the test.

A number of studies examined the effect and the extent of habituation. By and large they reveal a clear tendency for differential responsivity to decrease with repetitions. It is, however, difficult to draw practical conclusions from those studies because most of them did not include a systematic attempt to aggregate data across repetitions in order to estimate the optimal number GKT questions.

Lieblich, Naftali, Shmueli, and Kugelmass (1974) used a name-detection procedure, in which the subject's first name was presented to him along with four neutral control names. The sequence of five names was repeated ten times, and the order of the names within each repetition was determined randomly. The rate of name detection, based on skin conductance changes, tended to decrease across repetitions—from 60% to 48% in the low-motivation condition and from 55% to 50% in the high-motivation condition. However, even the rates obtained in the tenth trial were significantly larger than those expected by chance (20%), and aggregating data across the ten questions markedly increased detection rates—up to 96% and 93% in the low- and high-motivation conditions, respectively.

Ben-Shakhar et al. (1975) also used a name-detection procedure in which sequences were repeated five times using seven experimental conditions. Across experimental conditions there was a tendency for a small decrease in detection efficiency with repetitions of the question sequence, but in all repetitions detection efficiencies exceeded chance values. No attempt was made in that experiment to aggregate data across repetitions. Similar results were reported by Ben-Shakhar and Lieblich (1982) in four repetitions of a card-test procedure. In this experiment the decrease in detection efficiency was more pronounced than in the previous experiments, but significant detection was observed even in the fourth repetition.

Balloun and Holmes (1979) have conducted one of the few studies in which real-life conditions were approximated in the laboratory. Thirty-four subjects took a written intelligence test on which they were urged to cheat by confederates posing as other subjects. Both cheaters ($n=18$) and noncheaters were given a GKT polygraph interrogation which was repeated twice. Cheaters displayed larger electrodermal detection scores than noncheaters on both repetitions, but the differences between the two groups tended to decrease from the first to the second GKT. Furthermore, only in the first test were the detection rates based on the electrodermal measure significantly greater than rates expected by chance (61% of the cheaters were correctly identified in the first test, whereas only 17% were correctly identified in the second). Iacono, Boisvenu, and Fleming (1984) found similar results in a study of the effects of drugs on psychophysiological detection, using a series of ten GKT questions. While no drug effects were observed in this experiment, the difference in skin conductance response between relevant and control items tended to decline with each additional question.

All of the above-mentioned experiments (Balloun and Holmes, 1979; Ben-Shakhar and Lieblich, 1982; Ben-Shakhar et al., 1975; Iacono et al., 1984; Lieblich et al., 1974) demonstrated a decrease in detection efficiency with repetitions when detection was based only on the electrodermal measure. Elaad and Ben-Shakhar (1989) studied the effects of repetition in a GKT paradigm with three physiological measures. When the electrodermal measure was utilized, results were identical to those obtained in the other experiments. When respiration and cardiovascular measures were used, detection efficiencies were much lower than for the electrodermal measure, but no repetition effects were observed.

This series of experiments clearly shows that detection based on electrodermal measures under the GKT procedure is subject to a gradual decline when the question sequence is repeated. It must be emphasized that the repetition effect discussed here is not identical to the well-known phenomenon of habituation (e.g., Sokolov, 1963). While habituation refers to a simple reduction in responsivity with stimulus repetition, the detection studies reveal reduction of differential responsivity (i.e., a relative decline in the responses to the relevant items as compared with the responses to the neutral items). Direct practical implications are difficult to draw at this stage, because in spite of this decline in detection efficiency, there are indications that it is possible to detect information at better than chance levels even after as many as ten repetitions. Furthermore, there are indications (e.g., Lieblich et al., 1974) that aggregating data across repetitions can increase the accuracy of psychophysiological detection to very high levels. Careful parametric research must be designed in order to determine the optimal number of repetitions, beyond which no increase in detection efficiency would be obtained by aggregating data.

## Countermeasures

So far, we have discussed several procedural factors that may affect psychophysiological detection. Those factors are typically under the control of the polygraph examiner, who is free to choose the specific instructions given to the subject, as well as the number of questions and the number of alternative items per question presented to the subject in the course of the polygraph examination. There are, however, other factors that are under the control of the subject and might affect detection efficiency. One class of such factors falls under the topic of "countermeasures"—deliberate techniques that might be used by the subjects to alter their physiological reactions. Naturally, if such techniques could be shown to be effective, they might be used by guilty suspects attempting to appear innocent. Countermeasures could be performed in an attempt either to inhibit responses to the relevant items or to create excitation to the neutral items. Inhibiting responses to relevant questions is extremely difficult, and therefore most successful countermeasures are based on deliberate attempts to create responses to neutral items.

There are basically two types of countermeasures: physical countermeasures and mental countermeasures. Physical countermeasures are physical activities the subject does in order to avoid being detected. For example, subjects might try to inflict pain upon themselves by biting their tongues, or they might try to breathe heavily after a control question was presented, in order to create the impression of being more concerned with the control questions than with the relevant ones. Mental countermeasures refer to any mental activity the subject does in order either to create or to enhance physiological responding to the control (or neutral) questions, or to reduce responding to the relevant questions. Clearly, both types of countermeasures require some sophistication and a certain knowledge. However, by now there is an extensive literature in which polygraph procedures including effective countermeasures are described in great detail. Thus, the danger that interested individuals might gain the necessary understanding in order to use countermeasures is a real one.

In terms of practical applications, mental countermeasures are easier to conceal from an examiner. On the other hand, it seems that physical countermeasures are more effective in producing responses. It is curious that despite the obvious practical importance of the countermeasures issue, there are rather few experimental attempts designed to evaluate the various countermeasure techniques.

An early experiment conducted by Kubis (1962) tested both physical and mental countermeasures. Kubis reported that when subjects pressed their toes against the floor, detection rates were reduced to levels expected by chance. In another condition subjects attempted to mentally dissociate from the test items by ignoring the content of the questions and answering automatically. With this condition, the detection rates were the same as those obtained in a control condition in which subjects were not engaged in any countermeasures.

Lykken (1960) conducted one of the first experiments with the GKT procedure, and tried to teach his subjects various techniques to produce electrodermal responses to the neutral control items in order to fake the outcome of the GKT. Furthermore, subjects were provided with the opportunity to practice the production of voluntary electrodermal responses. At the same time, Lykken devised a special scoring system designed to overcome possible attempts at faking.[1]

Using this method, Lykken correctly identified all of the subjects on the basis of the electrodermal measure with twenty-five GKT questions, each containing one relevant and four neutral alternatives. This perfect detection was obtained in spite of the fact that the subjects were motivated to avoid detection and were instructed and trained to fake their results. Lykken (1960) concluded that "the

---

[1]This scoring system was based on the assumption that subjects attempting to fake will typically try to produce enhanced responses to a fixed number of neutral items in each question. If, for example, a subject is trying to produce artificial responses to two distractors in each GKT question, then the relevant alternative will typically produce the third largest response in each question. Lykken's scoring system was therefore based on deviations from a rectangular distribution of the ranked responses to the relevant alternatives of the various GKT questions.

GKT can yield extremely high validities, even with sophisticated defensive subjects, under conditions appropriate to its use" (p. 261).

Dawson (1980) used a mock crime paradigm in an attempt to study the validity of the CQT procedure, using 24 student actors trained in the Stanislavsky "method" of utilizing personal memories to create emotional states. The subjects were motivated and instructed to use the techniques taught at the Strasberg Theater Institute to appear innocent during the polygraph examination. It was believed that this choice of subjects and procedure would create "an opportunity to determine whether training in a type of mental countermeasure can be used by guilty subjects to successfully appear non-deceptive" (Dawson, 1980, p. 9). The results strongly indicated that this type of countermeasure is ineffective because no false-negative decisions were obtained.

Raskin and his colleagues have focused on the possible effects of physical countermeasures in several mock crime studies (e.g., Honts and Hodes, 1982a,b; Honts et al., 1985; Honts, Raskin, and Kircher, 1983). Rovner et al. (1979) demonstrated that providing subjects with detailed information about the CQT and with suggestions of possible countermeasures did not affect the outcomes of the CQT. However, when subjects were given a chance to practice with the polygraph and received feedback on their performance, some effects were obtained (25% of the decisions in that condition were erroneous, and 12.5% were inconclusive; whereas in the other conditions the error and inconclusive rates were 4% and 8%, respectively).

Honts et al. (1985) reported two mock crime experiments attempting to evaluate the effects of physical countermeasures on psychophysiological detection based on the CQT. In the first experiment, two of the three groups simulating the guilty condition were given information and training in the use of countermeasures. Subjects in one of those groups were asked to press their toes against the floor as soon as they recognized a control question. Subjects in the second countermeasure condition were asked to bite their tongues hard enough to produce pain. The results of this experiment did not reveal any effects from the countermeasure manipulations. The detection rates in both countermeasure groups did not differ from those obtained in a control group. In the second experiment, Honts et al. studied possible effects of multiple physical countermeasures. Subjects in one of the two groups simulating the guilty condition were asked to perform both types of countermeasures used in the first experiment. Furthermore, these subjects were given a practice examination containing questions similar to those used in the actual examination and were required to demonstrate their countermeasures for an assistant. The results of this experiment did show a strong effect from the countermeasure manipulation. There were marked differences in detection rates between the countermeasure condition and the control condition (countermeasure subjects produced 47% false negatives as compared with 0% false negatives for guilty control subjects). In fact, the pattern of physiological responses to the relevant and control questions in the countermeasure condition was undifferentiated from the pattern observed in a group simulating the innocent condition.

In both experiments, the examiners were unable to classify subjects as countermeasure users or nonusers at better than chance rates. Two studies conducted by Honts and Hodes (1982a,b) have produced results similar to those reported by Honts et al. (1985). It seems that multiple physical countermeasures can produce a substantial number of false-negative outcomes in a CQT-based polygraph interrogation. Honts et al. (1983) tried to assess whether the countermeasure effect obtained might be attributed to the low-motivation conditions in the Honts and Hodes (1982a) study. They conducted a similar experiment using high-motivation instructions and obtained a similarly powerful effect for the multiple physical countermeasure manipulation (while 78% of the guilty subjects who did not use countermeasures were correctly classified using standard CQT field practice, only 22% of the countermeasure subjects were correctly classified). However, Honts et al. (1983) reported that with the help of electromyographic recordings the examiner was able to identify most of the subjects using countermeasure techniques (80% of the countermeasure users were correctly detected, with no false-positive errors).

Elaad (1987) has recently examined the effects of mental countermeasures on the outcomes of a GKT polygraph interrogation. Subjects in one condition were instructed to count sheep throughout the entire test (continuous countermeasure). In a second condition subjects were instructed to count silently from 1 to 10 only when they heard the relevant item (relevant-specific countermeasure). The results for the first condition showed somewhat smaller electrodermal differentiation between relevant and neutral items than did those for a control group which was given no countermeasure instructions. The specific countermeasure condition, on the other hand, was associated with greater differentiation, presumably because in this condition the relevant item was singled out. It is notable that Elaad's (1987) results constitute the first demonstration that mental countermeasures have any effect on psychophysiological detection.

It is premature at this stage to draw conclusions about the extent to which psychophysiological detection is controllable by the subject. In general, though, it can be concluded that physical countermeasures have some effect, at least under certain conditions. The available countermeasure studies demonstrate that with enough information and practice, guilty subjects can mislead CQT polygraph examiners and produce physiological response patterns characteristic of an innocent subject. It seems that this is possible, though, only if subjects are given an opportunity to practice the physical countermeasures. One study demonstrated that these physical countermeasures may be detected by an examiner with the help of an electromyograph, but this device is not currently used in standard field CQT practice.

The practical implications of the current countermeasures research are rather clear: the danger of false-negative outcomes in CQT-based polygraph interrogations must not be neglected, despite the results of some mock crime experiments showing this type of error to be relatively rare (e.g., Podlesny and Raskin, 1978; Raskin and Hare, 1978). This danger might become even more serious if CQT results are to be used as evidence in a criminal court. Under such circumstances many criminals would be highly motivated to learn how to use effective countermeasure techniques—a task which might be achieved with only a little effort and investment.

It seems from the reviewed research that it is only the CQT which is vulnerable to countermeasure manipulations. As was demonstrated by Lykken (1960), the GKT can be made immune to such manipulations by adopting sophisticated scoring techniques. This conclusion must be qualified by the fact that research data are too scarce. In addition, it must be emphasized that all of the countermeasure research is based on laboratory experiments whose external validity is not clear.

## Effects of Drugs

Countermeasures are actions taken by the subject during the polygraph interrogation in order to avoid detection. Another possible means for avoiding detection could be employed by subjects prior to the test itself—the use of certain drugs that might be associated with physiological responding. If indeed such drugs are demonstrated to be effective in reducing differential responsivity to the relevant stimuli, their use might be more effective than the use of physical countermeasures because the use of drugs may be more difficult for the polygraph examiner to detect. In spite of its obvious practical importance, the issue of the effects of drugs in psychophysiological detection has received surprisingly little attention from researchers.

Waid, Orne, Cook, and Orne (1981) examined the effect of a tranquilizer (400 mg of meprobamate) on psychophysiological detection in a GKT paradigm. They reported a reduction in detection with the electrodermal measure as compared with no-pill and placebo subjects. The latter two groups showed clear differentiation between relevant and neutral items—9 out of 11 guilty subjects were correctly detected in the no-pill condition, and 8 out of 11 were correctly detected in the placebo condition. There was no indication of such differentiation in the meprobamate group; only 3 out of 11 guilty subjects were correctly detected, and this rate was not significantly different from the results obtained with innocent subjects. Furthermore, the polygraph examiner was not able to discriminate between subjects who took the drug and those who did not. It may be interesting to note that the drug seemed to cause a reduction only in differential responsivity to the relevant items but not in the general responsivity. More recently, Iacono et al. (1984) used diazepam instead of meprobamate as the antianxiety agent. The reason given by Iacono et al. (1984) for their choice was that diazepam is a more widely prescribed tranquilizer and is more easily available. In addition, possible effects of a stimulant (methylphenidate) were also examined in this study. In contrast to the previous study (Waid, Orne, Cook, and Orne, 1981), no drug effects were observed, and the subjects in both of the drug conditions showed differential response patterns to the relevant items which were similar to those observed under a placebo condition. In the 15 subjects who took diazepam, no false-negative errors were obtained, and only two and three false-negative decisions were made for each group of subjects ($n=15$) in the methylphenidate and placebo conditions, respectively. Iacono et al. (1984) dismissed possible objections to their study that might cast doubt that the drugs were administered properly. They claim that the doses of both drugs used in their study were several times the typical minimum known to be clinically effective, and that under the procedures used in the study, diazepam has been demonstrated to reach its peak effect. Furthermore, the investigators point out that both the experimenter and the subjects accurately perceived the effects of the diazepam. It is possible that either the choice of the antianxiety agent or some differences in the experimental design used may account for the difference between the results obtained in those two studies. However, without additional research it is not possible to determine the reasons for the differences or to draw conclusions regarding drug effects on psychophysiological detection.

An additional study examined the effect of Trasicor—a Beta blocking agent, on psychophysiological detection using a GKT paradigm. Elaad, Bonwitt, Eisenberg, and Meytes (1982) obtained a significant decrease in detection efficiency among subjects who took 40 mg. of Trasicor-80 as compared with a placebo group.

A single study has focused on the effects of alcohol on detection. Bradley and Ainsworth (1984) used the mock crime paradigm to examine the effects of alcohol consumption, both while enacting the mock crime and during the polygraph interrogation. Sixteen of the subjects simulating the guilty condition committed the crime while intoxicated, and the other sixteen "guilty" subjects committed the crime sober. These two groups were further subdivided so that half of the subjects in each group were interrogated while intoxicated and the other half were examined while sober.

The results revealed that only intoxication during the crime affected the outcome of the polygraph interrogation. Guilty subjects who committed the crime under the influence of alcohol were less detectable than those who committed the crime while sober. This effect was obtained for the electrodermal measure under both the CQT and the GKT. However, no alcohol effects were obtained for respiration. For the heart rate measure, the two factors interacted—when the GKT was used, guilty subjects who were intoxicated during both the crime and the interrogation tended to be less detectable. No effects were obtained for intoxication during the interrogation alone, implying that alcohol cannot be used as an effective countermeasure during polygraph interrogations. The obtained results may be due to the effect of alcohol either on the emotions of subjects committing the mock crime or on their memory for the relevant details.

# Subject-Dependent Factors

In the previous sections we discussed the effects of several variables on psychophysiological detection. All of the variables were those that could be experimentally manipulated (e.g., motivational instructions, feedback). Another class of variables that might be related to psychophysiological detection consists of individual attributes—traits characterizing the subject in general, independent of the administration of an experiment or a testing procedure.

In this section, we shall review the literature dealing with individual differences in relation to psychophysiological detection. The studies dealing with subject-dependent factors differ with regard to the source of the individual differences. Four types of such sources can be identified: (a) individual differences in psychophysiological reactivity (e.g., electrodermal lability), (b) age and gender, (c) ethnic and cultural factors, and (d) personality traits, usually measured by objective personality inventories. It must be emphasized that research based on individual differences is of a correlational type, and therefore does not allow for causal interpretations. Thus, for example, ethnic or personality factors may be associated with detection through their relationships with measures of psychophysiological reactivity (e.g., a certain ethnic group could be characterized by a greater tendency to show electrodermal responsivity than other ethnic groups, and this tendency may lead to a greater electrodermal detection in that group). Typically, all factors (ethnic, cultural, psychological, and psychophysiological) are intercorrelated; thus cause and effect cannot be ascertained.

## Individual Differences in Psychophysiological Measures

One source of individual differences is based on the autonomic measures monitored by the polygraph. Those measures typically display a great deal of individual differences, and to the extent that those differences are stable across situations, it might be reasonable to hypothesize that they will correlate with detection which is based on the same measures.

One characteristic of autonomic functioning that seems to be relatively stable is electrodermal lability (e.g., Crider and Lunn, 1971). This characteristic is usually defined either by the number of spontaneous electrodermal responses elicited while no specific stimulus was presented or by the frequency of responses to a series of mild standard stimuli (e.g., low-intensity tones). Waid and Orne (1980) conducted two mock crime studies designed to examine the relationship between electrodermal lability and the efficiency of detection based on the electrodermal measure. In their first experiment subjects simulating the guilty condition were instructed to memorize six code words of different semantic categories. All subjects were later tested using six GKT questions with four items each (the critical code word and three control words of the same category). The lability variables were defined on the basis of the number of nonspecific responses occurring during the interstimulus interval. The results revealed a statistically significant positive correlation (.56) between the number of nonspecific responses and the number of code words detected among "guilty" subject. The correlation among the "innocents" was also positive but not significantly greater than zero (.37). In their second experiment, Waid and Orne (1980) used a similar design with two changes: (a) the CQT was used in addition to the GKT, and (b) lability was defined by the number of nonspecific responses during a rest period. The results were similar to those of the first study, indicating positive correlations between electrodermal lability and electrodermal detection. The correlations obtained in the GKT test were .56 and .60 for guilty and innocent subjects, respectively; and under the CQT the respective correlations were .43 and .50. Waid and Orne concluded that electrodermally stabile guilty individuals are less susceptible to detection, at least when the electrodermal measure is being used. The results obtained with innocent subjects are, however, not clear, particularly with regard to the GKT. It seems that more labile innocent subjects tended to be falsely detected. Even if extremely responsive, there is no reason for the innocent to show greater responsivity to the critical items that are completely unfamiliar and undifferentiated from the control items (in the GKT). Waid and Orne did not provide a satisfactory explanation for this result.

In a subsequent study, Waid, Wilson, and Orne (1981) extended the previous study and examined the relationship between electrodermal lability measured on one occasion and three measures of detection (based on electrodermal, cardiovascular, and respiratory channels) taken one week later. This study utilized a mock crime procedure in which subjects simulating the guilty condition were instructed to memorize six code words. The results revealed significant effects of lability (defined on the basis of nonspecific skin conductance responses) on detection with all three measures when the CQT was used, but not when the GKT was used. "Guilty" stabile subjects were detected less frequently than labile ones. Among truthful subjects, the more labile were falsely detected as deceptive more frequently than their stabile counterparts. The correlations between electrodermal lability and the number of questions detected among "guilty" subjects were .35, .04, and .31 for the electrodermal, relative blood pressure, and respiration measures, respectively. The respective correlations among "innocent" subjects were $-.05$, .37, and .38.

More recently, Horneman and O'Gorman (1987) conducted an extensive study designed to examine relationships between different aspects of electrodermal responding and measures of detection. In the first phase of their study, Horneman and O'Gorman took 12 electrodermal measures during 4 tasks (e.g., habituation to tones, mental arithmetic). In a factor analysis of these data, two major factors emerged: (a) the first one, labeled "reactivity," accounted for 54% of the variance and was related predominantly to basic skin conductance level; and (b) the second factor, labeled "lability," accounted for 11% of the variance and was related both to the frequency of nonspecific responses during relaxation and to the number of skin conductance responses to tones. In the second phase of this experiment, subjects were exposed either to a card test or to a mock crime procedure (the GKT and the CQT were used to detect a series of code words). The results indicated that measures of electrodermal reactivity were moderately correlated with measures of electrodermal detectability. The authors suggested that the low reliability of the detection measures caused an attenuation of the correlations between electrodermal reactivity and detectability. A multiple regression analysis showed that electrodermal lability measures contributed significantly to the prediction of the detection scores. Horneman and O'Gorman concluded that their results are consistent with those obtained by Waid and Orne (1980) and by

Waid, Wilson, and Orne (1981). All of these studies demonstrated that "electrodermal lability is a correlate of the likelihood of detection in laboratory studies of PDD, and strongly suggest that this correlation cannot be accounted for simply in terms of a relationship with general reactivity of the system" (Horneman and O'Gorman, 1987, p. 329).

## Age and Gender Differences in Psychophysiological Detection

Only few studies have looked into possible gender differences in psychophysiological detection. Cutrow et al. (1972) studied nine physiological measures in three GKT tasks. None of their measures revealed any significant sex differences. Timm (1982) examined effects of placebo and feedback on electrodermal and respiration measures of detection in a mock crime procedure using the GKT. He used 135 female and 135 male subjects and did not obtain any significant difference between them in either measure of detection. Additionally, gender did not interact with the treatments examined by Timm. Similar results indicating that gender is unrelated to measures of differential responsivity in the GKT were reported by Gudjonsson (1982a), and by Furedy, Davis, and Gurevich (1988). Yet, it is possible that gender is related to psychophysiological detection, but in a more complex manner—through the interaction between the sex of the examiner and that of the examinee. No systematic attempts to study this possibility have been reported so far.

An interesting question arises regarding psychophysiological detection in children. It is not clear whether detection is possible with young children and whether psychophysiological differentiation between relevant and neutral stimuli develops with age and at what rate. Unfortunately, these issues were addressed only by a single study, and, therefore, only initial information is available. Lieblich (1971) examined 3- and 4-year-old children using six GKT conditions and the electrodermal measure for detection. The relevant information was not detected at a greater than chance rate in any of the conditions. Nevertheless, it was shown that psychophysiological differentiation could be manipulated even in young children. The various tasks used by Lieblich (1971) were ordered in terms of the amount of contrast between the critical item and the neutral ones (e.g., in one condition the critical item was the subject's name and the neutral control items were common names known not to be related to the subject; in another condition the subject's name was contrasted with names of persons from the child's immediate family circle). The signal-to-noise ratio (the ratio of the GSRs to the critical and the neutral stimuli) reflected the amount of contrast. These results can be compared with another study by Lieblich (1969) in which the very same procedure was implemented with adults (college students). The results obtained in the adult sample also indicated that differential electrodermal responsivity could be manipulated by changing the contrast between the critical and the neutral stimuli. However, the adults differed from the children in terms of the detection efficiencies—detection rates in the adult sample were significantly greater than chance in three out of the six conditions (the conditions in which a relatively high contrast between relevant and neutral stimuli was created). Lieblich (1971) reported that the poor psychophysiological detection in the young children did not result from small responsivity to the critical stimuli, but rather from their tendency to give relatively large responses to the neutral stimuli. Clearly, further research is needed to clarify the role of development in psychophysiological detection.

## Ethnic and Cultural Differences in Psychophysiological Detection

Kugelmass and his colleagues were the first to look into ethnic and cultural factors in the context of psychophysiological detection. In their first study, while examining the effects of stress on detection, Kugelmass and Lieblich (1966) observed clear individual differences in GSR reactions during the card test. Subjects of Near Eastern origin (born in the Moslem countries of the Mediterranean basin—Morocco, Yeman, Iraq, or Iran) displayed smaller responses to their chosen cards as compared with subjects of Western origin (born in European countries, in America, or in Israel). In a subsequent study, Kugelmass and Lieblich (1968b) focused on ethnic differences in psychophysiological reactivity. They used a sample of actual criminal suspects tested at the polygraph laboratory of the Israeli Police Force. Data were collected from a card test procedure incorporated into the standard polygraph examinations of 62 criminal suspects connected with serious offenses. The results agreed with the previous study and revealed significantly greater electrodermal responsivity to the relevant stimulus (a card chosen by the subject) among subjects of Western origin as compared with those born in Near Eastern countries. No such differences were obtained in the responses to the neutral stimuli. Kugelmass and Lieblich (1968b) then decided to collect additional data based on a sample of subjects who "approximate the phenotype of Near Eastern natives as closely as possible." (p. 160) Such subjects were available in Bedouin tribes living in Israel's Negev Desert. All ten subjects originally tested did not produce electrodermal responses to their chosen cards, and therefore their detection rate did not exceed chance expectancy levels. These ten subjects did produce, however, an orienting response (their mean reaction to the first item presented to them was 1000 ohms). Kugelmass and Lieblich (1968b) also reported on ethnic differences in basic physiological activity: the Bedouins displayed higher levels of skin conductance and lower pulse rates than the Jewish samples. This finding may reflect differences in physical fitness between the groups.

In an additional study, Kugelmass, Lieblich, and Ben-Shakhar (1973) examined another sample of 16 Bedouin subjects using 2 detection tasks (an object was chosen by the subject from a set of 6 objects, and the subject's first name was presented along with 5 additional first names). The results were very similar to those obtained by Kugelmass and Lieblich (1968b): responses to the relevant stimuli were generally small (e.g., half of the subjects gave no measurable GSRs to their own names), and the detection rates were at chance levels (only 12.5% of the Bedouin subjects were correctly detected in the name test, and 25% were correctly detected in the "object detection" task). In a second experiment reported by Kugelmass et al. (1973), an additional sample of 27 Bedouin subjects was tested. In contrast to the previous experiments in which Bedouin subjects were tested in their own locations, this time the subjects were brought to Jerusalem and were tested in more controlled laboratory conditions. The procedure included two name detection tasks (the name of the subject's wife and the name of his oldest son). Contrary to the previous findings, significantly greater than chance detection rates were obtained this time in both detection tasks (42% and 44% correct detections were observed in the "wife detection" and the "son detection" tasks, respectively). These rates were obtained despite the fact that GSR reactivity was as small as in the previous Bedouin samples, and basic skin conductance levels were also similar to those obtained in previous samples. Kugelmass et al. (1973) suggested two possible explanations for the different results obtained in the different Bedouin samples: (a) differences in the testing environment and procedures or (b) a sampling bias due to the greater ease of convincing Bedouins of higher status to make the trip to Jerusalem. In order to check for the first possibility, a subsample of the Jerusalem sample was retested under conditions similar to those used in the previous studies. This time a detection rate of 55% was obtained, effectively ruling out the first possibility. The authors raised the possibility that the Jerusalem sample had consisted of individuals with higher socioeconomic status within the tribe, as well as with higher levels of formal eduction (67% of the "Jerusalem sample" had some degree of formal education as compared with only 12% in the former Bedouin sample reported by Kugelmass et al.). This suggestion may be somewhat strengthened by an earlier observation of a positive relationship between years of schooling and card detection scores (correlations of .50 and .46 were reported in two samples of Jewish police trainees; see Kugelmass et al., 1973). The authors suggest that schooling may influence differential responsivity to relevant stimuli, because "concentrated attention to a particular task would be expected to develop within formal schooling" or because "socialization of a broader perceptual-cognitive style could underlie the relative extent of psychophysiological reactivity" (Kugelmass et al., 1973, p. 490).

Waid and Orne (1981) have suggested that the ethnic origin of the subjects might interact with the ethnic origin of the examiner. They demonstrated that American college students of Irish origin were detected less frequently (on the basis of the electrodermal measure) than students from other ethnic groups when the examiner was a former police captain of Irish heritage. However this result can be treated only as suggestive, because no systematic manipulation of the examiner-examinee ethnic origin was employed.

## Personality Differences in Psychophysiological Detection

A plausible source for the observed individual differences in detection is personality. Several researchers have looked into various personality dimensions, focusing on traits that are theoretically likely to be associated with psychophysiological reactivity (e.g., anxiety) or with deception and antisocial behavior (e.g., socialization, psychopathic tendencies). Giesen and Rollison (1980) examined the relationship between trait anxiety and psychophysiological detection using electrodermal measures and the GKT paradigm. They used a sample of 40 subjects selected for being electrodermal responders (by their self-report). The subjects were divided into high- and low-anxiety groups by their responses to an anxiety questionnaire (Lykken's Activity Preference Questionnaire); and both groups were engaged in either a mock crime or a neutral activity during which they were exposed to the relevant information. The results revealed significant effects on differential reactivity scores (responses to neutral stimuli subtracted from the responses to the relevant ones) for both the anxiety factor and the guilt-vs.-innocent treatment. Differential responsivity scores obtained in the guilty condition were larger than those in the innocent condition, and larger scores were obtained in the high-anxiety group than in the low one. Furthermore, those two factors interacted—while highly anxious subjects responded more strongly to the guilty rather than to the innocent treatment, practically no difference was obtained in the low-anxiety group. These results indicate that the relationship between trait anxiety and electrodermal responsivity is a complex one which may be revealed only in an emotionally laden situation when subjects are exposed to relevant stimuli. However, Honts, Raskin, and Kircher (1986) did not obtain any significant correlation between trait or state anxiety and CQT-based detection scores, either for subjects simulating the guilty condition or for those simulating the innocents. Similarly, Iacono et al. (1984) did not obtain significant correlations between measures based on the State-Trait Anxiety Inventory and electrodermal measures of detection based on a GKT task. On the other hand, Gudjonsson (1982a) reported that extreme levels of self reported tension during a card test experiment interfered with electrodermal differential responses.

Bradley and Janisse (1981b) examined a different personality dimension—extroversion/introversion—in the context of psychophysiological detection. They hypothesized that extroverted individuals who are believed to be more difficult to arouse cortically would be more easily detected than introverts because only the critical items would be cortically arousing for them. According to this hypothesis, introverts, who are more cortically excitable, would respond more to all interrogation questions, thus displaying less *differential* autonomic responsivity. A sample of 96 subjects was divided into extroverts and introverts by their responses to the Eysenck Personality Inventory. All subjects were engaged in a mock crime procedure such that half the subjects in each group were "guilty" and the other half "innocent." Subjects were interrogated using the CQT, and detection scores were based on the electrodermal measure. The results revealed a significant interaction between guilt/innocence and extroversion/introversion—extroverts were easier to detect than introverts; innocent extroverts scored in the more innocent direction and guilty extroverts scored in the more guilty direction. While 81% of the subjects classified as extroverts were correctly detected, the accuracy rate among the introverts was only 54% (as compared with a 50% chance detection rate). The authors account for the effects obtained by claiming that introverts are highly sensitive to potentially incriminating past-life questions, and, therefore, they responded strongly to the control as well as to the relevant questions. While this explanation may hold for the guilty subjects, it is not clear why innocent introverts should be less detectable than innocent extroverts. Gudjonsson (1982a,b) suggested that the relationship between extroversion and psychophysiological detection reported by Bradley and Janisse (1981b) is valid only for the CQT. Gudjonsson hypothesized that in a card test paradigm introverts will be better detected because "they are generally more susceptible to stimulus change than extraverts" (Gudjonsson, 1982a, p. 382). Gudjonsson obtained significant correlations between introversion scores and differential responsivity in three card test tasks only for normal males. However, in a more recent study based on a mock crime design, Steller, Haenert, and Eiselt (1987) extended the findings of Bradley and Janisse (1981b) and obtained a correlation of .32 between extroversion and electrodermal detection scores based on six GKT questions, among subjects simulating the guilty condition. The detection scores of subjects simulating the innocent condition were not correlated with the extroversion/introversion dimension. Iacono et al. (1984) on the other hand, did not obtain a significant correlation between extroversion scores, based on the Differential Personality Questionnaire, and GKT detection scores for subjects in the guilty condition.

Bradley and Janisse (1981b) examined another personality factor—neuroticism—but did not find it to be related to detection. A similar result was reported by Iacono et al. (1984). Gudjonsson (1982a), on the other hand, did obtain some significant correlations between neuroticism and differential responsivity on the electrodermal measure, but only for females and not for males. According to Honts et al. (1986), there is some indication that extroversion and neuroticism might be related to detection scores based on a CQT mock crime study. However, only some of the correlations reported in their study were statistically significant, and only for subjects simulating the innocents.

Another personality trait that was examined by Janisse and Bradley (1980) is Machiavellism. These researchers hypothesized that individuals who score high on the Machiavellian (mach) scale might have better control over their emotional reactions, which could be reflected by a smaller degree of autonomic differentiation. In this study, Janisse and Bradley employed a card test paradigm and used detection scores based on the pupillary response. No effects were obtained for the Machiavellian score—subjects scoring high on that scale were detected as effectively as low-scoring subjects. In a more recent study, Bradley and Klohn (1987) formulated a different hypothesis regarding the relationship between machiavellism and psychophysiological detection in the CQT. They assumed that subjects scoring high on the mach scale will better discriminate between relevant and control questions, and therefore will be more accurately classified than low mach scorers in CQT polygraph examinations. The results obtained by Bradley and Klohn (1987) provided only a partial support for their hypothesis—guilty high-mach scorers were more accurately detected than guilty low-mach scorers, on the basis of electrodermal and pulse rate measures, but no such differences were observed among the innocent subjects.

Several investigators have suggested that psychopathic tendencies might be correlated with psychophysiological detection. Psychopaths are considered to be conscienceless individuals who are not concerned about their wrongdoings. Therefore, it might seem reasonable to assume that they will show little emotional reaction when interrogated about such wrongdoings. Most studies dealing with this issue have utilized the CQT method for interrogating the subjects and the Minnesota Multiphasic Personality Inventory (MMPI) to identify psychopaths. Typically, subjects who scored high on the Pd (psychopathic deviate) scale of the MMPI were compared with low-scoring subjects. Barland and Raskin (1975b) studied criminal suspects using a mock crime procedure, while Raskin, Barland, and Podlesny (1977) examined suspects using a panel of legal experts to determine the criterion (i.e., guilt or innocence). The results of both studies did not reveal any relationship between psychopathic personality and detection scores—subjects with high Pd scores were detected as well as those scoring low on that scale. Barland and Raskin (1975b) reported a correlation of only .02 between Pd and detection scores. Raskin and Hare (1978) claimed that these negative results might have been caused by the inappropriateness of the MMPI as a clinical measure of the concept of psychopathy. Consequently, they conducted an additional mock crime study in which all subjects were prison inmates, and a clinical assessment procedure was used to categorize them into psychopathic and nonpsychopathic subgroups. These results were, however, similar to those obtained in the previous studies—psychopaths and nonpsychopaths showed similar detection scores based on respiration, electrodermal, and cardiovascular measures. This pattern was revealed both when each physiological measure was analyzed and when the measures were combined into a single numerical score. Recently, Patrick and Iacono (1989) conducted a constructive replication of the Raskin and Hare (1978) study and obtained similar results to all the previous studies. Almost identical accuracy rates for psychopathic and nonpsychopathic prisoner inmates were reported by Patrick and Iacono (1989), indicating no relationship between psychopathy and psychophysiological detection.

Balloun and Holmes (1979) claimed that it is difficult to draw conclusions from mock crime studies employing artificial "crimes." They conducted a study in which real-life conditions were approximated in the laboratory. Thirty-four subjects took a written intelligence test on which they were urged to cheat by confederates posing as other subjects. A GKT polygraph test was conducted for both cheaters ($n=18$) and noncheaters. The Pd scale of the MMPI was used to measure psychopathy. Detection scores based on the electrodermal measure were not affected by the Pd scores, indicating that psychopaths were detected as effectively as nonpsychopaths. Heart rate and finger pulse volume were also measured in this study, but failed to discriminate cheaters from noncheaters. The authors raise the possibility that the Pd scale is not a valid measure of psychopathy. Nevertheless, in light of the studies reviewed in this section we must conclude that no evidence was provided to demonstrate any relationship between psychopathic tendencies (whether measured by questionnaires or by clinical assessment methods) and psychophysiological detection. This conclusion contradicts theoretical approaches that emphasize guilt as the basic psychological process responsible for psychological detection.

Another personality variable, which is conceptually close to psychopathy and was considered as a possible determinant of psychophysiological detection, is the level of socialization. Waid et al. (1979a) argued that "the behavior patterns of poorly socialized individuals suggest that deception is not unusual for them and they might be less aroused while attempting deception and consequently less easily detected" (p. 15). In an additional article, Waid et al. (1979b) raised the possibility that "poorly socialized behavior develops as a result of insufficient physiological arousal in response to and in anticipation of stress" (p. 663). Waid et al. (1979a,b) used the socialization scale of the California Psychological Inventory (CPI) to classify their subjects into low- and high-socialization groups. All subjects participated in a mock crime experiment, with 15 subjects simulating the guilty condition and another 15 subjects simulating the innocents. The results clearly indicated that socialization is related to electrodermal responsivity to relevant and control questions and that low-socialization subjects might be more difficult to detect. In their first article (Waid et al., 1979a) the researchers reported, on the basis of four polygraph tests (two CQT procedures, a peak of tension, and a GKT test), that deceptive subjects who escaped detection tended to score lower on the socialization scale than subjects who were detected. Similarly, false-positive classifications were made among subjects who scored relatively high on the socialization scale. Among the subjects simulating the guilty condition, the SCRs to the relevant questions correlated .45 with socialization; and among "innocent" subjects, socialization correlated .56 with the mean SCR to all questions. Waid et al. (1979b) obtained significant correlations between socialization and SCRs to all questions, both when subjects were aware of the fact that their responses were monitored by the polygraph and when they were not aware. Furthermore, only high-socialization deceptive subjects gave SCRs that were significantly larger for the critical questions than for the noncritical ones. It is important to note that the two socialization groups did not differ in their electrodermal responses to routine questions.

The results reported by Waid et al. (1979a,b) do not agree with the results of studies which focused on psychopathy and used either the MMPI (e.g., Balloun and Holmes, 1979) or a clinical assessment procedure (Patrick and Iacono, 1989; Raskin and Hare, 1978) to classify subjects into psychopaths and non-psychopaths. The concepts of psychopathy and socialization are very similar, and it is not clear why only the latter measure produced a relationship with psychophysiological detection. It is possible that the differences are related to the different measures used for the personality factor. Waid et al. (1979a) discussed this issue and raised additional possible reasons for this discrepancy. However, in two more recent studies no significant correlations were obtained between measures of socialization and psychophysiological detection. Gudjonsson (1982a) reported near zero correlations between this personality dimension and differential responsivity based on the electrodermal measure in three card test tasks. Honts et al. (1986) presented, in an abstract form, the correlations of several personality variables with detection scores based on a CQT mock crime experiment. No significant correlations were obtained for the socialization scale of the CPI, neither in the group simulating the guilty condition nor in the one simulating the innocent condition.

It is difficult to summarize this section dealing with personality and psychophysiological detection, because too few studies were conducted for any given personality dimension and the results were often not conclusive and even contradictory. Nevertheless, it seems that some of the personality variables studied might turn out to be important in determining psychophysiological detection and in accounting for some of the individual differences in detection. In particular, socialization and psychopathy require further research to clarify the inconsistent results. The extroversion/introversion dichotomy, as well as level of anxiety, seem like promising predictors of psychophysiological detection.

# Comparing Different Physiological Measures for Psychophysiological Detection

An important question with obvious practical implications relates to the role of the different physiological measures used for the detection of deception. Typically, field practices make use of three or four measures — respiration, electrodermal activity, and cardiovascular measures (the most popular of which are changes in heart rate and relative blood pressure). Early descriptions of field procedures which focused primarily on the CQT emphasized respiration and blood pressure and tended to pay much less attention to the electrodermal measure (e.g., Inbau and Reid, 1953). On the other hand, the experimental work in this area from its outset used mostly the GKT and emphasized electrodermal measures (e.g., Ellson, Burke, Davis, and Saltzman, 1952; Lykken, 1959). It might seem as if electrodermal measures are more effective than other physiological measures when the GKT is being used, whereas respiration and cardiovascular measures are more effective under the CQT. As was detailed in Chapters 1 and 2, most field practices rely upon global, subjective, and intuitive evaluation of the polygraph charts. Under such procedures it is difficult to know how the different measures are weighted in the evaluation process. It is even possible that different examiners assign different weights to the different physiological measures. Wherever inference rules for reaching conclusions and making decisions on the basis of polygraph interrogation procedures are specified, equal weights are assigned to the different physiological measures (e.g., Backster, 1963; Kircher and Raskin, 1988). It is, however, far from clear that the different measures are equally efficient in detecting deception or that the relative efficiency of the different measures depends upon the polygraph method being used. In this section we will examine those questions and review a number of studies that provide data on the basis of which different measures can be compared. We shall examine whether different measures differ in their detection efficiency and whether such differences depend upon the specific polygraph method. In addition to the four popular measures mentioned above, some less conventional measures will be looked at (e.g., pupillary measures—Janisse and Bradley, 1980; evoked responses—Farwell and Donchin, 1986, 1988). Finally, attempts to apply a nonphysiological measure—voice analysis (e.g., Horvath, 1979)—will be discussed.

The number of studies that contain data relevant for comparing different physiological measures is fairly large. Therefore we shall present our review of the literature, separating studies that used a GKT paradigm from those that utilized the CQT method. At the end of the section we shall try to draw some general conclusions.

## Comparing the Validity of Different Measures for Psychophysiological Detection in the GKT

The first study that systematically compared different physiological measures for detection of deception was conducted by Thackray and Orne (1968b). They used a GKT paradigm and compared a total of eight measures: two respiration measures (breathing amplitude, BA, and breathing cycle time, BCT), two electrodermal measures (changes in skin resistance, GSR, and changes in skin potential, SPR), three cardiovascular measures (blood pressure, BP; finger volume, FV; and pulse volume, PV), and changes in the level of oxygen ($O^2$ S). The comparisons were based on several GKT questions related to personal items of the subjects' (e.g., the subject's first name) and two code words memorized by the subjects. Only three of the eight measures (GSR, SPR, and FV) produced detection rates that were consistently greater than rates expected by chance. Two measures (BA and $O^2$ S) produced significant detection rates in some of the tests. The two electrodermal measures were more efficient than the finger volume, with no consistent difference between them.

Cutrow et al. (1972) compared a total of nine physiological indices, including four of the measures used in the previous study and five additional ones. The measures used were BA, BCT, eye-blink rate (EBR), eye-blink latency (EBL), finger pulse volume (FPV), heart rate (HR), palmar galvanic skin response (GSRp), volar-forearm galvanic skin response (GSRv), and voice latency (VL). The comparison of the measures was based on a total of nine GKT-type questions (three questions referred to personal items, three referred to words memorized by the subject, and three were items involving money taken by the subject). In contrast with previous findings (e.g., Kugelmass and Lieblich, 1966; Thackray and Orne, 1968b), all nine indices produced better than chance detection efficiencies. The GSRp produced the best discrimination between relevant and neutral items, and the EBL produced the least effective outcome. However, no statistical tests were reported in comparisons of the measures. A combined score based on six of the measures (BA, BCT, EBR, FPV, GSRp, and VL) produced the most efficient result (it was significantly more effective than the best single index—the GSRp).

Both Thackray and Orne (1968b) and Cutrow et al. (1972) focused primarily on the issue of comparing physiological measures. To achieve this goal, they monitored several measures and conducted a systematic comparison between them. Many other studies, focusing on different issues, used more than one physiological measure and therefore may shed some light on the issue of the relative utility of different measures for psychophysiological detection.

Kugelmass and Lieblich (1966) compared measures of skin resistance and heart rate (the heart-rate measure was defined as the highest change in pulse rate within 5 seconds after stimulus presentation, independent of the direction of change) for card test detection under three stress conditions. In all three conditions the detection rates based on the GSR index were significantly greater than chance expectancy rates, whereas detection based on heart rate changes never exceeded chance expectation levels. The difference in detection efficiency between the GSR and the pulse rate measures was statistically significant.

In an additional study, Kugelmass, Lieblich, Ben-Ishai, Opatowski, and Kaplan (1968) compared the GSR measure to an index of relative blood pressure standardly used by field polygraph examiners. The main purpose of this study was to compare the different measures under realistic stress conditions, so the experiment was conducted in the Israeli police laboratories. It was based on the standard card test utilized in the course of the actual polygraph interrogation with suspects of actual crimes.

The results showed some advantage to the GSR measure (the rate of correct detections with this measure ranged between 52% and 56%) over relative blood pressure (47% of the cases were correctly detected), but these differences were not statistically significant and both measures yielded detection rates above chance level (1 in 6). As in their pervious study (Kugelmass and Lieblich, 1966), heart-rate changes did not produce detection rates greater than chance expectancy. In an additional report (Kugelmass and Lieblich, 1968a), which was based on the same data used by Kugelmass et al. (1968), the authors analyzed the respiration measure in addition to the GSR and blood pressure. The respiration measure was defined as the area under the breathing cycle waveform during the 5 seconds following stimulus presentation. This measure produced 44% correct detections (as compared with 52% for the GSR and 48% for the blood pressure measure). An attempt was made to combine the three measures. When a discriminant function was used (i.e., the optimal linear combination of the three measures), only a slight improvement was obtained (the detection rate was 54%). However, a nonparametric approach yielded a somewhat better result: when the responses to the different card numbers were ranked from highest to lowest for each measure and then the ranks were summed up to obtain a single measure, 61% of the cases were correctly detected.

Kugelmass and his colleagues examined the possibility that the blood pressure cuff might interfere with the GSR measure and reduce its efficiency. In standard field practice (at the time these studies were conducted) the blood pressure cuff was inflated to a pressure somewhat above the diastolic blood pressure (about 90 mm Hg), and this pressure is maintained during an interrogation period of about 2½ minutes. Kugelmass and Lieblich (1966) and Kugelmass et al. (1968) compared the efficiency of the electrodermal measure with and without the blood pressure cuff. In both studies the GSR was more effective under the no-cuff condition, but the difference reached statistical significance only on the first study.

Balloun and Holmes (1979) conducted a GKT polygraph test with 34 subjects, some of whom had actually cheated on an intelligence test (subjects were urged to cheat by confederates posing as other subjects). Three physiological measures were taken—skin resistance, heart rate, and finger pulse volume. Only the electrodermal measure produced significant discrimination between guilty and innocent subjects. In an additional study, Waid, Wilson, and Orne (1981) reported an advantage for the skin conductance measure over both respiration and blood pressure for psychophysiological detection under the GKT.

The pupillary response is a psychophysiological measure not commonly used for detection. This measure was demonstrated to produce significant detection rates in a card test procedure (Bradley and Janisse, 1979; Janisse and Bradley, 1980). In a subsequent study, these authors (Bradley and Janisse, 1981a) compared the pupillary response with more commonly used measures for psychophysiological detection. They obtained better detection efficiency in a GKT procedure with the skin resistance measure than with changes in either pupil size or heart rate. Nevertheless, the latter two measures produced significantly better-than-chance detection rates.

Timm (1982) examined the effects of placebo and feedback on the validity of the GKT. He used electrodermal and respiration measures and reported a significant advantage for respiration over skin resistance amplitude. Timm suggested two possibilities to account for this unusual result: (*a*) the electrodermal recording system contained in the field polygraph used by him was not as precise as the highly sophisticated laboratory equipment used in the other studies, and (*b*) the respiration measure used by Timm (total length of the respiration tracing) may be more valid than respiration measures that have been used in many other studies (e.g., respiration amplitude, respiration cycle time). In a subsequent study, Timm (1987) used similar procedures and similar measures and obtained significantly greater-than-chance detection scores with both electrodermal and respiration measures. Timm (1987) did not perform statistical tests to compare the measures, but inspection of his data suggests that the length of the respiration trace and skin resistance amplitude produced similar detection scores, with a slight advantage for the former measure.

Elaad (1987) conducted two GKT experiments using field polygraph setting and instrumentation. In both experiments the electrodermal measure turned out to be significantly more effective than either respiration or blood-pressure measures. While respiration produced better than chance accuracy rates, the blood-pressure measure produced accuracy rates at chance expectancy levels.

Several investigators have focused on a nonphysiological measure for detection—the analysis of tremors in the voice. The psychological stress evaluator (PSE) is a device designed to detect low-frequency tremors in the voice. The use of such a device for detecting deception is obviously very tempting because it can be employed without connecting subjects to polygraphs through electrodes, or even without the subject's awareness. However, in all the studies that used PSE

(Barland, 1975; Horvath, 1978, 1979; Nachshon, Elaad, and Amsel, 1985; Nachshon and Feldman, 1980) there is no single instance showing this measure to be a better-than-chance indicator of deception. Horvath (1978, 1979) conducted two studies in which the PSE was compared with the electrodermal measure in a card test paradigm. In his first study he reported an average of 24% and 21% correct detections with the PSE on two card test trials (against a chance expectancy rate of 20%). The average electrodermal detection rates were 69% and 43%. In his subsequent study Horvath (1979) obtained similar results. The average correct detection rates based on PSE recording were 20% and 17% in two card test trials. In contrast, electrodermal detection rates were 52% and 51% on the same card test trials.

Nachshon and Feldman (1980) conducted two experiments focusing on the validity of the PSE. In their first experiment, judges were unable to discriminate between critical and neutral stimuli at better-than-chance levels, either in a card test paradigm or in a horror picture test procedure. In their second experiment, they used a card test that was administered during an actual polygraph interrogation. The results were very similar to those obtained in the first experiment. In both experiments, not only a poor validity was obtained, but the interjudge reliabilities were very low (the average percents of interjudge agreements on the cards chosen by the subjects were 28.3 and 31.5 in the two experiments, respectively). Nachshon et al. (1985) conducted a further study focusing on the PSE, but in this study the judgments based on the PSE were compared with judgments based on other physiological measures without a criterion for ground truth. Therefore, it is impossible to draw conclusions from this study regarding the PSE's validity.

Horvath (1979) summarizes the PSE results based on his studies as well as previous studies by other investigators, saying: "detection rates obtained with the PSE have not been above chance level and when evaluated within similar contexts, have been greatly exceeded by field measures of GSR" (p. 329).

An additional measure which may be promising is the p300 component of the event-related potential. In two recent reports, Farwell and Donchin (1986, 1988) demonstrated how this measure can be applied for psychophysiological detection in the GKT paradigm. Their results are impressive, but they are based on small data sets; therefore more research is needed before potentials recorded from the brain can be used for psychophysiological detection.

## Comparing the Validity of Different Measures for Psychophysiological Detection in the CQT

A number of studies have reported on the validity of the CQT under controlled experimental conditions. Most of those studies were conducted by Raskin and his colleagues at the University of Utah (e.g., Barland and Raskin, 1975a; Kircher and Raskin, 1988; Podlesny and Raskin, 1978; Raskin and Hare, 1978). These studies employed the mock crime paradigm in which subjects in one group, simulating the "guilty" condition, are typically instructed by the experimenter to enter an office, after the secretary has left it, and take an envelope from a desk in the office, containing either money (e.g., a $10 bill) or some jewelry (e.g., a gold wedding ring). In the second stage, all subjects, both "innocent" and "guilty," are interrogated by a blind polygraph examiner. Typically these studies used several physiological measures; thus they may shed some light on possible differences between them.

Podlesny and Raskin (1978) examined both the CQT and the GKT using a mock crime paradigm. They utilized numerical field evaluations of the physiological measures as well as quantitative analysis of the data. With the field-scoring technique, only skin conductance and plethysmographic measures produced significant discrimination between "guilty" and "innocent" subjects. These effects were obtained under both the CQT and the GKT interrogation methods. Respiration and cardiovascular scores, on the other hand, did not produce significant discrimination between the two groups of subjects, but they did produce significant effects within the innocent group (i.e., a pattern of greater responsivity to control than to relevant questions). In their quantitative analysis, Podlesny and Raskin report on many different indices, but in general the results agree with those based on the field-scoring technique. Various electrodermal measures produced significant discrimination between guilty and innocent subjects for both interrogation methods. Similar results were obtained with the plethysmographic measure (finger blood volume and pulse amplitude). The respiration measures (respiration amplitude and cycle time) failed to produce any significant effects. The cardio measure (cardio systolic and diastolic pulse amplitude and heart rate) produced mixed results (some measures produce significant discrimination in some of the statistical analyses).

Dawson (1980) also conducted a mock crime experiment using the CQT with various physiological measures. Two versions of the CQT were used by Dawson: one in which subjects were instructed to respond verbally immediately following each question and one in which they delayed their verbal answer for 8 seconds following each question. A separate analysis of the physiological measures was employed for the question and for the answer in the delayed-answer condition. Both electrodermal and cardiovascular measures (changes from baseline measured at the diastolic portion of each pulse wave) significantly discriminated between "guilty" and "innocent" subjects under the immediate-answer condition and under the delayed condition when the physiological responses to the questions were used. The respiration measures (respiratory cycle time and amplitude) failed to produce significant effects under the immediate-answer condition and produced inconsistent effects under the delayed condition. The physiological responses to the answers in the delayed condition failed to produce significant effects with any of the physiological measures.

In a more recent study, Kircher and Raskin (1988) utilized similar mock crime procedures in an attempt to computerize various physiological measures in order to assess the probability of deception. They generated a discriminant function based on a standardization sample of 100 subjects (50 "guilty" and 50 "innocent" subjects). Five variables were selected for the discriminant function from a large set of physiological measures. The selection of variables was based on maximization of the differences between the two subsamples (guilty and innocent). Three of the five variables selected for the discriminant function were derived from the electrodermal channel (skin conductance amplitude, skin conductance full recovery time, and electrodermal burst frequency). The other variables were blood pressure amplitude and length of the respiration tracing. The three electrodermal measures accounted for more than 70% of the predictable variance in the criterion. The skin conductance amplitude was the single best measure and was the most heavily weighted variable in the discriminant function (the relative weights of the five variables were .61, .11, −.01, .11, and .17 for skin conductance amplitude, recovery time, burst frequency, blood pressure amplitude, and respiration length, respectively). The simple correlations of the skin conductance amplitude with the criterion of guilt vs. innocence were .77 for the standardization sample and .82 for a cross-validation sample. Blood pressure amplitude also produced robust correlations with the criterion (.61 in the standardization sample and .66 in the cross-validation sample). Respiration length turned out to be a much less valid and robust predictor (it correlated −.55 with the criterion in the standardization sample but only −.27 in the cross-validation sample). Kircher and Raskin (1988) concluded that "skin conductance response is the most useful measure for discriminating between truthful and deceptive subjects" (p. 299).

## A Summary of the Measures Comparison Literature

Several conclusions can be drawn from our review of the literature dealing with comparisons between different measures for psychophysiological detection. Contrary to what might have been expected from early accounts, no differences emerge between laboratory and field studies or between studies using the GKT and those using the CQT. Almost all the studies that employed a systematic comparison between physiological measures of detection demonstrated a clear advantage to electrodermal over all other measures used. This result was obtained in GKT studies (e.g., Cutrow et al., 1972; Thackray and Orne, 1968b) as well as in CQT mock crime studies (e.g., Kircher and Raskin, 1988), in laboratory studies, and in studies conducted in real-life situations (e.g., Kugelmass et al., 1968). The only instance in which electrodermal measure was of inferior validity to some alternative measure (respiration) was provided by Timm (1982), but was never replicated. Moreover, the electrodermal channel is the only one that produced significant discrimination between relevant and neutral stimuli (or between guilty and innocent individuals) in all the studies reviewed. Other physiological measures seem to produce better-than-chance accuracy levels as well, but the results are not uniform. For example, respiration was demonstrated to be relatively valid in some studies (e.g., Kugelmass and Lieblich, 1968a; Timm, 1982, 1987), but not in others (e.g., Thackray and Orne, 1968b); blood pressure produced better than chance accuracy levels in some studies (e.g., Kugelmass et al., 1968), but not in others (e.g., Elaad, 1987; Thackray and Orne, 1968b). The only nonphysiological measure that was studied, the PSE, does not seem to be a valid measure for psychophysiological detection.

CHAPTER 5

# The Detection of Deception: A Psychophysiological, Specific-Effects-Oriented Perspective

In this chapter we would like to take a fresh look at the problem of evaluating polygraphy, or the "detection of deception." Our starting point will be the psychological process of deception and we shall base our discussion on the science of psychophysiology, conceived as that part of the science of psychology which uses unobtrusively measured physiological functions to measure and differentiate between psychological processes (Furedy, 1983).

We view psychology itself in a nondualistic framework, which is to say that the same deterministic, cause-effect logic is applied to physical, physiological, *and* psychological events. Contrasted with this monist, deterministic framework (see, e.g., Maze, 1983) is the currently more popular dualist, teleological approach, according to which teleology is appropriate for things psychological, while normal cause-effect mechanisms are reserved only for the physical.

Though popular, this sort of dualism is philosophically unsound as a scientific approach, because it consigns not only the teleological realm but also the relationships between the psychological and physical realms beyond cause-effect explanation, which is to say that these aspects are consigned to scientific oblivion (see, e.g., Anderson, 1962). On a more applied level, this sort of dualism is evident in those who would argue that, for psychological treatments, placebo factors can be considered as positive evidence for treatment efficacy, on the grounds that psychological processes are purposive and hence not subject to normal cause-effect logic (e.g., Critelli and Neumann, 1984). This approach, in the long run, is technologically retrogressive, in that long-term improvements in psychological treatments cannot be made. So we get the psychotherapists who run antismoking clinics ending up with the (honest but) lame advice that they can only stop you from smoking if you have the willpower to do so.

In the monist, deterministic view, all applications, whether they be psychological or physiological or involve (as is most usual) some interaction, need to be evaluated in terms of a specific-effects logic. The paradigm case for this sort of evaluation is that used in pharmacology for evaluating drug effects. In those tests of efficacy, the drug is pitted against a no-drug condition in a double-blind arrangement. This ensures that the presence vs. absence of the drug is the *only* difference between the experimental and control conditions. This procedure controls for placebo factors, which are held constant between the two conditions, so that a difference between the conditions is interpretable as being due to the specific (beneficial) effect of the drug being tested.

The following two sections will apply the specific-effects perspective to two purported applications of psychophysiology: biofeedback and polygraphy. A detailed consideration of the former application is useful, because the issues have emerged clearly in recent papers, at least partly because there have been a number of interchanges between proponents and opponents of the specific-effects approach. Similar interchanges have only begun to emerge in the case of the polygraph (see Furedy and Heslegrave, 1989b).

# Biofeedback

The central assumption behind this purported application of psychophysiology is that if the patient is supplied with temporally fine-grained information about changes in physiological functions that are not available to consciousness, then this information, in itself, will improve the patient's control over those functions. So, for example, if heart rate deceleration is the desired target behavior, then providing patients with information about beat-to-beat (or second-to-second) changes in heart rate should improve the patient's ability to decrease heart rate.

Biofeedback has been employed in a wide range of situations, and for a considerable variety of physiological functions. The situations have ranged from laboratory animal research with curarized rats (e.g., Miller, 1969) to field human therapeutic programs for relieving various psychosomatic symptoms such as headaches and for controlling events associated more specifically with physical medicine (e.g., paroxysmal atrial tachycardia). The physiological functions have included those predominantly under autonomic control (e.g., heart rate, blood pressure, GSR), motor-controlled functions not normally under voluntary control (e.g., muscular tension), and centrally controlled functions (e.g., the alpha component of the EEG). It is also the case that while psychophysiological *research* on biofeedback has been conducted on both sides of the Atlantic, applications have been much more popular in the U.S., which, as in the case of the polygraph, was the origin of biofeedback (in the early sixties). One indication of the extent of American biofeedback enthusiasm up to the mid-eighties is the fact that no less than two societies existed until then, each with its own official journal: the American Biofeedback Society (originally the American Biofeedback Research Society from the late sixties to the early seventies) and the American Association of Biofeedback Clinicians (AABC).[1]

---

[1] In 1988, the American Biofeedback Society (official journal: *Biofeedback and Self-Regulation*) changed its name to the Association for Applied Psychophysiology and Biofeedback, while the AABC has ceased to exist, along with its official journal (*Clinical Biofeedback and Health: An International Journal*). These signs of waning in biofeedback's popularity are paralleled (some might say prophesied) by the earlier-reported decrease in strength of the *laboratory* curarized-rat biofeedback phenomenon reported by Miller and Dworkin (1974).

Such an apparent waxing and waning in popularity, coupled with geographical differences in popularity, suggests that biofeedback's efficacy has not been primarily evaluated on scientific, evidential grounds. In what follows, we present the logic of evaluation as demanded by the specific-effects perspective and consider some arguments that have arisen from the debate concerning biofeedback's proper evaluation.[2]

## Definition of the Phenomenon and Derivation of the Proper Control Condition

The essence of the biofeedback phenomenon is the *contingency* between the moment-to-moment changes in the target physiological function (e.g., beat-to-beat changes in heart rate) and the moment-to-moment changes in the information (e.g., corresponding beat-to-beat changes in tone frequency) fed *back* to the patient. The phenomenon itself may be said to occur if and only if this contingent feedback information results in an improvement in the ability to control the target physiological function in the direction desired (e.g., heart rate deceleration).

It is important to distinguish such a biofeed*back* phenomenon from a related, but quite different, phenomenon—biofeed*forward*. The feedforward phenomenon occurs when noncontingent, nontemporally fine-grained information about the target physiological function is conveyed to the patient. For example, the patient may be told that certain stressors lead to heart rate acceleration and should therefore be avoided if the aim is to learn to decelerate. Or, more directly, the patient may be advised to breathe at a slower and more regular rate in order to produce heart rate deceleration. This sort of *instructional*, feedforward, information may be quite effective in producing the desired target behavior, but it is not biofeedback. The distinction, moreover, between feedback and feedforward is not merely an academic one of purely scientific importance. It is of considerable practical import. Specifically, the provision of feedforward information by the therapist requires none of the psychophysiological and computer-associated hardware and software skills that are needed in most feedback applications.

The demonstration of the occurrence of the biofeedback phenomenon requires showing that the *contingency* between the physiological function and feedback produces an improvement in the target behavior. This means that the experimental or treatment condition must differ from the control or no-treatment condition *only* with respect to the contingency and nothing else. Treatment evaluations that contrast an explicit biofeedback condition with an explicit no-feedback condition do not satisfy this requirement, assuming that the treatment to be evaluated is

---

[2]For more detailed arguments for the specific-effects position with respect to biofeedback, see Furedy (1979, 1984a,b; 1985; 1987b,c), Furedy and Riley (1982), Furedy and Shulhan (1987), and Furedy, Shulhan, and Levy (1989). For some opposing views, see Green and Shellenberger (1986), Lehrer (1984a,b), Mulholland (1982), and Shellenberger and Green (1987). Finally, for some more neutral commentary on the debate, see Carlson (1987) and Rosenfeld (1987).

biofeed*back*. The problem with the explicit no-feedback control is that it differs from the explicit feedback condition in respects other than the contingency. Specifically, there is additional (feedforward) information provided in the feedback condition, where such information has to be understood to contain motivational factors (i.e., you are being treated as a more important person since you are being given the latest in therapeutic technology: biofeedback). In other words, any difference between the experimental and control conditions may be due to placebo factors unrelated to biofeedback itself.

Accordingly, the only adequate way of evaluating biofeedback is the use of a double-blind arrangement which is analogous to the pharmacological procedure, so that it is *only* the contingency that is being varied between the two conditions. It is true that the exact procedures used for drug testing need not be repeated. In those procedures, the treatment is varied between groups of patients (with some receiving the drug and the others the placebo) and is varied on an all-or-none basis (drug vs. no drug). For evaluating biofeedback, as detailed elsewhere (Furedy, 1985, 1987b), all patients can be given (long) periods of accurate feedback and (much shorter) periods of no feedback. Moreover, to avoid patient recognition of the contingency variation, the contingency may be varied merely between close (highly accurate feedback) and less close (less accurate feedback). These modifications leave the essence of the evaluation unchanged: any difference in performance between the experimental and control conditions is due only to the *contingency* difference between them, i.e., to the specific biofeedback effect.

In this sort of evaluation, the question is not whether the treatment in question works. All treatments work to some extent. Rather, the question is formulated in terms of technological treatments that are genuinely based on scientific principles rather than on placebo factors: does biofeedback have a specific, beneficial effect on the target physiological functions of interest? However, the specific-effects orientation is by no means commonly accepted, even among researchers who have advanced the view that evaluation of biofeedback should be in the "package" mode (see, e.g., Furedy, 1987c).

## Package Evaluation Arguments

One form of the package evaluation view favored by many clinicians is the argument that biofeedback should be evaluated against the best alternative treatment (BAT). The BAT control appears clinically attractive when set against the specific-effects-oriented inaccurate feedback control. The latter is difficult to institute, and those clinicians who assume that it can only be used in a between-groups arrangement argue that it involves depriving some patients of an effective treatment. Finally, the inaccurate feedback control involves an element of deception since patients are not told of this procedure. In contrast, the BAT seems to provide *all* patients with a reasonably effective treatment (i.e., biofeedback or the BAT). Nevertheless, even on strictly applied grounds, the BAT control's advantages are more apparent than real.

One problem is that the etiology of symptoms that biofeedback is used to alleviate is not well enough understood to allow determination of what the actual *best* alternative control is. In reality, any particular BAT indicates a given clinician's individual preference (which itself cannot be comparatively evaluated against other preferences), rather than being derivable from the available literature. A logically relevant literature, indeed, would probably be impossible to produce even in principle, because these treatments are each packages made up of unspecifiable components which include the therapist's bedside manner, as well as the patient-therapist relationship.

Accordingly, any biofeedback/(purported)BAT comparison involves comparing the differing placebo effects associated with biofeedback and the BAT, where both sorts of placebo effects themselves vary over time (as a function of society's awareness of, and feelings toward, biofeedback and the BAT) and place. In addition, the attitude of the therapist toward the treatments, as well as the therapist-patient relationship, is also a factor that affects the nature of placebo effects. Such placebo-contaminated comparisons, therefore, are of no informative value in the evaluation of any treatment. This applies, of course, to the evaluation of unstandardized polygraphic interrogations, which have the same sorts of unspecifiable placebo effects operating.

Another form of the package argument is the view that biofeedback's effectiveness can be evaluated in terms of its costs relative to other treatments. For example, Lehrer (1983) cited evidence (Lehrer, 1982) which compared biofeedback to progressive relaxation treatments using live or tape-recorded instructions. Because only the (more expensive) live relaxation was superior to biofeedback and because biofeedback machines are decreasing in price "while the cost of professional time is increasing," the conclusion was that "biofeedback actually may have some financial advantages" (Lehrer, 1983, p. 825). However, "snake oil may have been quite cheap, but because it had no demonstrable specific effects, it had no place in even nineteenth-century, *scientifically-*based medicine" (Furedy, 1984a, p. 524). No matter how cheap a treatment may become, it is worthless if it has no demonstrated specific *beneficial* effect. Moreover, there may also be specific *detrimental* effects which can be temporarily masked by ephemeral but locally powerful placebo influences. Accordingly, while the snake oil analogy may be offensive and certainly should not be taken to suggest that biofeedback *is* snake oil (see, e.g., Green and Shellenberger, 1986), the analogy does indicate that the snake oil *logic* of evaluation applied to biofeedback is not scientifically based, and it results in technology that, in the long run, is ineffective.

Still, there is the view that even if the specific-effects evaluation is appropriate for laboratory research, there are insurmountable practical difficulties involved in adopting this approach for clinical (field) evaluation. In our view, however, the notion that the difficulties are insurmountable stems from a misunderstanding of the specific-effects position. Accordingly, we turn to some clarifications of that position in the light of some difficulties that have been raised (see, e.g., Green and Shellenberger, 1986; Shellenberger and Green, 1987).

## Some Clarifications of the Specific-Effects Position as Applied to the Evaluation of Clinical Biofeedback

Many clinicians consider that instituting a contingency-based control condition to evaluate biofeedback is both unethical and unfeasible. It is true that there are serious problems if the pharmacological evaluation procedure is applied without any modification, that is, if accurate feedback is given only to one group and not to another (the pharmacological placebo control group) and if the other group receives totally inaccurate feedback (the pharmacological no-drug condition). The between-groups manipulation raises ethical problems, because it deprives one group of patients from what may be the most desirable treatment.[3] The false-feedback condition, at least with respect to some target behaviors (e.g., tonic heart rate change), is unfeasible because it can be *detected* by many patients, so that feedback ceases to be the only difference between the two conditions. However, as detailed elsewhere (Furedy and Riley, 1982), the pharmacological evaluation method can be modified for biofeedback evaluation, while preserving the essential logic of the comparison, namely, that the only difference between the two conditions is the degree of *contingency* between feedback and target behavior. The method is the within-subject, *degraded* contingency control procedure (see also Furedy, Shulhan, and Levy, 1989, for some concrete examples).

It is also important to recognize that the requirement made by the specific-effects position is that of elimination in the scientific sense of that term,[4] namely, the "elimination of *differential* influences of factors unrelated to the factor under evaluation (i.e., the one being 'manipulated')" (Furedy, 1987b, p. 178). Similarly, in the pharmacological evaluation paradigm, there is no elimination of the placebo influences themselves, but only an elimination of any *differential* influences between the drug and placebo conditions.[5]

We turn now to the application of the specific-effects position to polygraphy.

---

[3]Another view is that while the efficacy of a candidate treatment has not been demonstrated, depriving patients of its (so-far doubtful) benefits does not constitute a serious problem.

[4]The meaning of "eliminate," when used to refer to the influence of placebo factors in the evaluation of biofeedback, has not always been clear. An early formulation of this requirement (Furedy, 1985) may have been interpretable as requiring elimination in the common-sense usage of that term, which would mean that the purportedly beneficial factor in biofeedback (the information) would need to be shown to work *in isolation*, without any of the therapeutic context (Green and Shellenberger, 1986). This requirement is nonsensical, and irrelevant to the clinic, where biofeedback is in a thoroughly therapeutic context. It is also the reason why laboratory evaluations of biofeedback can never be directly relevant to clinical (field) evaluation issues.

[5]For a working through of this elimination argument using a hypothetical question raised by Green and Shellenberger (1986)—whether information from stopwatches helps running performance—see Furedy (1987b, pp. 177-179).

## Polygraphy

The specific-effects position's implications for polygraphy are similar to its implications for biofeedback. According to this position, the central assumption behind *this* purported application of psychophysiology is that if the examiner is supplied (through the machine) with information about changes in physiological functions in the examinee that are not observable to the examiner without the machine, then this information, in itself, will improve the examiner's ability to detect deception in the examinee. In what follows, we elaborate on the specific-effects perspective applied to polygraphy.

### Definition of the Phenomenon and Derivation of the Proper Control Condition

The essence of the polygraphic phenomenon is the information supplied by the machine to the examiner. The phenomenon itself may be said to occur if and only if this information results in an improvement in the examiner's ability to detect deception (or guilt). As in biofeedback, there is a contingency involved, but in polygraphy the contingency is between the examinee's physiological changes (as registered on the machine) and the accuracy of the judgment made by the polygrapher. Because of advances in modern electronics, the *electronic* accuracy (i.e., the accuracy with which the machine registers the examinee's physiological changes) is close to 100%, but the question remains whether this sort of accuracy has any beneficial effect in increasing the examiner's *detection* accuracy.

This question can only be resolved by employing a comparison where only the electronic accuracy differs between the two conditions. In the case of the polygraph, which involves a single decision at the end of the procedure rather than continuing control (as in biofeedback), the comparison has to be made between subjects (i.e., examinees), and the examiners have to be blind to whether they are using the high- or low-accuracy machine. If, under these arrangements, the higher electronic accuracy also results in higher detection accuracy, then a specific effect of the polygraph will have been demonstrated.

It is important to recognize that in this perspective, there has been a switch from considering accuracy assessed against a 50% chance level to accuracy of the procedure with the physiological information assessed against the procedure without the physiological information (but equal in all other respects). This switch is analogous to the biofeedback case, where we moved from considering whether a given treatment worked to whether a given treatment worked better with than without feedback. Just as all treatments probably work to some (difficult-to-specify) extent, so human procedures for detecting the guilty are probably better (by some difficult-to-specify extent) than chance. The issue, however, is whether there is an *improvement* in the accuracy of that detection that is attributable to the specific effect of the physiological information supplied to the examiner about the examinee.

## The Current Accuracy Debate

For most experts, the accuracy issue has centered on comparing the polygraph against chance (50%) and perfect (100%) accuracy. This approach is most clearly illustrated by the debates between Lykken (e.g., Lykken, 1974) and Raskin (e.g., Raskin, 1978), with the former (opponent) contending that the accuracy is no more than 70% and the latter (proponent) contending that it is closer to 90%. This debate does not appear to be close to resolution. One factor that contributes to the difficulty of resolving this sort of accuracy issue is that, as indicated above, the CQT procedure is too unstandardized (and therefore operator-dependent) to be characterizable in terms of (operator-independent) accuracy figures. Because of this problem, the debate, in these terms, is a matter of mere opinion, no matter how expert that opinion may be. In addition, however, from a specific-effects perspective, the debate is also irrelevant to the central issue, which is whether the physiological information supplied by the machine increases detection accuracy. It will be noted that whether the CQT polygraph procedure as a whole is less than 70% accurate or closer to 90% does not speak to the improvement-in-accuracy issue, just as the question of how effective biofeedback therapies are as a package does not bear on the question of whether biofeedback itself produces an improvement in therapeutic effectiveness. In the final section, we discuss specific aspects of the specific-effects approach for evaluating the CQT polygraph.

## Specifics of the Specific-Effects Approach to the Polygraph[6]

From a purely psychophysiological perspective that stresses the study of psychological processes, the essential problem is one of *differentiation* (Furedy, 1986; Furedy, Davis, and Gurevich, 1988) between deception and truthfulness. From this perspective, neither the CQT nor the GKT is really concerned with deception as such. Rather, both procedures aim to *detect* the guilty. However, field polygraphy is a branch of applied psychophysiology rather than pure science, and for the applied endeavor it matters little that the process of deception is not studied, as long as the guilty can be detected.

Still, if the psychophysiological detection technology is going to be scientifically based, then it must be shown, as a first step, that physiological information improves the examiner's detection ability. That ability, however, has to be assessed in the full, admittedly contaminated, context of the typical North American CQT polygraph, just as biofeedback therapy needs to be assessed in the full clinical context. The so-called blind-scoring control (where the scorer is not the examiner and is not familiar with the case) and the blind-examiner control

---

[6]Many of the arguments in this section stem from, and are elaborated in, the treatment of the polygraph by Furedy and Heslegrave (1989a,b), the latter being a reply to comments by Ben-Shakhar (1989), Iacono (1989), Lykken (1989), Raskin and Kircher (1989), and Saxe and Cross (1989).

(where the examiner is not familiar with the case) are both procedures that provide interesting information about certain *components* of the polygraph, but neither procedure evaluates the central question of whether the physiological information adds anything to the detection ability of the examiner in the actual, complex, contaminated situation that constitutes the North American CQT.[7] So the "blindness" has to be with respect to the electronic-accuracy manipulation (as indicated above), rather than with respect to the information which examiners believe, rightly or wrongly, is an essential part of the CQT detection process.

Only after some positive evidence was obtained to demonstrate the beneficial effects of the physiological information in the field (and so far, by the way, no such evidence has been gathered for the CQT polygraph even in the simpler situation of the laboratory) would it be appropriate to consider doing research on other detection-related factors such as countermeasures, individual differences, and effects of drugs. In the absence of such positive evidence of efficacy, based on proper evaluative studies, research into these other factors cannot yield interpretable results which can take us beyond mere speculation. Just as in science, the hypotheses about a given phenomenon can only be sensibly taken up *after* the phenomenon in question has been demonstrated, so in science-based technology, a procedure can be further refined only *after* proper evaluative studies (i.e., sound clinical trials) have established its credentials.

---

[7]Contamination could affect not only the measurement of the physiological charts, but also the responses themselves through the way in which the questions are formulated *and* presented to the examinee by a "hostile" vs. a "friendly" examiner.

CHAPTER 6

# Theoretical Issues in Psychophysiological Detection

This book, like most other discussions of psychophysiological detection, focuses primarily on applied issues related to polygraph-based interrogations. However, the phenomenon of psychophysiological differentiation between relevant and irrelevant stimuli is interesting and challenging from a theoretical perspective. In this chapter we shall review several theoretical accounts that have been formulated to deal with psychophysiological detection and related phenomena. The focus of this discussion will be on the GKT, because this method is the basis for most of the research and theorizing in this area of psychophysiology and because it is the only standard and controlled detection procedure. As described in previous chapters, the alternative methods (e.g., RIT, CQT) are not standardized and are problematic in their use of control questions. As a result, it is difficult to provide theoretical interpretations for experimental effects and phenomena based on them.

The different theoretical approaches to be discussed in this chapter can be classified into two major classes: (*a*) theories that emphasize motivational and emotional factors as the important determinants of psychophysiological differentiation (e.g., feelings associated with deception, fear of the consequences of the polygraph test's results, motivation to deceive) and (*b*) theories that are based on cognitive factors (e.g., knowledge and awareness of certain information, attentional mechanisms that operate while processing the questions).

## Motivational-Emotional Approaches

An early attempt to classify the alternative theoretical accounts in the area of psychophysiological detection was made by Davis (1961). He listed three possible mechanisms for the detection phenomenon: the conditional response theory, the punishment theory, and the conflict theory.

Orne and his colleagues (e.g., Gustafson and Orne, 1963, 1965a) have stressed the concept of motivation for a successful performance of the task at hand. In the typical real-life interrogation context this would normally mean motivation to appear innocent (not deceptive), but in experimental setups it is possible to manipulate the subject's perception of the task and, accordingly, the type of motivation. Gustafson and Orne (1963, 1965a) studied the role of motivation by manipulating subjects' perception of the detection task. It is important to note that the different approaches are not mutually exclusive; rather, they emphasize different factors which can, in principle, operate together to determine psychophysiological detection.

## The Conditional Response Mechanism

This theory rests on the assumption that the relevant questions (or items in the GKT) produce differential physiological responsivity because they were conditioned to the subject's past experience (e.g., crime). According to this account, the more serious the crime, the stronger the reactions that would be evoked by the relevant questions. This theory seems intuitively plausible in the context of police interrogations in which the relevant questions are associated with a past experience loaded with strong emotions. It provides, however, no good explanation for the results of many laboratory experiments which demonstrate the successful detection of the card number picked by a subject, a situation which does not seem to involve any strong emotions.

## The Punishment Mechanism

This account focuses on the consequences of the polygraph procedure, rather than on its antecedents. It rests on the assumption that the enhanced responses elicited by the relevant questions are due to fear of the consequences of the subject's failure to deceive. Again, fear of the consequences of the polygraph examination's outcome may be characteristic of the field setup where the subject is interrogated using the polygraph because he or she is suspected of a certain crime and therefore might bear the consequences of failing the examination. The typical experimental procedure (the card test), on the other hand, does not involve serious consequences for the subjects, and yet quite high detection rates can be observed in this situation (e.g., Gustafson and Orne, 1964; Kugelmass, Lieblich, and Bergman, 1967). Furthermore, Kugelmass and Lieblich (1966) have manipulated the perceived consequences of a polygraph test, and demonstrated that similar detection rates were obtained in a situation involving strong realistic stress (a sample of policemen were told that their ability to control their emotions was being tested and that only those able to achieve such control and pass the test could qualify to serve in the police force) and in a situation that was nonstressful (the test was presented as an attempt to examine whether the apparatus was functioning properly).

In a more recent study, Bradley and Janisse (1981a) manipulated threat of punishment in a mock crime experiment using both the GKT and the CQT. Half of the subjects in both "innocent" and "guilty" groups were threatened with an electric shock if classified guilty. This threat did not affect detection efficiencies based on heart rate, electrodermal, and pupillary measures, either in the GKT or in the CQT, although heart rate changes of both guilty and innocent subjects tended to receive scores more in the guilty direction under the threat. Another experimental result not compatible with the punishment theory was reported by Thackray and Orne (1968a). They employed a GKT procedure and obtained significant detection rates with a group of subjects unaware of the fact that they were being tested by the polygraph. Moreover, no significant difference was obtained in that experiment between the "aware" and the "nonaware" conditions. However, Thackray and Orne (1968a) suggested that this result should be treated cautiously because it was not entirely certain that the "unaware" situation was indeed created.

## The Conflict Approach

This theory postulates that the enhanced physiological reactions evoked by the relevant items reflect the conflicting response tendencies inherent in those items (i.e., lying vs. telling the truth). The conflict between two incompatible response tendencies that are simultaneously aroused leads to an emotional reaction that may be reflected by the physiological measure monitored by the polygraph. This idea can be related to the early work of Luria (1932) on human conflict. He even suggested a different type of detection method based on the measurement of hand tremors, where subjects would be instructed to respond "yes" or "no" to each question by pressing a bar (e.g., a right-hand bar for a "yes" response and a left-hand bar for a "no" response).

The conflict idea is supported by an experiment conducted by Gustafson and Orne (1965b), which demonstrated that verbal lying increased card detection rates. In this experiment, one group of subjects was instructed to answer "no" to all questions, and thus lied when asked about their chosen card, whereas another group was instructed to respond with a free association to each question. A third group was instructed to remain silent while the questions were presented. The higher detection rates obtained in the first group support the conflict theory, because conflicting responses (the true one, "yes," and the one instructed by the experimenter, "no") were evoked only in that case. Nevertheless, the detection rates obtained in the silent group were significantly greater than chance, indicating that differential physiological responsivity is possible even without verbal responses. Kugelmass et al. (1967) dealt with a similar question, but used a different design—one group of subjects was instructed to answer "no" to all questions, whereas the other group was instructed to respond "yes" to every question. Thus the second group gave a truthful answer to the relevant question, and no conflicting response tendencies were evoked by that question. The results indicated that the relevant stimuli were detected in both groups (at significantly better than chance levels) with no difference between them. Janisse and Bradley (1980) dealt with the same problem using a modified design. Subjects in two experimental conditions tried to conceal their chosen card. In one of these groups subjects were instructed to answer "no," whereas in the other condition they remained silent. Subjects in a third condition did not attempt to conceal information and showed their choices to the experimenter before questioning. This third group was tested under a silent condition. Janisse and Bradley (1980) used changes in pupil size as the physiological measure and obtained significantly greater than chance detection rates in each of their experimental conditions. No significant differences in detection rates between the three groups were obtained.

These results are incompatible with the conflict theory, as well as with any other theory that attributes the detection phenomenon to the act of lying. In two recent studies (Elaad and Ben-Shakhar, 1989; Horneman and O'Gorman, 1985), however, the result obtained by Kugelmass et al. (1967) was not replicated. In both studies more efficient detection of card numbers was obtained under a "no" response condition than under a condition of "yes" response. In fact, it seemed that the "no" response was more effective than any of the other response types that were examined (see Elaad and Ben-Shakhar, 1989). It should be noted, though, that both Elaad and Ben-Shakhar (1989) and Horneman and O'Gorman (1985) reported significantly better-than-chance detection rates under all response conditions, including a condition where the subjects were instructed to remain silent.

The studies of Horneman and O'Gorman (1985) and Elaad and Ben-Shakhar (1989) may revive the conflict hypothesis, but this theory cannot fully account for the detection phenomenon, because their experiments as well as those conducted by Kugelmass et al. (1967) and Janisse and Bradley (1980) clearly demonstrate that detection is possible in a nonconflict condition (e.g., the "yes" condition). Thus, conflict may add to the differential responsivity evoked by relevant stimuli, but it is not a necessary condition for such responsivity.

## Motivation and Psychophysiological Detection

An early experiment by Gustafson and Orne (1963) utilized a card-test procedure in an attempt to demonstrate the role of motivation on psychophysiological detection. One group of subjects was given motivational instructions. They were told that the goal of the experiment was to see how well they could conceal information from the experimenter and that it is an extremely difficult feat which can be successfully performed only by people of superior intelligence and emotional control. Furthermore, they were promised an extra dollar if they would succeed. A second group of subjects—the control group—was told that the only purpose of the study was to find out how normal subjects reacted physiologically to a series of numbers and letters. The results revealed a significantly higher detection rate in the motivational than in the nonmotivational condition. Furthermore, in the nonmotivational condition the detection rate was not significantly higher than the rate expected by chance alone.

In a subsequent study Gustafson and Orne (1965a) extended their 1963 study by adding variables and experimental conditions. They manipulated the motivation factor, leading one group of subjects to believe that only highly intelligent individuals with more than the usual amount of control are able to fool the lie detector (i.e., motivation to deceive); whereas a second group was led to believe that it is extremely difficult and even impossible for normal, well-adjusted individuals to prevent themselves from giving certain physiological reactions when they lie (i.e., motivation to be detected).

No significant effect was obtained for the type of motivation in an initial card test procedure (i.e., the detection rates were 75% and 69% in the motivation-to-deceive and in the motivation-to-be-detected conditions, respectively). However, the most striking aspect of Gustafson and Orne's experiment was the strong interaction that was obtained between the motivational instructions and the feedback provided to the subjects following the initial series of card test questions. Regardless of the actual outcome of this first card test, half of the subjects in each motivational group were informed that their chosen card had been detected by the polygraph (positive feedback). The other subjects were informed that they must have chosen a blank card (though they did not), thus leading them to believe that detection was avoided (negative-feedback group). The interaction indicated that detection rates in a second series of card test questions were high whenever the feedback contradicted with the subject's motivation (e.g., when subjects motivated to be detected were led to believe that their chosen card was not detected in the initial card test procedure). Detection rates in the second card test were much lower when the feedback indicated to the subjects that their first task was successfully performed (i.e., an avoidance of being detected for the motivation-to-deceive group and a successful detection for the motivation-to-be-detected group). Gustafson and Orne (1965a) concluded that the perceived failure in the first round increased those subjects' motivation in the second round, and this increased motivation to succeed caused the enhanced detection rates obtained in the second card test. Subjects believing they had succeeded in the first round lost their motivation and thus did not show great responsivity to the relevant questions during the second card test. In other words, according to Gustafson and Orne (1965a), the interaction between the demand characteristics of the experimental task and the perceived success in it determines to a great extent the physiological responsivity to the various questions and the resulting rate of detection of relevant information.

This approach is similar to the punishment idea, mentioned earlier, in that both are related to the consequences of the polygraph test. However, Gustafson and Orne's formulation is somewhat more general because it emphasizes the concept of motivation to succeed in the detection task. Avoiding punishment is just one instance of succeeding in this task, and as Gustafson and Orne (1965a) demonstrated, task perception can be manipulated.

However, several studies conducted in the late sixties and seventies are incompatible with the motivation theory. The Kugelmass and Lieblich (1966) experiment, described earlier, indicates that detection rates were not affected by the manner in which the test was presented to the subjects. Similar rates were obtained when the outcome of the test carried personal consequences for the subject and in a neutral condition. Davidson (1968) manipulated the motivation factor by varying the amount of monetary reward that was offered to the subjects for a successful outcome (avoiding detection) in a GKT procedure. He obtained extremely high levels of detection accuracy in both experimental conditions (92%

of the guilty subjects and 100% of the innocent subjects were correctly detected). However, the null result in Davidson's experiment could be accounted for by a ceiling effect.

Horvath (1979) conducted a card-test experiment in which one group of subjects was motivated to avoid detection and a second group was motivated to be detected. When the electrodermal measure was used, significantly higher detection rates were obtained in the motivation-to-be-detected condition. Furthermore, Horvath compared this result with the result of a previous experiment (Horvath, 1978) in which no motivational instructions were given. The detection rate in the no-motivation condition was similar to the rate obtained in the motivation-to-be-detected condition. It is, however, difficult to interpret these findings, because between-experiment comparisons may introduce uncontrolled confounding factors. Furthermore, the effect obtained within the second experiment is not very clear because both groups were motivated. One possible explanation offered by Horvath (1979) for this effect is that subjects motivated to be detected manipulated their physiological responses deliberately to produce the desired outcome.

Lieblich et al. (1974) manipulated the level of motivation using a procedure similar to that of Gustafson and Orne (1963), but did not obtain an effect for the motivation factor. They suggested that differences in the stimuli used in the two experiments may account for the differences in their results. While Gustafson and Orne (1963) used neutral stimuli (card numbers) that were made relevant to the subjects through instructions, Lieblich et al. (1974) used the subject's name as the relevant stimulus. However, in a more recent study Elaad (1987) used a GKT procedure and obtained a robust effect for the motivation-to-deceive factor with neutral stimulus material, similar to the stimuli used by Gustafson and Orne (1963). High level of motivation to avoid detection was associated with enhanced detection efficiency in four independent experiments conducted in standard experimental laboratories as well as in the Israeli Police laboratories. The effect of motivation on detection was observed when detection was based on both electrodermal and respiration measures and on the use of different verbal response conditions. It should be emphasized, though, that in contrast to the early findings of Gustafson and Orne (1963), significant detection was obtained by Elaad even in a condition of low motivation. Thus it seems that motivational instructions are an additional factor contributing to psychophysiological differentiation, but like the conflict factor, it is not a necessary condition for differential responsivity to relevant stimuli.

## Cognitive Approaches

The theories discussed so far stressed emotional and motivational factors as underlying the process of psychophysiological detection. The major problem with all of those approaches is the difficulty in accounting for significant detection rates under mild conditions, when subjects are not specifically motivated to avoid detection (e.g., Davidson, 1968; Elaad and Ben-Shakhar, 1989; Horvath, 1978; Lieblich et al., 1974), when deception is not required (e.g., Elaad and Ben-Shakar, 1989; Horneman and O'Gorman, 1985; Kugelmass et al., 1967), when subjects are not attempting to conceal the relevant information (Janisse and Bradley, 1980), and even when subjects are unaware of the fact that their responses are monitored by the polygraph (Thackray and Orne, 1968a).

These facts have led several researchers to formulate different approaches — approaches that focus primarily on cognitive factors associated with the perception and processing of the stimuli presented to the subjects in the course of the polygraph test.

## The Concept of Guilty Knowledge

The concept of guilty knowledge was introduced by Lykken (1959, 1960, 1974) to describe a procedure that has been used by polygraph examiners for many years under different labels (e.g., peak of tension, stimulation tests). Nevertheless, the concept of guilty knowledge is important because it implies an interesting theoretical perspective.

Lykken (1974) made the assumption that the guilty knowledge, which constitutes the basis for distinguishing between innocent and guilty subjects, is sufficient for creating enhanced responsivity to the relevant items in subjects possessing this guilty knowledge. This assumption rests on the extensive research dealing with the orienting reactions (ORs). The OR describes a complex of physiological reactions evoked by any novel stimulus or by any change in stimulation (e.g., Berlyne, 1960; Sokolov, 1963). In principle, each item presented to the subject, whether guilty or innocent, in the course of the GKT is capable of evoking an OR. Naturally these ORs will display a habituation process — a gradual decline in response magnitude with repeated presentations of the stimuli (Sokolov, 1963). The interesting feature of orientation which provides this concept with an explanatory power for the detection phenomenon is that significant stimuli (i.e., stimuli that have acquired a signal value) evoke enhanced ORs. Lykken (1974) made the connection arguing that: ". . . for the guilty subject only, the 'correct' alternative will have a special significance, an added 'signal value' which will tend to produce a stronger orienting reflex than that subject will show to other alternatives" (p. 728). In other words, it is assumed that the guilty knowledge provides a subset of the items with significance, or signal value, and therefore those items evoke stronger ORs. Clearly, for subjects who do not possess the guilty knowledge, all items are equivalent and evoke regular ORs that will habituate with repetitions. If the psychophysiological differentiation in the GKT is mediated through a mechanism of orientation, then the enhanced responsivity to the relevant items should not depend upon deception, motivation, or fear of punishment. Indeed, Lykken (1974) argues along these lines when he refers to an individual possessing the guilty knowledge: "Whether he is high or low in reactivity, whether he has confidence in the test or not, whether he is frightened and aroused or calm and indifferent, we can still expect that his response to this significant alternative will be stronger than to the other alternatives as long as he recognizes which alternative is 'correct'" (p. 728). We have labeled Lykken's approach as "cognitive," because it depends only on the assumption that some individuals possess a certain "guilty knowledge" whereas others do not. The emphasis here is on the fact that an individual knows something, rather than on the individual's emotions, fears, conditioned responses, or deception. This cognitive approach is compatible with findings that demonstrated how relevant information can be detected even under mild conditions where no motivational instructions were given to the subjects and where no verbal response was required (e.g., Ben-Shakhar, 1977; Ben-Shakhar and Lieblich, 1982). It is compatible also with the surprising detection-without-awareness effect reported by Thackray and Orne (1968a).

There is, however, some evidence that is less favorable to this purely cognitive approach. The recent findings of Elaad and Ben-Shakhar (1989) and Horneman and O'Gorman (1985) suggest that the actual verbal response does have an effect and that a deceptive verbal response enhances the differentiation between relevant and irrelevant stimuli. The early work of Gustafson and Orne (1963) together with the more recent study of Elaad and Ben-Shakhar (1989) suggests that increased motivation to avoid detection is associated with enhanced detection rates. It seems from these studies that although factors such as deception and motivation to deceive are not necessary for detection, they may increase detection efficiency. These facts should be incorporated into the theoretical approach based on the mechanism of orientation, if this approach is to provide a full account of psychophysiological detection.

Several investigators (Bradley and Warfield, 1984; Giesen and Rollison, 1980; Stern et al., 1981) reported experimental results that can be interpreted as incompatible with the idea that guilty knowledge is sufficient to produce psychophysiological differentiation between relevant and irrelevant stimuli. Both Giesen and Rollison (1980) and Stern et al. (1981) utilized mock crime experiments in which the "innocent" subjects were exposed to the relevant information, though in an innocent context. In spite of this procedure it was possible to discriminate between "guilty" and "innocent" subjects on the basis of the electrodermal measure, and very few false-positive results were obtained (none in the Giesen and Rollison study and 3 out of 26 in the Stern et al. study). Bradley and Warfield (1984) included in their experiment four groups of subjects simulating "innocent conditions," but unlike the typical innocent group in mock crime experiments, the subjects in three of these groups were exposed to the relevant information. They either witnessed the "crime," were told the crime details, or carried out innocent activities involving crime-related information. An additional group of innocent subjects had no crime-related information.

The results of this experiment indicated that subjects simulating the guilty condition showed greater physiological differentiation between the relevant and irrelevant items than the subjects in the three innocent conditions who were exposed to the crime-relevant information. These results could be interpreted as a contradiction of the guilty-knowledge approach because significant differences in detection were obtained between different groups of subjects all possessing the guilty knowledge. It should be pointed out, however, that despite the significant differences between the guilty group and the informed innocent groups, significant levels of detection were obtained even with the informed innocent subjects.[1] In other words, Bradley and Warfield's (1984) results, like the results of many other experiments, are compatible with the basic guilty-knowledge assumption. The experiment indicates, however, that additional factors (e.g., actual involvement with the crime vs. mere guilty knowledge) may play an important role in determining the degree of psychophysiological differentiation between relevant and irrelevant information.

## Attention and Information Processing

Waid and his colleagues have suggested that psychophysiological detection may depend on the way subjects process the stimuli presented to them in the detection task (e.g., Waid and Orne, 1981; Waid et al., 1978). The assumption is that the physiological response to a stimulus reflects the degree to which the stimulus was attended to. Accordingly, subjects can avoid detection by ignoring the stimuli presented to them and by responding mechanically to each stimulus rather than "deeply" processing it (Craig and Lockhart, 1972). This approach is supported by studies demonstrating positive correlations between orientation during stimulus presentation and later recall of the stimulus material (e.g., Corteen, 1969).

Waid et al. (1978) examined the relationship between electrodermal responsivity and recall in a GKT task. Subjects learned a list of code words, which were subsequently subjected to a GKT procedure in which they were presented, together with control words. Detection of the code words was positively correlated with the number of words recalled after the administration of the GKT. Moreover, recalled items were more likely to evoke an electrodermal response.

In a subsequent study Waid, Orne, and Orne (1981) extended the previous one and included a CQT procedure in addition to the GKT. Both relevant and "control" questions that were later recalled produced larger SCR amplitudes than non-recalled questions. For the guilty subjects a positive correlation ($r = .40$) was found between the number of questions detected using the electrodermal measure and a measure of differential recall (number of relevant questions recalled minus number of control questions recalled divided by the total number of questions, both relevant and control, recalled). This finding indicates that the greater the guilty subject's tendency to recall relevant rather than control questions, the more likely the subject is to be detected on the basis of the electrodermal measure. This same correlation, however, was not statistically significant when computed for

---

[1] In a reanalysis of Bradley and Warfield's (1984) data, we tested whether the mean detection score of informed innocent subjects was greater than a chance expectation score. Using a normal approximation to the detection index distribution, we found that the mean detection score based on the pooled data of all three informed innocent groups was significantly greater than chance ($z = 2.30; p < .05$).

the blood pressure and respiration measures. Additionally, this study revealed a significant positive correlation ($r = .48$) between the number of irrelevant questions a guilty subject recalled and the rate of detection via the electrodermal measure. A positive correlation ($r = .53$) between the ability to recall items of a videotaped crime and differential SCR responsivity to the critical items was also reported by Iacono et al. (1984).

The results of both studies (Waid et al., 1978; Waid, Orne, and Orne, 1981) were interpreted in terms of the "depth-of-processing approach" (Craig and Lockhart, 1972). The physiological responses evoked by a given stimulus are assumed to reflect the processing of that stimulus—the deeper the processing, the larger the responses elicited. "The more actively a subject attends to a given question, whether irrelevant, relevant or control, the larger the SCR it evokes, and the more likely it is to be recalled later" (Waid, Orne, and Orne, 1981, p. 230). Thus the individual differences in the physiological responsivity to the different questions are explained in terms of the amount of attention paid to them. Recall of irrelevant questions in the CQT and of control questions in the GKT may serve as an independent index of the subject's general alertness. These questions are innocuous and nonthreatening to the subjects; therefore their recall may indicate that the subject was attentive to the test in general and that all the test questions were processed. This deep processing of the questions should increase the likelihood of psychophysiological differentiation.

It must be stressed, however, that all the above-mentioned studies (Iacono et al., 1984; Waid et al., 1978; Waid, Orne, and Orne, 1981) present correlational data to support the depth-of-processing approach. It is possible, therefore, that the relationship between psychophysiological responding and memory is not a causal one and that other factors have affected both the responses to the various questions and their subsequent recall. Future research along these lines should attempt to manipulate attention to different items and examine whether such manipulations affect differential psychophysiological responsivity.

In a recent study Elaad and Ben-Shakhar (1989) have argued along the line of Waid, Orne, and Orne (1981). They assumed that under natural conditions the motivation of an individual possessing guilty knowledge is to avoid detection. To achieve this goal, guilty subjects must establish a mental dissociation from the relevant information (by not paying attention to these items). However, creating a mental dissociation is not an easy task, and it may be influenced by several factors. Many of the factors mentioned earlier (e.g., motivational instructions, reward for "beating the polygraph," a deceptive verbal response, an actual involvement with the event) could be associated with psychophysiological differentiation via their influence upon the level of attention toward the test questions in general and toward the relevant items in particular. An innocuous laboratory situation where no motivational instructions are given and no verbal response is required may facilitate a state of mental dissociation from the stimuli and may help the guilty subject ignore the relevant items. This may account for the relatively low levels of psychophysiological differentiation usually obtained under such conditions (e.g., Elaad and Ben-Shakhar, 1989; Gustafson and Orne,

1963; Horneman and O'Gorman, 1985). However, as most of the experiments demonstrate, even under these mild conditions, some psychophysiological differentiation may be expected as long as the subject recognizes the relevant information.

## The Dichotomization Approach

Another approach that stresses cognitive rather than emotional factors as the important determinants of psychophysiological detection was developed by the Jerusalem group (e.g., Ben-Shakhar, 1977; Lieblich, et al., 1970). Like Lykken's guilty knowledge concept, the dichotomization notion is based on mechanisms of orientation and habituation. It originated from observations demonstrating detection of information under mild conditions (Kugelmass et al., 1967) and from the effect of stimulus set size on differential physiological responding (Lieblich et al., 1970).

The basic assumption of the dichotomization approach is that the stimulus set is differentiated into two distinct categories: relevant vs. irrelevant stimuli. Furthermore, it is assumed that habituation generalizes within each of these categories, with little or no carryover across categories. In other words, it is assumed that subjects possessing guilty knowledge are paying attention to just one aspect of the stimuli presented to them during the polygraph test—whether they belong to the relevant or to the irrelevant stimulus category—and that they ignore all other aspects of the stimuli (i.e., features distinguishing between different stimuli of the same category). In terms of Sokolov's theoretical formulation (e.g., Sokolov, 1963, 1966), it is postulated that a single neuronal model (a central representation of the stimulus input) is formed for each stimulus category (the relevant and the neutral categories).

Several predictions follow from this approach. The first is that increasing the stimulus frequency of just one category will yield more habituation of the stimuli in that category, without affecting the responsivity to the stimuli in the other category. Thus, the relative overall responsivity to stimuli in a given category should be a decreasing function of the relative frequency of the stimuli in that category. Thus, the greater the relative frequency of the relevant stimuli in the stimulus set, the less psychophysiological differentiation expected. This prediction was found to be valid, with the predicted effect being quite robust. Several experiments demonstrated that psychophysiological detection depends on the relative frequency of the relevant stimuli in the stimulus set presented to the subject (e.g., Ben-Shakhar, 1977; Ben-Shakhar, et al., 1975, 1982; Lieblich et al., 1970).

It should be pointed out that the dichotomization model does not necessarily depend on the assumption that the relevant stimuli in the GKT are signal stimuli that produce enhanced ORs. As long as the relevant stimuli are relatively rare (are presented at a relative frequency of less than 50%), they are expected to produce greater physiological responsivity than the irrelevant stimuli, according to the dichotomization model. Ben-Shakhar (1977), indeed, demonstrated that if the irrelevant stimuli are presented with a low frequency (1 to 8), then they yield a greater responsivity than the relevant ones, thus demonstrating a "negative detection" (detection of the irrelevant rare stimuli). The differential responsivity obtained by Ben-Shakhar (1977) in the two conditions (i.e., a condition of rare relevant stimuli and a condition of rare irrelevant stimuli) was, however, asymmetrical: rare relevant stimuli produced much stronger differential responsivity than rare irrelevant stimuli. Therefore, it was suggested that the relevant items do have a signal value which is an additional factor contributing to the increased physiological responding evoked by these items.

The second prediction that follows from the dichotomization model is that the response magnitude to a given stimulus (from either category) should be determined by its serial position within its own category. Thus, for example, if the sixth stimulus presented to the subject in a GKT test is the second relevant stimulus, it should elicit a response magnitude characteristic of a second stimulus in a habituation function. This prediction was tested and to a large extent corroborated by Ben-Shakhar (1980).

The approach also assumes a generalization of habituation within each category. This third prediction was partially tested by Ben-Shakhar (1977). In one condition the stimulus set consisted of two stimuli — a relevant stimulus that was presented at a relative frequency of 1 to 8 and an irrelevant stimulus presented at a relative frequency of 7 to 8. In a second condition the single relevant stimulus was presented at the same frequency as in the first condition, but there were seven different neutral stimuli, each presented at a relative frequency of 1 to 8. The results revealed the predicted pattern of essentially identical levels of detection efficiency under the two conditions. Thus the differences between the neutral stimuli in the second condition did not affect the electrodermal responsivity measured in that experiment, corroborating the notion of within-category generalization of habituation.

The physiological responsivity, according to the dichotomization approach, is determined only by the serial position of the stimulus within its own category. Thus if a single relevant stimulus is included in a stimulus sequence presented to subjects undergoing a GKT test, the differential responsivity evoked by this relevant stimulus should not depend on its serial position within the sequence. The single relevant stimulus is the first stimulus in its category, regardless of its serial position in the sequence.

Two studies tested this prediction and produced inconsistent results. Ben-Shakhar and Lieblich (1982) did not confirm this prediction of the dichotomization model, and obtained more enhanced electrodermal responding with earlier presentations of the relevant stimulus than with late presentations. Consequently, Ben-Shakhar and Lieblich (1982) suggested a revision of the account according to which some generalization of habituation occurs across the two categories. In a more recent study, Ben-Shakhar, Asher, Poznansky-Levy, Asherowitz, and Lieblich (1989) obtained similar electrodermal responding to early and late presentations of the relevant stimulus. They tried to account for the differences in the results obtained in the two experiments in terms of differences in the degree of similarity between the relevant and neutral stimuli. They argued that in the first experiment the relevant stimulus had a clear common component that was shared with all other stimuli in the set, whereas in the second experiment it had a clear distinctive component. Thus, according to this formulation, the process of dichotomization may depend upon common and distinctive features of the two stimulus sets. Indeed, the role of common and distinctive stimulus features in determining electrodermal responsivity to relevant stimuli was demonstrated in a series of experiments by Ben-Shakhar and Gati (1987).

It may be hypothesized that the dichotomization process is affected by a number of factors. For example, factors such as motivation and deception, discussed in the previous section, may affect psychophysiological differentiation and detection efficiency through their influence on the process of dichotomizing the stimulus set into clear and distinct categories of relevant vs. neutral stimuli. This formulation is similar to the one suggested by Elaad and Ben-Shakhar (1989) which focuses on the ability of the subject to ignore the familiar relevant stimulus. A clear distinction between the two categories corresponds to a state where it is difficult to ignore the relevant stimulus. Current research is not sufficient, however, to discriminate between the two alternative hypotheses: (*a*) that situational factors (e.g., motivation to deceive, deceptive verbal response, involvement in the situation) affect detection because they are associated with a larger level of responsivity to the relevant stimuli, and (*b*) that those situational factors affect detection through their influence on the dichotomization process. Thus, according to this hypothesis, a situation involving a high level of motivation to deceive will be associated not only with larger detection rates, but also with less generalization of habituation across categories, and with a stronger stimulus set size effect and a weaker serial position effect. Further research might shed some light on this question.

## Summary and Conclusions

Two classes of theoretical approaches were reviewed in this chapter. One class stressed emotional-motivational factors such as fear of the consequences of the test's outcome, deception, conflicting response tendencies, and motivation to avoid detection. The other class focused on cognitive factors such as the way the stimuli are perceived and categorized and the degree to which they are attended to by the subjects.

The results of many experiments mentioned in this chapter, as well as in Chapter 4, suggest that no single theory or single theoretical approach is capable of providing a full account for the data. Rather, an integration of the different approaches is needed in order to achieve a better understanding of the mechanisms involved in psychophysiological detection. For example, the data suggest that motivation to avoid detection is an important factor that may facilitate detection, but it is not a necessary condition for detection, because detection was repeatedly demonstrated under low-motivational conditions. Likewise, dichotomization of the stimuli into relevant vs. neutral stimulus categories may be an important factor under certain circumstances (e.g., when the two stimulus categories are clearly differentiated), but this process may depend on motivational and emotional factors. Thus a deceptive verbal response or motivational instructions may facilitate the dichotomization process and thus contribute to an enhanced detection efficiency. Emotional factors may also contribute to psychophysiological detection by affecting the processing of the stimuli presented to the subject during the polygraph interrogation. These examples demonstrate that psychophysiological differentiation is a complex phenomenon which is determined by the interaction of many factors, affective and cognitive, operating together.

CHAPTER 7

# International Usage Contrasts: Cultural Factors

There are marked differences in usage of polygraphy between various countries. Many of these differences are of limited interest, because polygraphy requires a certain level of technical development and resources to support the reliable measurement of physiological changes, and many underdeveloped countries do not have the necessary resources. In addition, countries that do not strongly protect individual rights are not likely to use polygraphy, because other third-degree methods are available, and the question of guilt vs. innocence can be decided on the political grounds of what is in the best interests of the state.

This still leaves the set of technologically advanced democracies, and within this group of countries there remain considerable differences in the extent and sort of polygraph usages. The similarities in technical development and political systems render these usage differences of considerable interest, because they suggest the operation of cultural factors on a procedure which, purportedly, is a scientifically based technology that should be independent of such cultural influences.

In this chapter, we shall consider these marked contrasts between developed democratic countries, and we shall offer some sociological hypotheses (of a necessarily speculative sort) to account for these contrasts. We restrict our attention to only four contrasts, because our purpose is not to present a complete survey of usages (any such survey, in any case, would be dated by the time this book is published[1]), but rather to illustrate how powerful cultural factors can be, and to begin the task of attempting to understand these factors. The contrasts are discussed relative to the modern polygraph's place of origin and of widest current use: the U.S.

---

[1] For additional information on specific countries' polygraphic practices, as they were a few years before the publication of each paper, there are a number of sources. For Israel, see Harnon (1982); for the U.K., see Gale (1987, p. 1); for Canada, see Furedy (1989).

## The United States Versus Continental Western Europe

As we have already seen, polygraphy in the U.S., though controversial, is quite seriously considered as at least a potentially scientifically accurate way of detecting deception, when in the hands of qualified professionals. Accordingly, there are many states in which polygraphic evidence is admissible in criminal courts of law, although in most of the states consent of either the prosecution or the defense, or both, is required (i.e., "stipulated" admission). This means, of course, that the examiner can be either "hostile" (e.g., police polygrapher) or "friendly" (e.g., hired by the defense), so there is plenty of scope for polygraphic examinations to occur.

It is also worth noting that even the recent legislation (Employee Polygraph Protection Act, 1988) passed to outlaw polygraphy's industrial use is not as restrictive as it may appear. Its use *is* permitted in those industrial contexts where employees are suspected of a crime, so the event-related version (i.e., the CQT) has had its credibility bolstered by this legislation. Also, event-free usage of polygraphy continues in security (broadly defined) organizations. Finally, as is evident from American newspaper headlines, in more general societal conflicts involving the truth (e.g., salaries offered to leading sports figures), one or both sides in a conflict will offer to subject their credibility to the polygraph. Like the duel in earlier times, the polygraph is therefore viewed as the arbiter of truth, but with science rather than divinity as the basis of that arbitration.

Countries like Holland and West Germany in continental Western Europe are currently as active and well-developed in the science of psychophysiology as the U.S. Yet there is no evident research interest in the psychophysiological detection of deception, and academics appear to be totally uninterested in the topic.[2] Polygraphy's criminal use has been specifically outlawed in several of these countries such as West Germany. In West Germany, first the Bundesgerichtshof (1950), which is the supreme court, and later the Bundesverfassungsgericht (1981), which is another supreme court that has constitutional rights as a special concern, ruled against polygraphy's criminal use. Moreover, presumably on the basis of these judgments, there is also no industrial polygraphy in West Germany (Boucsein, 1989, personal communication). In these countries, then, the North American event-related CQT is practically unused by either forensic authorities or security organizations. Similarly, the polygraph is not used in civil disputes as a scientific arbiter.

---

[2]One of us (JJF) has found that lectures on the polygraph draw larger American and Canadian audiences than any other topic in psychophysiology (e.g., conditioning, orienting, cognitive stress), whereas in Holland, West Germany, Norway, and Sweden the suggestion to talk about polygraphy has uniformly been rejected in favor of other psychophysiological topics.

Our speculative explanation for these differences is that Americans tend to be taken in more by pseudoscientific, technically based, shortcut[3] procedures than Europeans. Some support for this view comes from the case of that other recent purported application of psychophysiology—biofeedback.[4]

As detailed in Chapter 5, the polygraphic application's basic, and totally unevaluated, assumption is that providing physiological information about the examinee to the examiner will improve the examiner's ability to detect guilt in the examinee. The biofeedback application's basic, and almost totally unevaluated, assumption is that providing physiological information about the patient *to* the patient will improve the patient's ability to control certain physiological functions.

In North American research on psychophysiology, biofeedback's star has waned, as judged by publications in the foremost empirical journal, *Psychophysiology*. The 1987 issue contained *no* biofeedback papers, as compared with six, seven, and ten in the 1982, 1977, and 1972 volumes, respectively. However, biofeedback continues to be widely used by both medical and nonmedical American practitioners, although recently, as indicated in footnote 1 in Chapter 5, the applied enthusiasm has also shown signs of waning.

The American psychophysiological biofeedback boom of the seventies heard little echo in Western Europe. There were, of course, psychophysiological laboratories that investigated biofeedback phenomena, and there were even European research conferences (subsequently published) devoted to the topic that were organized by Europeans acting as primary (e.g., Birbaumer and Kimmel, 1979) and secondary (e.g., Beatty and Legewie, 1976) editors. However, no biofeedback institutes or societies were formed of the sort that flourished in the U.S. in

---

[3] Faith in shortcut or "quick-fix" methods appears to be particularly strong in the U.S. Where truth is concerned, this could well be a delusion, because in many cases there is no definitive answer, even *after* exhaustive investigations have occurred. It is only a strong faith in technology that would suggest that it is possible, through gadgetry, to reliably uncover deception, and hence the truth. Certainly, there is no evidence from the science of psychophysiology to support this assumption.

[4] An observation that seems to contradict our speculative explanation for the European-American difference is the widespread use of handwriting analysis (graphology) in some European countries such as West Germany and Holland. In contrast, this procedure is rarely used in North America. Graphology is used mainly for personnel selection (applicants being invited to apply in handwriting), despite the fact that its validity has never been demonstrated. Recent reports, indeed, have indicated that graphology adds nothing at all to intuitive predictions of on-the-job performance (Ben-Shakhar et al., 1986; Neter and Ben-Shakhar, 1989). It is interesting to note that the main reason for the use of graphology in personnel selection seems to be the belief that honesty is reflected in certain features of handwriting. So it appears that graphology has played a role in certain European countries that is similar to that of polygraphy (in its event-free usage) in the U.S., although the pseudoscientific trappings may be more marked in the case of the polygraph (because of the electronic machinery) than in that of graphology.

the seventies (again see footnote 1, Chapter 5, for developments in these American societies). In Western Europe, apparently, more rigorous evaluation of new techniques is demanded before one surrenders to their charms.

## The United States Versus Japan

One set of polygraphic procedures consists of the event-free "tests" of honesty. These "tests" are administered mainly for hiring purposes, but they are also considered useful for employee screening; until recently, they formed the main staple of American polygraphic activity and, as well, were quite common in Canada.[5] These honesty-assessment polygraphic procedures are completely unstandardized, and usually quite brief, in order to cut costs for the (employer) user. With the banning of these "tests" in the U.S. noted above (in Section 1), and similar bans imposed in most Canadian provinces, these event-free procedures have only recently effectively disappeared from the private sector.

The predominant event-related North American procedure is the CQT. Especially if administered for at least 90 minutes, and by a qualified polygraphic practitioner with at least 6 months of training (but no prior background in psychology or psychophysiology—a high school diploma is usually the only background requirement), the CQT is regarded, at least in terms of congressional law, as a scientifically sound way of detecting deception. Even in states where polygraphic evidence is not directly admissible as evidence in a court of law, the CQT still retains its usefulness in purely criminal contexts, industrial-criminal contexts (e.g., employee suspected of a crime "voluntarily" submitting to the polygraph in order to clear his or her name), and security contexts.

However, although most examinees consent only to the detection function of the CQT, a major element is a confession-inducing component, and in this regard the procedure serves an interrogatory rather than a detection function. For many police interrogators, it is this confession-inducing component that is considered to be most useful, with the physiological information and machinery serving more as a prop in the interrogation procedure. Aspects which serve this interrogatory function include questions during the pretest interview, which elicit information useful for the later inducement of confessions but which are irrelevant for the detection function of the procedure; the direct oral communication of the results of the "test" to the examinee by the examiner following a waiting period when the examinee is left alone to stare at the wall, in contrast to the usual practice with genuine psychological tests like IQ tests where the results are communicated in written form and without any examinee waiting (softening-up?) period; and the extended post-test interview, i.e., interrogation—the sole purpose of which is to elicit a confession. In any of the three contexts (industrial,

---

[5]In Toronto in the late seventies, fast-food firms employing student casual labor routinely required prospective employees to "take a polygraph," and in those days of relatively high unemployment, most applicants complied.

industrial-criminal, and security), an examinee who consents to the CQT's detection function may end up being subjected to an interrogatory post-test interview that can last several hours, or as long as it takes to produce a confession.

In Japan, polygraphy is carried out only by the police. Even though the polygraph has been used at least as far back as the late forties, there never has been any industrial use, in contrast to the burgeoning private polygraph industry in the U.S. So in contrast to the steady increase in American polygraphic examinations up to 1987 (and many of these examinations were the event-free honesty "tests" provided to employers by private polygraphers), the rate of (police-polygrapher) examinations in Japan has remained at about 5000 per annum for the last decade (for 1975-1979 figures, see Fukumoto, 1982, p. 237). The Japanese police employ individual testers with an undergraduate major in psychology, who are part of the police science office. These police polygraphers, moreover, do only polygraphic testing, and no other police work such as interrogation or investigation. In addition, many of the polygraphers regularly get 6-month research leaves and conduct laboratory investigations that are reported both at their annual research conference[6] and in journals.

The control question technique employed by these Japanese police polygraphers differs in a number of important respects from the North American CQT. One such difference is that no interrogation is involved, and the results are reported in written form to the authorities for the purpose of detection, rather than orally to the examinee for the purpose of confession inducement. Another difference is that in the Japanese CQT the control questions refer to crimes of the same gravity as the relevant questions, but crimes of which the examinee is not suspected by the police, so in this respect this technique is similar to Reid's (1947) "guilt-complex" technique.

In principle, then, it is possible to develop a situation in the Japanese CQT where the only difference between the relevant (experimental) and control questions for the guilty is that the examinee is deceptive about the relevant question and truthful (but otherwise equally concerned) about the control question. For the innocent, there is no apparent difference between the two, and the innocent should be equally concerned about both questions. So in principle, this version of the CQT does have a control in the normal, scientific sense of that term.

In practice, however, it is extremely difficult to convince an examinee that he or she is equally under suspicion of having committed the hypothetical crime as of having committed the real one. Accordingly, in practice, the Japanese CQT

---

[6]At a recent (1985) conference, one of us (JJF) found two interesting audience reaction to an invited paper which attacked the American CQT. One reaction was that, in contrast to any other group of polygraphers in the world, this group appeared to share the misgivings concerning the American CQT and strongly preferred the GKT. The other, even more academic, reaction was a comment by one polygrapher, who said that since JJF's arguments raised irrefutable difficulties for all current detection methods, he should therefore consider whether what he has been doing so far may be wrong. This sort of self-criticism by a professional of his own methods is rare even in more basic-research, academic circles.

does not seem to be a particularly valid way of detecting the guilty. Nevertheless, it is important to recognize that the Japanese CQT does not have the unstandardized, interrogatory-interview components of the North American version, and the control involved is, at least in principle, of the normal scientific sort.

The most significant American-Japanese difference, however, is in the respective use made of the GKT. It is true that the American CQT often includes the card test, which is a form of the GKT. However, the use to which this form of the GKT is put by the CQT examiner is not the detection of guilt, but rather the convincing of the examinee by the examiner that the polygraph is infallible. As to field use for detection purposes, at the time of writing, the GKT has rarely been employed to this end by American polygraphers.

In contrast, Japanese police polygraphers are extensive field users of the GKT. Cooperation between police and news media is such that almost 50% of the cases allow employment of the GKT.

It bears emphasis, however, that on such aspects as dependent-variable measurement and even administration, it is not known how rigorous the actual administration of the GKT is in Japan. Still, more extensive research backgrounds of Japanese polygraphers coupled with the more scientific and potentially standardizable nature of the GKT suggest that the administration of this procedure may approximate those of IQ tests in terms of reliability. The validity issue in the field remains in doubt, however, because the usual problems of establishing independent and accurate criteria exist.

In considering reasons for the various American-Japanese differences, probably the one that is most readily explained is the lack of any industrial polygraphic activity in Japan.[7] This is simply due to the greater degree of trust that holds between Japanese employers and employees. This relation is typically long-term, and is similar to that in a family. In this context, it would be unthinkable to subject either prospective or current employees to such an insulting procedure as the polygraph.[8]

The better scientific background of Japanese police polygraphers compared with that of their American counterparts, as well as the increased level of specialization (i.e., the fact that Japanese police polygraphers are not engaged in other sorts of police work), is probably attributable to differences in the history of polygraphic development. The American development, as described in Chapter 1, occurred relatively independently of the sciences of psychophysiology and psychology. Even the leading figures in the American Polygraph Association generally did not have a strong scientific background in these subjects, in terms of doctoral degrees, independent research activities, and so on. In contrast,

---

[7]Much of our comments on the Japanese situation are based on a number of interviews conducted with Japanese polygraphers by JJF, as well as a private written communication to him by Professor Yo Miyata concerning Japanese polygraphic practices.

[8]Another piece of evidence that trust rather than legislation is involved is that, in contrast to the American 1988 congressional act, in Japan "there are no regulations restricting commercial use of the polygraph" (Fukumoto, 1982, p. 237).

Japanese polygraphy had its origins in academic institutions in the thirties (e.g., Akamatsu, Uchida, and Togawa, 1933) and only began to be applied on a large scale in the late forties. Even then, however, the academic connections remained, inasmuch as the application was in the context of the police sciences division (for an account of Japanese developments up to the seventies, see Fukumoto, 1982), and examiners, as we have indicated, have psychological and psychophysiological backgrounds.

This greater background in the principles of psychological testing is evident in both Japanese polygraphic writings and practice. Consider, for example, the claim by a Japanese polygrapher that, in Japan, the "polygraph test is considered as a psychological test or psychological procedure, in contrast to its use as an interrogative technique in America" (Fukumoto, 1982, p. 237). This shows a more rigorous understanding of the term "test" than is evident in American writings, as well as a greater attention to elementary principles of psychological testing.

In practice, too, the Japanese polygraphic procedures appear to be more consistent with psychological testing principles. Even the (Japanese) CQT appears to be less contaminated with interrogatory components than the American CQT.[9] More importantly, the GKT, which is now being widely used in Japan, is fully consistent with psychological and psychophysiological principles, even though it does not actually measure deception and may not be practicable in many circumstances. What is noteworthy, however, is that none of the interrogatory skills are needed, or are even sensible, with the GKT.

Finally, there are two other differences that may account for the more detection-based approach to polygraphy in Japan, as compared with the more interrogatory-based American CQT procedure. Firstly, as indicated in footnote 9, Japanese police may be able to use more extensive methods of confession inducement through nonpolygraphic methods than can American police. Secondly, the Japanese conviction rate is over 98%, as compared with the 60% American rate. Accordingly, the "psychological rubber hose" (Furedy and Liss, 1986), confession-inducing function of the polygraph is of less relative value to Japanese than to American prosecutors.

## The United States Versus Australia

In general, American technological innovations are taken up completely by Australian society with no more than a lag of a few years. Both in its industrial and criminal (police) use, the polygraph represents a marked exception to this general transfer rule.

---

[9]It should not be thought that we are suggesting that interrogation plays less of a role in Japanese than in American police work. There is, indeed, evidence to suggest that Japanese interrogatory methods are more intrusive, and more contrary to basic human rights (see e.g., Futaba, 1984). Our point is merely that the polygraphic detection function is not contaminated by interrogatory components, as is the case in the American CQT.

Concerning industrial use, Australians are quite familiar with enthusiastic American business opinion. For example, a Law Reform Commission (1983) dealing with lie detection cites a business commentator's view that these "new tools will provide useful correlative substantiation for backgrounding data currently available. They may even help us determine when the good apple begins to sour" (p. 164). However, the commission's opinions are clearly contrary to the polygraph's industrial use. A survey by an Australian psychophysiologist (White, 1985) of attorneys general of the Australian states (and the Northern Territory) revealed a uniform opposition to industrial use, although in some cases the opposition did not need to be explicitly formulated, because no such industrial use was apparent.[10]

A 1985 interview with Wayne Evans (a former police prosecutor in Sydney and currently a barrister and a lecturer in the police academy) suggested that the polygraph's industrial use was simply "not on" in Australian society, because the procedure would not be interpreted as a "fair" one and the unions[11] would walk out. This view was uniformly confirmed in other interviews with Australians. The concept of "fairness" is very strong in Australian society, so the charge of unfairness is a very serious one.

Concerning criminal use by the police, this has also been practically nonexistent in Australia. In Mr. Evans's view, if the police asked to use the polygraph (in its American CQT form), the request would be denied on the grounds that it is psychologically coercive. It is noteworthy that in Australia there is a prohibition, on the grounds of "unfairness," against interviewing (i.e., interrogating) a juvenile even with the lawyer present. It is necessary to have the parent there as well. Such a foursome arrangement is, of course, incompatible with polygraphy, which requires a one-on-one arrangement.

The sense of fairness which is involved is a rather unique one, and can be characterized as following "Marquis of Queensberry Rules." The relation between the police and criminals, indeed, is commonly viewed as any other game, to be played (as all games) fairly according to a set of rules. Third-degree methods (provided they are relatively mild) are considered more permissible by the public than any procedure which tricks or "psychologically coerces" the subject, as CQT polygraphy does with its various deceitful manipulations. In

---

[10] We are indebted to Dr. White for supplying copies of the survey to JJF during a 1985 trip to Australia. Much of the following material was also obtained by JJF during interviews, and we are indebted, in particular, to Wayne Evans for interesting comments.

[11] The unions are a very powerful force in Australian society and extend their activities well beyond what would be considered to be strictly industrial issues in other countries. For example, before the outbreak of the war with Japan, the Australian Prime Minister, Robert Menzies, wished to export pig iron to Japan, but the Dockworkers Union successfully prevented the ships from being loaded on grounds which seem to be political rather than industrial. They succeeded in their political act, and were also successful in hanging on Menzies (later Sir Robert) the nickname "Pig Iron Bob," a name which stuck with him for the rest of his career. A walkout by the unions over an issue like the polygraph would almost certainly be a completely effective deterrent against its industrial use in Australia.

other words, giving the suspect "one or two belts" is one thing, but being sneaky is intolerable.

Consistent with the gamelike perception of the police-criminal relationship is the very low (about 40%) conviction rate in Australia. Such a low rate does not seem to cause public concern, perhaps because the fear of (violent) street crime is not as prevalent and strong as it is in U.S. In addition, the criminal as hero is a view that is more common in Australia than in any other country, and it has persisted from the days of Ned Kelly (the nineteenth-century highwayman) to those of Darcy Duggan (who made several escapes from prison in the late fifties and early sixties and received wide public support). No doubt Australia's beginnings as a convict colony has something to do with this rather unique set of cultural values.

## The United States Versus Israel

Polygraphs are frequently used in Israel, mostly for event-related purposes. The bulk of the examinations are done by government agencies, most notably by the police department, which carries out most polygraph interrogations.

These polygraph-based interrogations are similar to those in the U.S. Most leading Israeli polygraphers have received at least part of their training in American polygraph schools or in Israeli schools that apply similar methods and ideas to those used in the U.S. Many Israeli polygraphers are members of the American Polygraph Association.

Nevertheless, there are a number of important differences between the polygraph practices in the two countries. First, there is a much greater tendency in Israel to use the GKT in addition to the CQT, at least as far as the police polygraphers are concerned. This tendency seems to be growing. In the past four years, some 1,000 polygraph examinations employed the GKT.

The importance of the GKT is emphasized in the course of routine police investigators' training. Furthermore, investigators are trained to search for appropriate items that could be utilized in a GKT-type interrogation, and not to disclose those items. An Israeli police polygrapher (E. Elaad, personal communication) cites an interesting recent example to illustrate the importance attached to GKT-based polygraphy. In a television news broadcast, the minister of police asked a police officer investigating a murder case about the type of gun used for the murder. The investigator refused to disclose this information to his superior on the grounds that this item was secret and that a break in secrecy could interfere with the investigation.

A second American/Israeli difference is that in Israel polygraphs are rarely used for personnel selection.[12] There are many private polygraph agencies that

---

[12]The reason for this may be related to the marked popularity of handwriting analysis in Israel. Ben-Shakar et al. (1986) have estimated that graphology is the single-most popular personnel selection tool in that country. One reason for this is that graphological

operate throughout the country, but they typically deal with event-related applications. Of these applications, an interesting one which is very common concerns insurance claims. Insurance companies will often offer a polygraph examination to a person claiming compensation as a condition for rapid settlement. The reason for such an offer is presumably to avoid false complaints, but the offer is of dubious propriety. False-positive errors are frequent in CQT polygraph (most private investigators utilize the CQT), so that even for the honest claimant there is a considerable risk involved in meeting the insurance company's offer. From the company's perspective, of course, the polygraph could well be an indirect, but effective, way to avoid having to make payments.

The legal status of polygraph-based interrogations in Israel was discussed at length by Harnon (1982), and little has changed since then. Basically, polygraph-based testimony is inadmissible in the criminal courtroom, but it can be used in civil cases by joint prior stipulation.

---

"analysis" of one or two pages of handwriting is much cheaper than polygraphic analysis, with its attendant psychophysiological software and hardware costs. The point made in footnote 4 applies here: the fact that polygraphs are not used for personnel selection is not necessarily a sign of increased scientific sophistication. One has to look very carefully at usage of alternative pseudoscientific methods before assuming that a lack of polygraph use indicates progress in scientific sophistication.

CHAPTER 8

# Beyond Validity: Utility and Legal Considerations in the Application of Psychophysiological Detection

Proponents as well as opponents of the polygraph concentrate almost exclusively on the question of validity, although they usually rely on different data sets and arrive at different conclusions (e.g., Lykken, 1978a,b, 1979; Podlesny and Raskin, 1977, 1978; Raskin, 1978; Raskin and Hare, 1978; Raskin and Podlesny, 1979). Even more neutral reviews of the detection literature refer to validity as the major issue (e.g., Saxe et al., 1985).

Although positive validity is a necessary condition for any application of polygraphy, other factors must also be considered, such as costs associated with the different outcomes of polygraph-based decisions, or prior probabilities of guilt. Furthermore, it is not clear how valid a test needs to be to justify its use. It has been repeatedly demonstrated that even highly valid tests could be of no value for some decisions; similarly, tests of moderate- or even low-validity coefficients could be extremely valuable for other decisions (e.g., Brogden, 1949; Cronbach and Gleser, 1965; Meehl and Rosen, 1955; Schmidt, Hunter, McKenzie, and Muldrow, 1979).

Despite their neglect in the polygraph literature, these factors nevertheless significantly affect the *utility* of psychophysiological detection. In the first part of this chapter we shall distinguish between different uses of polygraphy and examine them from a decision-theoretical perspective. In the second part of the chapter we shall discuss some legal considerations which transcend the issue of utility. Specifically, we shall focus in this section upon the risks involved in any attempt to use polygraph-based classifications as admissible evidence in the criminal court.

## The Concept of Utility and Its Importance for Evaluating Psychophysiological Detection

The basic concept we shall be using in this discussion is that of "utility," by which we mean the gains (or losses) associated with an outcome of a given decision. Those gains could be expressed in monetary units, or on some other numerical scale as long as it correctly represents the relations between the different outcomes. The overall utility of a given decision is the weighted average, or the expected value, of the utilities associated with all possible outcomes of the decision. In order to assess whether a test is useful for a given purpose, a comparison must be made between the expected utility of the optimal decisions based on the test and the best possible decisions made without the benefit of the test (by the best a priori strategy). For a thorough discussion of these issues, see, for example, Cronbach and Gleser (1965). It should be noted that utilities are subjective, and they need not be the same for the various parties associated with the polygraph interrogation: the examiner, the subject, the client, or society at large.

## Utilities Associated with the Different Outcomes of a Polygraph-Based Decision

The polygraph test,[1] like any other test, yields at least two possible outcomes (e.g., involved vs. not involved in a given crime), either of which may be either true or false. The payoff structure of the test is related to the joint occurrence of the test's outcome and the true state of the world. Thus, in the simplest case, where both the test's outcome and the true state of the world are dichotomized into two categories, the payoff structure can be described by a $2 \times 2$ matrix with four cells. Table 8.1 illustrates a payoff matrix of a polygraph test applied to a criminal investigation.

The four entries of this matrix represent the following outcomes: (1) a hit or correct identification (CI) (e.g., a guilty suspect was identified by the test as involved in the crime under investigation); (2) false positive (FP) (e.g., an innocent suspect was falsely identified by the test as involved or deceptive); (3) miss (M) (e.g., a guilty suspect was falsely classified as not involved with the crime under investigation); (4) correct rejection (CR) (e.g., an innocent suspect was correctly classified as not involved with the crime, or as nondeceptive). Of course, the matrix may be of a higher order, for example, $2 \times 3$ if we allow for an inconclusive decision category. Each possible cell has consequences for the

TABLE 8.1. Four outcomes resulting from the joint occurrence of the polygraph test result and the true state of the world.

| | Polygraph test outcome | |
|---|---|---|
| State of the world | Involved (deceptive) | Not involved (not deceptive) |
| Guilty | Correct identification (CI) | Miss (M) |
| Innocent | False positive (FP) | Correct rejection (CR) |

---

[1] For the purpose of this chapter's discussion we will be using the term "test" to apply to both the GKT and the CQT, although the latter is not really a test (see Chapter 1).

individual tested as well as for society in general. There is an extensive literature on the strategies of translating such qualitative consequences into numerical values, usually labeled as costs and utilities (e.g., Cronbach and Gleser, 1965; Edwards and Tversky, 1967; Schmidt et al., 1979). Such quantification, although quite problematic, is essential for a proper application of tests in decision making. As was so aptly pointed out by Rorer, Hoffman, and Hsieh (1966, p. 368):

However difficult the process of quantifying one's values may be, there is no avoiding it if one is to defend his procedure as "rational" or "scientific." . . . It must be recognized that if an individual is unable to construct a table representing his values with regard to specific decision outcomes, then he has no rational basis on which to make that decision, with or without the test. [In our case the polygraph.]

A decision-theoretical analysis of polygraph results was conducted by Lieblich, Ben-Shakhar, Kugelmass, and Cohen (1978) for the GKT and by Ben-Shakhar, Lieblich, and Bar-Hillel (1982) for different applications of the CQT. Under standard assumptions it can be shown (see Ben-Shakhar and Beller, 1983; Ben-Shakhar, Lieblich, and Bar-Hillel, 1982) that the payoff matrix can be represented by a single parameter—the cost ratio of the two possible errors (FP and M). Let us label this parameter $r = C(\text{FP})/C(\text{M})$, where $C$ is a cost function. Thus, $r > 1$ implies that a false-positive error is more costly than a miss, and vice versa. Furthermore, $r = 3$ implies that the decision maker considers three misses as equivalent to a single false-positive error (i.e., the decision maker is willing to tolerate up to three misses in order to avoid a single false-positive error). If we are to base decisions on the outcomes of polygraph tests, we ought to pay close attention to the parameter $r$. For example, if $r$ is very large (i.e., if a false-positive conclusion is considered far worse than a miss), then the decision maker should require very strong incriminating evidence, in the form of very large differences between the responses to the relevant questions and the controls, before making an "involved" or "deceptive" evaluation. Similarly, when $r$ is very small (i.e., a miss is much more to be feared than a false positive), even the slightest incriminating evidence should be used to reach an "involved" decision.

The whole question of the utility and the usefulness of the polygraph depends on the payoff structure, such that extreme values of $r$ in either direction may mean that the test is useless. Recall that the larger the value of $r$, the larger the difference between the responses to relevant and control questions that is required in order to incriminate a given suspect. Thus, an extremely large value of $r$ may yield an incriminating criterion with very low frequency of occurrence. In extreme cases (e.g., actual frequency of reaching the criterion is 1 in 100 tests), the test would be practically useless, and the cost of administering it might exceed its benefits, even if the test's validity is relatively high. Similarly, if the $r$ value is extremely small, the incriminating criterion might be extremely frequent. A test that yields extremely frequent incriminating decisions is useless, just like a test that almost never incriminates anyone (for a further elaboration of this point, see Ben-Shakhar, Lieblich, and Bar-Hillel, 1982).

## Prior Probabilities, or Base Rates

Another parameter that ought to be considered when applying the polygraph (or any other test) for decision making is the prior probabilities of the different possible outcomes. For example, there is a marked difference between a dispute between two individuals where it is certain that one of them is lying (i.e., the prior probability that any one of them is deceptive is .5) and a situation where something was stolen from a large company and many individuals (e.g., 20) could have done it (in which case the prior probability that a given individual is the thief is 1 in 20). The term "prior" is used to indicate that the probability is measured without the benefit of the information provided by the test (the polygraph). Clearly, this probability can be estimated, as in the examples mentioned above, on the basis of the relative frequency of individuals who could be involved with the event under investigation. But in some circumstances it could be based on prior information (e.g., intelligence), which would make some individuals more likely than others to be involved in the event.

The role of prior probabilities in determining the usefulness of the test is very similar to the role of the cost ratio ($r$) discussed in the previous section. The more extreme the prior probabilities (in either direction), the less useful the test. To make this point clear, consider the following extreme example in which there is a single guilty individual in a group of 1000 suspects. The prior probability of guilt in this case is .001, meaning that without the benefit of the polygraph one can reach a rate of 99.9% correct decisions just by classifying all suspects as innocents. In order for the polygraph to be useful in this case, it needs to produce better accuracy rates than those produced by the a priori strategy (unless, of course, the costs associated with a miss are much greater than those associated with a false-positive error). Clearly, it is unlikely that any psychological test will produce accuracy rates that come anywhere near the 99% figure. Similarly, it could be demonstrated that a situation characterized by an extremely high value of prior probability of guilt is also not likely to benefit from the information provided by the polygraph. Other examples for the role of prior probabilities in decisions based on tests are given by Meehl and Rosen (1955) and more recently by Ben-Shakhar, Bar-Hillel, and Lieblich (1986, p. 469).

## A Decision-Theoretical Analysis of Polygraph-Based Decisions

In order to reach optimal decisions and to determine the usefulness of a given test, the different parameters of the decision problem—the cost ratio, the prior probabilities of the different outcomes, and the test's validity—must be mathematically integrated. We shall not present a technical description of this integration process, but instead shall base the present discussion on the analyses conducted by Lieblich, Ben-Shakhar, Kugelmass, and Cohen (1978) and by Ben-Shakhar, Lieblich, and Bar-Hillel (1982), without describing their details. The interested reader is referred to those sources, as well as to more general discussions of the decision-theoretical approach as applied to testing (e.g., Cronbach and Gleser, 1965).

It is interesting to note that most description of polygraph procedures completely ignore the issues discussed in this section. Even the relatively advanced approaches to polygraphy—approaches that include quantification of the physiological responses and attempts to suggest quantified decision rules (e.g., Backster, 1963; Podlesny and Raskin, 1977, 1978)—do not take costs, payoffs, and prior probabilities into account. Because of this, the decision rules advocated by those polygraph experts are completely rigid (e.g., a total score greater than 5 leads to an "innocent" decision, a score less than $-5$ leads to a classification of the suspect as deceptive, while a score that falls between those two values results in an inconclusive decision). This procedure is recommended and applied regardless of the characteristics of the specific decision situation—the number of suspects, the prior information available to the examiner, and the costs associated with the different types of errors (false positive and false negative). Clearly, no single symmetrical decision procedure could be optimal for all possible combinations of $r$ values and prior probabilities of guilt. The analysis employed by Ben-Shakhar, Lieblich, and Bar-Hillel (1982) indicates that if it is assumed that polygraph examiners are operating as efficient decision makers, then they are clearly biased in favor of correctly identifying guilty suspects. In other words, they regard a miss as much more costly than a false-positive error. This type of payoff structure sharply contradicts claims made often by polygraph proponents according to which the CQT procedure is designed to protect the innocent. If, on the other hand, polygraph examiners are not maximizing expected utility, there is not much sense in belaboring their payoff considerations. In this case, the high rates of false positives might reflect the fact that relevant questions, as claimed by Lykken (1979), are more physiologically arousing than control questions even for innocent suspects.

In Chapter 1, we presented several situations to which the polygraph might be applied, such as criminal trials or personnel selection. Those applications may be characterized by very different values of the parameter $r$, as well as by different distributions of prior probabilities. Ben-Shakhar, Lieblich, and Bar-Hillel (1982) employed a decision-theoretical analysis of the potential contributions of the polygraph. They used published accuracy rates as a basis for estimating the validity of the CQT (though they explained there why these may well be too high), and estimated the prior probabilities of deception and the social costs of both types of erroneous classifications of suspects in three polygraph applications: pre-employment screening, police interrogation, and criminal trials. They concluded that from a strictly utilitarian perspective, polygraph-based decisions in the latter two contexts could often be worse than default decisions (that is, decisions made on the basis of prior probabilities and costs alone without appeal to any specific information). Although the use of the polygraph as evidence in criminal trials is very rare, some experts have strongly recommended it, arguing that the truth-finding process could greatly benefit from its use (e.g., Ploss, 1978; Stephens,

1981). The criminal trial context is typically characterized by a large value of $r$. This is because the standard of proof in such trials ("beyond a reasonable doubt") reflects the notion that false-positive error—convicting the innocent—carries a much heavier cost than a miss error—acquitting the guilty (Kaplan, 1968). Based on attempts to quantify the "burden of proof" (Cullison, 1969; Simon and Mahan, 1971), Ben-Shakhar, Lieblich, and Bar-Hillel (1982) reasoned that in criminal cases a false-positive error is about six times as costly as a miss. With such a nonsymmetrical cost structure (a large value of $r$), the incriminating criterion would be met in extremely rare cases, and CQT-based decisions would likely be worse than decisions based on alternative evidence, even if the validity of the CQT is as high as its proponents claim. Thus, decisions based on the CQT polygraph test are unlikely to add anything to the utility of the fact-finding process.

This decision-theoretical analysis must be qualified because it is based on the assumption that decisions are made solely on the basis of the polygrapher's evaluation. However, even nonexclusive usage of the polygraph is unjustified unless it is possible to assure that it will be given no more (and no less) than its proper weighting vis à vis the other evidence. Ben-Shakhar, Bar-Hillel, and Lieblich (1986) listed several reasons showing why this may be difficult or even impossible to achieve, and why often polygraph evidence would be overweighted.[2]

A different application of polygraphy that has been quite popular is preemployment screening and periodic honesty checks (see Sackett and Decker, 1979; U.S. Congress, 1983). As in criminal trials, the preemployment screening context is also characterized by a nonsymmetrical cost structure, but this time $r$ is typically much smaller than 1, because employers are highly averse to accepting candidates who are possibly dishonest. Rejecting honest candidates, however, is usually considered of much smaller consequence by most employers. The decision-theoretical analysis employed by Ben-Shakhar, Lieblich, and Bar-Hillel (1982) demonstrates that because of the nonsymmetrical cost structure, CQT-based polygraph evaluations will rarely be useful for personnel selection.

These decision-theoretical considerations are important because they demonstrate the distinctions between different applications of the polygraph test. Specifically, the conclusion drawn from this line of reasoning is that any application characterized by a nonsymmetrical payoff structure (by an extreme value of the parameter $r$) is unlikely to benefit from polygraph tests. Indeed, Ben-Shakhar, Lieblich, and Bar-Hillel (1982) argued that one of the few situations in which polygraph tests could be of positive utility is the police investigation context. This

---

[2] Our reservations notwithstanding, Cavoukian and Heslegrave (1980) studied the effect of adding to the evidence in a simulated criminal trial a polygrapher's testimony that the defendant is *not* guilty. They found that this information increased the proportion of subjects who judged the defendant innocent, but that the polygrapher's evaluation did not completely dominate the evidence, since some subjects nonetheless judged the defendant to be guilty.

would be a case where the test's results could not be used as admissible evidence in court, and where the outcome would only be a decision of the sort of whether to continue the interrogation of a given suspect or to release the person and concentrate on alternative leads. Thus, the cost of a false-positive error is considerably smaller than in the case of a court decision, and the $r$ value is likely to be much closer to 1.

# Legal Considerations

In the first two chapters of this book we described the rationales of the different methods of psychophysiological detection. We presented several arguments showing why the most prevalent method of polygraphy, the CQT, is highly problematic from both theoretical and logical perspectives. In Chapter 3 we focused exclusively on the issue of validity and concluded that the available research is insufficient for estimating the validity of psychophysiological detection techniques in realistic settings. In the previous sections of this chapter we argued, following Ben-Shakhar, Lieblich, and Bar-Hillel (1982), that even if the more optimistic validity estimates of the CQT are assumed, it is still unlikely that testimony based on this method will be of positive utility. This conclusion was based primarily on the premise that false-positive errors carry much greater costs than misses in criminal trials. But there are additional reasons not to use evidence based on psychophysiological detection methods in criminal trials. These arguments, which are derived primarily from Ben-Shakhar, Bar-Hillel, and Lieblich (1986), go beyond the issues of validity and utility because they seem to hold true irrespective of how accurate the polygraph-based interrogation system may be.

## The Polygraph Interrogation as a Contaminated Procedure

It will be recalled that CQT polygraph examiners are exposed to a great deal of non-physiological information (see Chapters 1 and 2 for a description of the CQT procedure), such as information provided to them by other examiners and impressions formed during the pre-test interview and during the test itself. It is impossible to differentiate between the impressions formed by this prior information and those gained from the purely physiological data obtained during the so-called test phase of the polygraph interrogation procedure. This feature, which characterizes all types of polygraph-based interrogation procedures, but in particular the CQT, has been labeled "contamination" (Ben-Shakhar, Bar-Hillel, and Lieblich, 1986), meaning that judgments and conclusions derived from the physiological information are contaminated with various kinds of nonphysiological information. Contamination is inherent to the CQT because this procedure is not based strictly on the psychophysiological data, but rather on the whole examiner-subject interaction, including the pre-test interview. Furthermore, CQT polygraphers believe that it is essential that the same investigator construct the questions during the pre-test interview and administer them during the test phase of the interrogation. Typically, the same person evaluates the polygraph charts and draws the final conclusion on the basis of all the information available to him or her. The main problem with contaminated tests is that the sources of the conclusions drawn from that test cannot be known, and they can be very different from those believed to underly the inferences made on the basis of the test.

One implication of the contamination feature of CQT polygraph techniques is that the weight of the strictly physiological information in the polygraph examiner's conclusion is not known, and in principle can be very small or even nil. The following two demonstrations may illustrate why the contamination factor is crucial for understanding how polygraph examiners operate in practice. Barland (1975) found that in only 2 out of 19 cases did polygraph examiners give final evaluations that differed from those solicited just before the administration of the polygraph test (e.g., on the basis of the prior information available to the examiner). A second, quite powerful demonstration was provided by a CBS production of a *60 Minutes* broadcast in 1986. Three different polygraph firms were independently called to test an alleged theft of a camera and lens from a photography magazine office employing four employees. In fact nothing was stolen from the office, but the polygraph examiners were told that it could have only been done by one of the four employees. Each polygraph examiner was told that "it might be _____," with a different employee being fingered in each case (a decidedly weak fingering). In each case, the polygraph examiner identified the "fingered" employee as deceptive, and did so with complete confidence in his decision. This demonstrates not only that polygraph examiners can go wrong, but that there is a systematic and powerful source of bias in these types of interrogation procedures, a bias caused by contamination.

Clearly, the nonphysiological information can, in some instances, add to the accuracy of the polygrapher's final judgment, but it has little to do with the device's ability to detect deception. If we confuse the polygrapher's validity with that of the polygraph, we may end up with highly inflated validity estimates for the latter. On the other hand, if one is interested in the human ability of detecting deception, rather than detection by a machine, then a host of additional problems surface—problems which are particularly revelant for the legal applications of polygraphy.

Contamination of the polygraph results cannot be completely eliminated even if charts are scored by "blind evaluators" with no a priori information, as is often done in experimental research (e.g., Podlesny and Raskin, 1978). This is so because contamination not only may affect the evaluations made by the polygrapher, but also may affect the way the whole test is administered. This more subtle kind of contamination might be introduced into the charts through the "interpersonal expectancy effect" (Rosenthal and Rubin, 1978). This effect was first discovered in the context of psychological experiments and refers to the fact that experimenters often elicit from their subjects behavior that tends in the direction of their hypothesis, a sort of self-fulfilling prophecy. In the context of polygraph interrogations, it translates to the possibility than an interrogator who has formed an opinion about a suspect's guilt before the initiation of the test is likely to elicit from the suspect a psychological response pattern supporting that opinion (Ben-Shakhar, Lieblich, and Bar-Hillel, 1982; Ben-Shakhar, Bar-Hillel, and Lieblich, 1986; Sackett and Decker, 1979).

## The Legal Implications of Contaminated Polygraph Procedures

If, as we have argued throughout this section, the accuracy of CQT polygraph results is due, in whole or in part, to the human polygrapher administering the test, rather than to purely physiological information, then expert testimony of a polygraph examiner represents only that polygrapher's own, possibly valid, opinion. On a scale of expert testimony that runs from the subjective impressions of a well-trained police detective to "hard" evidence such as fingerprints, polygraphers' evaluations fall much closer to the former end. But the problem with polygraphers as expert witnesses is not just their subjectivity. Many other types of experts can be characterized as subjective. The law of evidence often deliberately binds the hands of the judge in seeking out the facts. No such limitations bind the polygrapher, who has access to any information which the police have their hands on. The legal or ethical guidelines constraining the polygrapher's interaction with the suspect are much fewer than those binding the judge or jury. The polygraph interrogation is conducted outside the presence of the suspect's legal counsel, unlike courtroom interrogations. Allowing polygraph test results into the court might deprive suspects of many of the protections provided to them by due process. It opens a back door for all kinds of inadmissible evidence, including those obtained by unsavory means or worse, which may enter, unchecked and unchallenged, through their influence on the knowledgeable polygrapher's evaluations and conclusions. In other words, accepting polygraphers as expert witnesses may be a way of "laundering" inadmissible evidence, because such inadmissible evidence might influence the polygraph examiner, even without the examiner's awareness, and there is no way for the judge to differentiate between the different factors that may have led the polygrapher to a given conclusion. Particularly insidious in this context is the high confidence that polygraph examiners can manifest in completely erroneous and contaminated evaluations—as documented in the *60 Minutes* report.

This argument transcends the issue of validity, and it holds even if CQT-based polygraph interrogations are as valid as proponents of the CQT claim (e.g., Raskin, 1986). Clearly, if polygraphy was indeed an accurate tool, it would make the polygraph-based testimony relevant. But relevance is a necessary but not a sufficient condition for admissibility, and entire categories of possibly relevant evidence are routinely excluded from the courtroom. The grounds for such exclusion are based either on norms (as when U.S. courts refuse to admit illegally obtained information) or on the inherent weaknesses of certain kinds of evidence, such as vulnerability to distortion (e.g., hearsay evidence) or possible prejudiciality (e.g., character testimony). By allowing uninhibited, even if accurate, impressions to influence the court, the legal system may be working against its own aims and purposes. The appearance of objectivity and "scientificness" imparted to lie detection by the use of polygraphs obscures the fact that polygraphy, in standard practice, is at best a clinical skill. Lie detection is a somewhat mysterious and opaque process, but the mystery exists not in the working of the polygraph, but in the workings of the polygrapher's mind. Once this is acknowledged, the question arises whether there are any grounds to believe that as *human* lie detectors, polygraphers are superior to other people in general, and to judges or juries in particular.

In the above discussion of polygraph admissibility, we focused primarily on the CQT. We did this because (*a*) the bulk of polygraph interrogations are carried out through the CQT, and (*b*) contamination is an inherent feature of this technique. Clearly, the GKT can also be administered in a contaminated manner, that is, by an overly informed polygrapher. Unlike the CQT, however, the GKT can be fairly easily decontaminated simply by using double-blind procedures characterizing scientific experimentation settings. Lykken (1981) demonstrated how this can be achieved by the use of a pedagogical detective story. Decontaminated polygraph procedures could be designed simply by differentiating between the different stages of the interrogation and by making them independent. The person constructing the questions must of course be familiar with the details of the crime, but not with the suspects. In fact, there is no need for this person to see any of the suspects or to know anything about them. The actual administration of the test can be relegated to a second person, a technician trained for the task but requiring no special investigative skills. It becomes a purely mechanical procedure, and the questions can even be administered by a tape recorder. The interpretation of the charts could be carried out by a third, independent person, who knows nothing about the suspect or the case. Preferably this stage could be carried out mechanically by a computer program, just as in psychophysiological experiments. Such a decontaminated polygraph procedure could be designed with the GKT, but it would undoubtedly meet with great opposition from most proponents of the CQT who see the very power and essence of their technique in the interaction between the suspect and the interrogator.

By saying that GKT-based polygraph interrogations can be designed in a decontaminated manner, we do not wish to imply that this method in its present state is ready to become admissible evidence in the criminal court. No data exist today from which sound estimates for the GKT validity in real-life setups can be generated. But there are dangers other than random errors that should be taken into account before allowing even GKT polygraphy into the courtroom. The GKT is heavily dependent on the assumption that the details of the crime are kept secret from all suspects. Any leakage of relevant information to the suspects may increase the risks of making false-positive errors. Such a leakage is possible by a mistake made at some stage of the interrogation, but it could also happen by a deliberate attempt to convict one of the suspects. Some comforting evidence was provided by a few studies which demonstrated that exposing innocent subjects to the guilty knowledge had very little effect on the false-positive rate (Bradley and Warfield, 1984; Giesen and Rollison, 1980; Stern et al., 1981). These experiments were conducted in laboratory conditions, and in most cases the innocent subjects were exposed to the guilty information in an innocent context. Further research is therefore required to seriously assess the impact of exposing innocent suspects to the guilty information in real-life situations.

There are additional factors differentiating the simulated from the realistic situation that might affect the outcomes of the GKT. Recall that this method depends on the assumption that the relevant items were perceived by the guilty person and that this individual remembers them at the time of the test. Unfortunately, all GKT studies used a very simple task in which the experimenters guaranteed that all the relevant items were perceived and learned by the subjects. Furthermore, the subjects are typically tested immediately after being exposed to guilty information; thus memory does not play an important role in the experimental situation. In real life, things might be entirely different. The guilty suspect is faced with a complex scene, and it might be much more difficult to assume that all details were indeed noticed, processed, and stored in memory. Criminal suspects are very rarely tested immediately after committing the criminal act. Typically, they may be tested days, weeks, and sometimes months after the crime was committed. These factors might affect the false-negative rates (e.g., the rate of false-negative error might be larger in real-life applications of the GKT than in experimental situations). On the other hand, it could be argued that crime-related information is very likely to be perceived and remembered, because of its great relevance to the perpetrator of the crime. It is, of course, unknown whether and to what extent these factors might affect the GKT efficiency, and future research addressing these questions should be conducted before GKT-based testimony is allowed in court.

## Conclusions

The evaluation of the polygraphic procedures has been a central issue of this book. In the first two chapters, different methods of psychophysiological detection were assessed with respect to their rationales and underlying logic. We argued that only one method—the GKT—stands on solid logical and theoretical grounds. In the third chapter, the methods were evaluated using standard criteria of reliability and validity, and we concluded that these parameters cannot be accurately estimated on the basis of the available data, at least not if by validity one means the ability of detecting deception in realistic settings.

In this chapter we assessed polygraphic procedures from a social and legal standpoint. In the first section, consideration of decision-theoretical criteria led to a conclusion that such an assessment must be done separately for each application of polygraphy, because the different usages might differ drastically with respect to the basic features of the decision situation (i.e., costs, payoffs, and prior probabilities). By analyzing three types of polygraph applications it became clear that both the industrial application and the criminal court usage of polygraphy are unlikely to add to the utility of decisions made in those contexts. This conclusion holds true even if one accepts quite favorable estimates of the polygraph's validity. A third application that was examined is the use of the polygraph within law enforcement agencies. This application might benefit from psychophysiological detection procedures because it is characterized by a more symmetrical cost structure than the other applications, in that costs associated with misclassifying an innocent suspect as deceptive are much smaller in the police investigation setup than they are in the criminal courtoom.

The issue of contamination was the focus of the second section of the chapter. We argued that polygraphic procedures as typically used are contaminated as a result of the examiner knowing much more than what is revealed by the polygraph charts; therefore, it is not known whether, or to what extent the examiner's conclusions are based on the physiological responses to the questions. Contaminated procedures should not be used as admissible evidence in the criminal court because they could be a conduit into the courtroom for inadmissible evidence, unchecked and unchallenged, through their influence on the examiner's evaluations. The different methods of polygraphy differ with respect to the contamination issue. Although contamination seems to be an inherent feature of the CQT, the GKT can be fairly easily decontaminated. We described how this can be achieved, but concluded, nevertheless, that even the GKT should not be used as admissible evidence in criminal courts until further evidence showing its efficiency in real-life settings accumulates.

CHAPTER 9

# Future Perspectives

All predictions are conditioned by the context of the predictors. Our particular context is a psychophysiological orientation that insists on the evaluation of psychological treatments in terms of their specific effects. Nevertheless, in addition to these logical considerations (that are invariant across cultures), there are, as we have indicated in Chapter 7, cultural factors that play a powerful role in determining both the nature and the perceived scientific status of methods of detecting deception. These cultural factors are more difficult to analyze in logical terms, but their influence still has to be recognized in any analysis or prognosis. In this final chapter, we shall consider future applied and basic research from a logical, scientific point of view, and will end with a more speculative consideration of potentially relevant societal influences.

## Applied Research

In considering the future of applied research in the area of psychophysiological detection, we begin by delineating that which is researchable. Next, we raise the basic evaluative issue of whether the psychophysiological information obtained does improve detection, and we analyze the prospects of obtaining positive evidence for this claim with the various detection methods used. We then consider conditions that affect accuracy, raise the problems associated with various pitfalls, and finally comment on prospects of future improvements in dependent-variable measurement.

### Restricting the Domain of Applied Psychophysiological Detection-of-Deception Research

To the extent that applied research is grounded in scientific methodology (without which the information gleaned is of little practical use), standardization is an essential requirement. In other words, the instrument in question must be reasonably constant from competent operator to competent operator. Such constancy is not possible for those forms of the CQT that use confession inducement, because the content of the questions, the way in which the questions are put, and the duration of both the pre-test and (especially) the post-test interviews vary as a function of the examiner's confession-inducing purposes. Accordingly, applied research must be restricted to the GKT and to those forms of the CQT that do not use confession inducement.

The most salient effect of this restriction is that it excludes the North American CQT from consideration as being evaluatable as a scientifically based, *psychophysiological* means of detecting deception. This leaves open the possibility that individual *interrogators* who employ the polygraph as part of their interrogating procedure may become extremely accurate as deception detectors, but the same may be said of individual fortune-tellers who use other props to ply their trade. That possibility granted, it is still the case that no matter how accurate the North American CQT may be in the hands of some individual operators (and so far, by the way, *independent* evaluations have generally failed to confirm the high-accuracy claims made by some individuals), no systematic research can be informative about the procedure as used by the "average" competent operator, because the procedure is too unstandardized.

## The Basic Evaluative Issue: Does It Work?

It follows from the specific-effects orientation detailed in Chapter 5 that if the question posed in this section's title is to be answered affirmatively, evidence must show that the technique being evaluated has a specific, beneficial effect on the ability of the users to achieve their purpose; in this case, that purpose is the detection of guilt. Other orientations may accept, as evidence, expert *testimonial* evidence of the form, "In my vast experience it has worked well for me." However, the specific-effects orientation requires expert *evaluative* evidence which demonstrates that the psychophysiological information provided by the polygraph does, indeed, improve detection accuracy.

No such evidence is currently available for even the GKT, but it is not too great a leap of faith to predict that when such evidence is gathered, it will be clearly positive for this technique. This prediction is supported by two considerations: first, the GKT has been shown in numerous studies to be a much-better-than-chance detector of guilt; secondly, and unlike the CQT, it contains little non-psychophysiological information in the procedure, so that any detecting ability is likely to be due to the psychophysiological information obtained.

The Japanese version of the CQT (which is similar to the American "guilt-complex" procedure) discussed in Chapter 7 is at least free of the interrogatory nonpsychophysiological contamination of the American CQT, and so it may also prove to "work" in the sense defined here. However, the problem here is that while, *in principle*, the contrast between experimental (relevant) and control questions is methodologically sound, it is *in fact* very difficult in real-life settings to construct question pairs that are equal in emotional impact. The difficulty is that the context usually makes the crime of which the suspect is accused more threatening than the (purportedly equivalent) hypothetical crime. Because of this difficulty, it is not likely that much systematic work will be done with the Japanese CQT, and hence extensive positive evidence for its "working" is unlikely to be obtained in any large amounts. For the remainder of this chapter, therefore, our discussion will be restricted to the GKT.

## Subsequent Evaluative Issue: Factors Affecting Accuracy

Any scientifically based instrument which "works" in the sense of improving baseline (without-instrument) performance is affected in the degree of this improvement by various factors. In the case of the GKT, the accuracy level is likely to be affected by such factors as the number of relevant/control comparison questions that can be generated, the comprehensibility and lack of ambiguity in the questions, the characteristics of the examinees, the seriousness of the crime, and the accuracy of the physiological measures employed. Whether relevant field studies are performed depends largely on whether the GKT comes into common use in North America.

An important aspect of such studies is that they should separately consider the two types of error: false-positive and false-negative errors. A purely scientific reason for this consideration is the fact that the two sorts of errors are in a trade-off relationship: reducing one sort may lead to some increase in the other. In the GKT, increasing the number of relevant/control comparisons (through repetition and/or through increasing the number of questions asked) may lead not only to a reduction in the false-positive rate but also to some increase in the false-negative rate.[1] Therefore, statements regarding the effects of various factors on accuracy will have to be qualified as to which *sort* of errors are involved.

In addition, important nonscientific considerations relate to the distinction between false-positive and false-negative errors. These considerations have to do with the *value* placed on the two kinds of errors, which in turn is determined by the severity of the crime as well as the relative value placed by society on balancing the rights of the accused with those of the victim. It is probably also true that this relative value differs from examiner to examiner, which makes it even more important that the detection-of-deception procedure be as free of examiner bias as posssible. Such freedom from bias is, at least in principle, possible with a standardized test like the GKT.

## Practical Pitfalls

Even if applied research establishes the conditions under which the GKT is most accurate, there will still be practical problems to be faced in specific situations. These problems center on sources of unconscious bias in the examining situation.

---

[1] It is possible to increase the number of questions without increasing the false-negative rate by adjusting the decision rule for determining whether a particular subject is deceptive or truthful, but without such adjustments, a decrease in the false-positive error rate does generally result in an increase in the false-negative error rate.

One such source of bias occurs when the examinee is unwittingly provided with (at least partial) knowledge about details of the crime which, allegedly, have been kept secret from innocent suspects. It is important to recognize that such knowledge need not be fully explicit for it to bias the GKT. A critical contribution of applied research in this area will be information on how to minimize this source of bias.

Another biasing source can occur if the examiner has a strong opinion about the guilt of the suspect, coupled with knowledge about details of the crime. In that case, even unwittingly, the examiner may put the relevant questions with more emphasis and thereby increase the false-positive error rate of the GKT. One way of avoiding this pitfall is to have the examiner as ignorant about the crime as are innocent suspects, but this would minimally require someone other than the examiner to construct the questions. Another possibility is to *evaluate* the gravity of this sort of bias, by having examiners rate the examinees' guilt before administration of the GKT and determining whether such prior guilt expectations are correlated with GKT (physiological) outcomes. Finally, it may be feasible to eliminate this source of bias by recording the questions before the examinee enters the room to be tested.

## Dependent-Variable Improvements

The most obvious source of potential improvement lies in the choice of dependent variables. The traditional three measures of the CQT polygraph (GSR, respiration, and blood pressure) may not be optimal. Sensitivity relative to detection accuracy needs to be assessed in terms of the following considerations: which measure is best on its own, what combination is best, and which added elements contribute a significant amount to increasing accuracy.

There is also the possibility that, for each measure, there are aspects other than the traditional ones that will yield more information. For example, in the case of respiration, quantitative methods have usually examined only frequency and amplitude.[2] There is some unpublished laboratory GKT evidence from Japan that suggests that the *apnea* duration following inspiration may provide better information than frequency or amplitude, perhaps because voluntary control of this aspect of respiration is more difficult.

However, the most exciting recent potential extensions have emerged in studies that have used the EEG evoked reaction potential (ERP) in laboratory GKT procedure using the "odd-ball paradigm" (Farwell and Donchin, 1986, 1988). These studies have sometimes reported accuracy rates of 99%, which is far higher than those achieved with traditional, autonomic measures. Part of the reason for this may lie not in the measure, but in the fact that the ERP paradigm permits trials to be given every few seconds rather than at longer intervals of

---

[2]Studies conducted by Timm (1982, 1987) constitute exceptions to this rule. In those experiments, the total length of the respiration tracing was used, and as detailed in Chapter 4, this respiration measure yielded significant detection results.

some 20 seconds. More generally, however, the ERP paradigm offers the possibility of a purely *cognitive* measure of deception, because the onset latency of the ERP (usually the P300) is far shorter than the onset latency of an automatically controlled response like the GSR. Nevertheless, from a practical point of view, there are enormous problems of software expertise and costs in developing a version of the ERP GKT which would be usable in the field. A minimum requirement for field use is that the ERP GKT be demonstrated to be far more accurate than the conventional autonomic-based GKT. At this stage, it bears emphasis that the ERP GKT results not only are strictly laboratory-based, but also have yet to appear in full-length form, in addition to being replicated in other laboratories.

## Basic Research

The controlled conditions of the laboratory offer opportunities to study questions that cannot be addressed in the field. This also means that direct inference from laboratory to field is impossible, even though the principles established in the laboratory may provide useful hypotheses for field use. In this section we consider two areas of laboratory research that may yield fruitful insights.

### The Nature of the Psychological Process of Deception: The Differentiation-of-Deception Paradigm

From a basic-research psychophysiological perspective, the primary interest lies not in the *detection* of deception in individuals, but in the *differentiation* of deception as a psychological process from other psychological processes. From this perspective, as indicated earlier, even the experimentally sound GKT does not measure deception.

The demonstration of deception as a psychophysiological phenomenon requires a comparison of physiological responses to two conditions (experimental and control), which differ only with respect to deception. Neither the CQT nor even the GKT provides such a demonstration, because, at best, the difference between the two conditions is the presence of guilt rather than that of the process of deception itself.[3] The differentiation-of-deception paradigm (DDP) uses relatively neutral autobiographical items as questions. Differential question significance, which is confounded in the CQT, with respect to isolating deception, is controlled through employing questions of equal (and low) significance. Differential fre-

---

[3]For an elaboration of the thesis that, contrary to the claim suggested by the phrase "detection of the deception," deception, in fact, is not detected either by the CQT or by the KGT, see Furedy (1986) and Furedy and Heslegrave (1989a). A related point is that it is important to distinguish between the applied aim of *detecting* deception as being present or absent in a given individual and the scientific aim of *differentiating* deception from other related but different psychological processes. The former aim is necessarily a between-subjects discrimination, whereas the latter can be both a within- as well as a between-subjects discrimination.

quency of occurrence, which is confounded in the GKT with respect to isolating deception, is controlled through using 50% each of honestly and deceptively answered questions. An electrodermal (GSR) form of the differentiation-of-deception phenomenon has recently been reported (Furedy et al., 1988), following some earlier conference-abstract reports (Hemsley, Furedy, and Heslegrave, 1980; Heslegrave, 1982). Specifically, Furedy et al. (1988) found that GSRs to questions answered deceptively exceeded GSRs to those answered honestly, where the only difference between experimental (deceptive) and control (honest) conditions was the presence of deception. In our view, despite the many laboratory reports of detection-of-deception studies, the DDP represents the first relatively unequivocal demonstration of deception as a psychophysiological phenomenon.

The demonstration of a phenomenon should be followed by explorations into factors affecting it, which in turn should yield possible explanations of the phenomenon in terms of hypothetical mechanisms. In the case of the deception phenomenon, factors that probably should be explored include levels of incentive motivation to deceive (manipulable, for example, by differential money incentives) and more intrinsic motivation concerning whether the ability to deceive is a desirable one (manipulable, for example, by instructions).

Clues concerning possible mechanisms may be obtained by extending the range of dependent variables studied. Heslegrave's (1982) preliminary report suggested that deceptive items were differentiated from honest items not in heart rate acceleration, but in *deceleration*. Moreover, no differential sympathetic changes were observed for these items. This pattern of results suggests that deception involves parasympathetic withdrawal ("hiding") rather than a sympathetic activation (fight-or-flight response). It is interesting to note that field detection-of-deception procedures use relative blood pressure *increase* as an index, which is contrary to the above parasympathetic-withdrawal interpretation of deception.

## GKT Laboratory Parameters

The GKT lends itself well to laboratory studies, and as detailed in Chapter 4, there have been many explorations of various motivational, cognitive, and emotional factors related to the GKT. These are likely to continue, and to yield results of interest not only for detection of the guilty, but also for issues such as the role of response habituation in such detection.

Moreover, manipulation of factors such as perceived accuracy will be of interest to the applied community, if only because many (CQT-oriented) polygraphers believe that high perceived accuracy is essential for detection. However, the results from these laboratory studies can at best be only suggestive for field conditions, there being many differences between the two.

Of these differences, the most obvious is that subjects undergoing real-life polygraphic interviews are likely to be considerably more aroused and concerned than those subjects involved in laboratory experiments. In addition, in field situations, subjects would vary in many ways: subjects would view the examination, the examiner, and the purpose of the test differently; they would probably be more heterogeneous and vary from laboratory subjects in such factors as age, background, intelligence, and personality; the events preceding the examination would differ as well as the time period between the critical event and the examination; in the field, the guilty subjects would be more motivated to deceive; and the anxiety or stress levels of guilty and innocent subjects may differ more extensively in the field than in the laboratory.

It should also be noted that although a number of factors have been listed that may differ from the laboratory to the field situation, the *direction* of these effects has not been specified. This is because our present state of knowledge does not allow us to predict with any confidence the directional influence (if any) of these factors on detection accuracy. Accordingly, hypotheses about factors affecting field accuracy can only be adequately evaluated in the field itself, even though laboratory studies can provide a fruitful source for formulating such field-related hypotheses.

## Societal Considerations

In this final section, we consider two societal aspects of the polygraph which, in our view, will in the future become increasingly relevant.

### Effects of Reduction of Direct-Evidence Use of the CQT Polygraph

It may seem quite plausible to think that whenever the polygraph is denied evidential status in the criminal courts (as occurred, for example, in the 1987 Supreme Court decision in Canada), the influence of the polygraph is thereby diminished. The grain of truth in this belief is that the scientific status of the procedure is, indeed, decreased, and hence professional polygraph associations are displeased by such developments.

However, there are grounds for suggesting that the *indirect* influence of the polygraph may actually increase when its direct-evidence use is denied. In the hands of police interrogators, the polygraph becomes an even more useful confession-inducing instrument, because the events occurring during the polygraph "test" are no longer subjected to critical scrutiny by defense counsel, since the procedure is no longer deemed relevant. This leaves the police polygrapher even more freedom to ply the "psychological rubber hose" in the privacy of the one-on-one situation demanded by the polygraph, knowing that it is not likely that what goes on during the confession-inducing phase of the examination will ever be critically examined by the defense.

### Cultural Credibility Factors: Possibilities for Education

Although the argument is necessarily speculative, there may be a case for suggesting that an inverse measure of a society's level of civilization is the degree of credulity in superstitious, psuedoscientific procedures, and that this measure is more accurate than the extent of technical gadgets available. The inverse credulity measure would place ancient Greek civilization above that of Rome, because although the latter had much more efficient plumbing and military systems, it was also far more steeped in superstition in the conduct of everyday affairs (e.g., the testing of entrails before every battle). Similarly, pseudoscience-based technologies like astrology, graphology, and CQT polygraphy enjoy considerable status in technically sophisticated American society, not only in legal contexts but also in other areas where there is a dispute about credibility between contending parties.

Part of the reason for this, in our view, is that the Greek concern for defining terms has been replaced by the Roman pragmatic notion of getting on with the job and not worrying about terminological disputes as long as the procedure "works." This sort of pragmatism extends beyond the lay community to the professional one. For example, the American Psychological Association, which has a separate committee dealing with psychological tests, has continued to treat the North American CQT as a test despite the fact that, as noted earlier, psychological textbook definitions of what a test is (e.g., Anastasi, 1988), contradict this treatment. Under these circumstances it is difficult to see how educating the public about the polygraph will be effective, because without clarity of concepts, such "education" is no more than political indoctrination. Once education is politicized in this way, the strength of competing vested interests determines the outcome. In the case of the CQT polygraph, there are many vested interests which are strongly in its favor. Accordingly, without a determination to confront basic terminological issues, it is not likely that the forces opposed to polygraph use will succeed in the U.S.

A recent case in point that, in our view, illustrates the problem is the 1988 U.S. Congressional ban on the industrial use of the polygraph. This, on the surface, looks like a great step forward in the antipolygraph campaign, and the American Psychological Association, which acted as a supportive information source, is considered by most to have struck a blow for science-based technology.

It is true that this legislation eliminates a large proportion of polygraphic examinations of the event-free sort and that these examinations are even looser than the event-related CQT. So the *number* of polygraph tests (and therefore of practitioners) has been reduced, especially in the hiring context. However, because the bill permits "specific-incident" (i.e., event-related) polygraphy under certain "restrictions," it can be viewed as providing positive support for the CQT. One consequence of this support is that it is likely to increase the dangers of polygraphy for individual employees *in* the workplace. This is because the distinction between "industrial" and "criminal" is not a valid one. Cases where there have been alleged criminal acts in industry are ones that are wide open to event-related, CQT, polygraphic "investigation."

For the individual employee (especially if he or she is in a relatively high position), the stakes are much higher than in the case of initial hiring. It is one thing not to get a specific job for unjust reasons. It is another to lose a job (or to be stigmatized), and thereby possibly ruin one's career, through failing a CQT polygraph.

For psychological organizations like the American Psychological Association, the polygraph represents a severe test of scientific credibility. Even if the CQT were a test rather than an unstandardized interrogatory interview, the predominant view of psychologists is that it is a test of questionable validity. In that case, the "severe restrictions" placed on the use of the polygraph by the 1988 bill, namely, that the "test" last at least 90 minutes, that the examinee get the questions in advance, and that the examiner have at least 6 months of training, are all restrictions which, on examination, are less than impressive once what is actually involved in the CQT polygraph is considered.

The more-than-90-minute requirement is no help. It may even exacerbate the detection problems, because the increased time may be employed for the confession-inducing function of the CQT, a function which is, necessarily, a subjective one. Ensuring that the employee get the questions in advance similarly has no clearly positive effect on validity. Indeed, in the CQT, this condition is *impossible* to fulfill with respect to the so-called control questions, since these are made up in discussion between examiner and examinee *during* the polygraph procedure at the so-called pre-test interview. And the 6-month training requirement for examiners is relevant only if the procedure is a valid test. After all, if it is agreed that tea-leaf reading is not a valid procedure for determining the future, then requiring tea-leaf readers to have 6 *years* of experience would not resolve the scientific validity problem inherent in the tea-leaf reading enterprise.

Of course at a purely political level, it is obvious why such conflicts are ignored in the quest for the compromise necessary to get a bill through Congress. However, such short-term expediency is satisfied at the cost of long-term confusion, and encourages a move toward superstition in the particular society that takes such an expedient approach to its problems and ignores basic terminological issues about what constitutes a test and what is a genuinely scientifically based technology.

# References

Akamatsu, P., Uchida, Y., and Togawa, Y. (1933). The measurement of PGR(1). *Phylosophia*, *3*, 230–241. (In Japanese.)

Anastasi, A. (1988). *Psychological Testing*, 6th ed. New York: Macmillan.

Anderson, J. (1962). *Studies in Empirical Philosophy*. Sydney: Angus & Robertson.

Backster, C. (1962). Methods of strengthening our polygraph technique. *Police*, *6*, 61–68.

Backster, C. (1963). Polygraph professionalization through technique standardization. *Law and Order*, *11*, 63–64.

Balloun, K.D., and Holmes, D.S. (1979). Effects of repeated examinations on the ability to detect guilt with a polygraphic examination: A laboratory experiment with a real crime. *Journal of Applied Psychology*, *64*, 316–322.

Barland, G.H. (1975). *Detection of Deception in Criminal Suspects: A Field Validation Study*. Ph.D. dissertation, University of Utah.

Barland, G.H., and Raskin, D.C. (1973). The use of electrodermal activity in the detection of deception. In W.F. Prokasy and D.C. Raskin (Eds.), *Electrodermal Activity in Psychological Research*. New York: Academic Press.

Barland, G.H., and Raskin, D.C. (1975a). An evaluation of field techniques in detection of deception. *Psychophysiology*, *12*, 321–330.

Barland, G.H., and Raskin, D.C. (1975b). Psychopathy and detection of deception in criminal suspects. *Psychophysiology*, *12*, 224 (abstract).

Barland, G.H., and Raskin, D.C. (1976). *Validity and Reliability of Polygraph Examinations of Criminal Suspects*. Report No. 76-1, Contract No. 7599-0001, Law Enforcement Assistance Administration, United States Department of Justice.

Beatty, J., and Legewie, H. (Eds.) (1976). *Biofeedback and Behavior*. New York: Plenum.

Ben-Shakhar, G. (1977). A further study of the dichotomization theory in detection of information. *Psychophysiology*, *14*, 408–413.

Ben-Shakhar, G. (1980). Habituation of the orienting response to complex sequences of stimuli. *Psychophysiology*, *17*, 524–534.

Ben-Shakhar, G. (1989). Future prospects of psychophysiological detection: Replacing the CQT by the GKT. In J.R. Jennings, P.K., Ackles, and M.G.H. Coles (Eds.), *Advances in Psychophysiology, vol. 4*. Greenwich, Conn.: JAI Press.

Ben-Shakhar, G., Asher, T., Poznansky-Levy, A., Asherowitz, R., and Leiblich, I. (1989). Stimulus novelty and significance as determinants of electrodermal responsivity: The serial position effect. *Psychophysiology*, *26*, 29–38.

Ben-Shakhar, G., Bar-Hillel, M., Bilu, Y., Ben-Abba, E., and Flug, A. (1986). Can

graphology predict occupational success? Two empirical studies and some methodological ruminations. *Journal of Applied Psychology, 71*, 645–653.
Ben-Shakhar, G., Bar-Hillel, M., and Lieblich, I. (1986). Trial by polygraph: Scientific and juridicial issues in lie detection. *Behavioral Sciences and the Law, 4*, 459–479.
Ben-Shakhar, G., and Beller, M. (1983). An application of decision-theoretical model to a quota-free selection problem. *Journal of Applied Psychology, 68*, 137–146.
Ben-Shakhar, G., and Gati, I. (1987). Common and distinctive features of verbal and pictorial stimuli as determinants of psychophysiological responsivity. *Journal of Experimental Psychology: General, 116*, 91–105.
Ben-Shakhar, G., and Lieblich, I. (1982). The dichotomization theory for differential autonomic responsivity reconsidered. *Psychophysiology, 19*, 277–281.
Ben-Shakhar, G., Lieblich, I., and Bar-Hillel, M. (1982). An evaluation of polygrapher's judgments: A review from a decision theoretic perspective. *Journal of Applied Psychology, 67*, 701–713.
Ben-Shakhar, G., Lieblich, I., and Kugelmas, S. (1970). Guilty knowledge technique: Application of signal detection measures. *Journal of Applied Psychology, 54*, 409–413.
Ben-Shakhar, G., Lieblich, I., and Kugelmass, S. (1975). Detection of information and GSR habituation: An attempt to derive detection efficiency from two habituation curves. *Psychophysiology, 12*, 283–288.
Ben-Shakhar, G., Lieblich, I., and Kugelmass, S. (1982). Interactive effects of stimulus probability and significance on the skin conductance response. *Psychophysiology, 19*, 112–114.
Benuossi, V. (1914). Die Atmungsymptome der Luge. *Archive fur die Gesampte Psychologie, 31*, 244–273.
Berlyne, D.E. (1960). *Conflict Arousal and Curiosity.* New York: McGraw-Hill.
Bersh, P.J. (1969). A validation study of polygraph examiner judgment. *Journal of Applied Psychology, 53*, 399–403.
Birbaumer, N., and Kimmel, H.D. (Eds.) (1979). *Biofeedback and Self-Control.* Hillsdale, N.J.: Erlbaum.
Bradley, M.T., and Ainsworth, D. (1984). Alcohol and psychophysiological detection of deception. *Psychophysiology, 21*, 63–71.
Bradley, M.T., and Janisse, M.P. (1979). Pupil size and lie detection: The effect of certainty on detection. *Psychology, 4*, 33–39.
Bradley, M.T., and Janisse, M.P. (1981a). Accuracy demonstrations, threat and the detection of deception: Cardiovascular, electrodermal and pupillary measures. *Psychophysiology, 18*, 307–315.
Bradley, M.T., and Janisse, M.P. (1981b). Extraversion and the detection of deception. *Personality and Individual Differences, 2*, 99–103.
Bradley, M.T., and Klohn, K.I. (1987). Machiavellianism, the control question test and the detection of deception. *Perceptual and Motor Skills, 64*, 747–757.
Bradley, M.T., and Warfield, J.F. (1984). Innocence, information, and the guilty knowledge test in the detection of deception. *Psychophysiology, 21*, 683–689.
Brogden, H.E. (1949). When testing pays off. *Personnel Psychology, 2*, 171–183.
Bundesgerichtshof (1954). *St. 5*, 333. (In German.)
Bundesverfassungsgericht (1981). *2*, 166 (In German.)
Carlson, J.G. (1987). Comments on the Furedy/Shellenberger-Green debate. *Biofeedback and Self-Regulation, 12*, 223–226.
Cavoukian, A., and Heslegrave, A.J. (1980). The admissibility of polygraph evidence in court. *Law and Human Behavior, 4*, 117–131.

Church, R.M. (1964). Systematic effects of random error in the yoked control design. *Psychological Bulletin*, 62, 122–131.
Cook, T.D., and Campbell, D.T. (1979). *Quasi-Experimentation: Design and Analysis Issues for Field Settings*. Boston: Houghton Mifflin.
Corteen, R.S. (1969). Skin conductance changes and word recall. *British Journal of Psychology*, 60, 81–84.
Craik, F.I.M., and Lockhart, R.S. (1972). Levels of processing: A framework for memory research. *Journal of Verbal Learning and Verbal Behavior*, 11, 671–684.
Crider, A., and Lunn, R. (1971). Electrodermal lability as a personality dimension. *Journal of Research in Personality*, 5, 145–150.
Critelli, W., and Neumann, K.F. (1984). Placebo: Conceptual analysis of a construct in transition. *American Psychologist*, 39, 32–39.
Cronbach, L.J., and Gleser, G.C. (1976). *Psychological Tests and Personnel Decisions* (2nd ed.). Urbana: University of Illinois Press.
Cullison, A.D. (1969). Probability analysis of judicial fact finding: A preliminary outline of the subjective approach. *Toledo Law Review*, 538–548.
Cutrow, R.J., Parks, A., Lucas, N., and Thomas, K. (1972). The objective use of multiple physiological indices in the detection of deception. *Psychophysiology*, 9, 578–588.
Davidson, P.O. (1968). Validity of the guilty knowledge technique: The effects of motivation. *Journal of Applied Psychology*, 52, 62–65.
Davis, R.C. (1961). Physiological responses as a means of evaluating information. In A.D. Biderman and H. Zimmer (Eds.), *The Manipulation of Human Behavior*. New York: Wiley, pp. 142–168.
Dawson, M.E. (1980). Physiological detection of deception: Measurement of responses to questions and answers during countermeasure maneuvers. *Psychophysiology*, 17, 8–17.
Desroches, F.J., and Thomas, A.S. (1967). The police use of the polygraph in criminal investigations. *Canadian Journal of Criminology*, 27, 43–66.
Edwards, W., and Tversky, A. (1967). *Decision Making*. Baltimore: Penguin Books.
Elaad, E. (1987). *Psychophysiological Detection in the Guilty Knowledge Test*. Unpublished Ph.D. thesis, The Hebrew University of Jerusalem, Israel.
Elaad, E., and Ben-Shakhar, G. (1989). Effects of motivation level and verbal response type on psychophysiological detection in the guilty knowledge test. *Psychophysiology*, in press.
Elaad, E., Bonwitt, G., Eisenberg, O., and Meytes, I. (1982). Effects of beta-blocking drugs on the polygraph detection rate: A pilot study. *Polygraph*, 11, 225–233.
Elaad, I. (1981). *The Effect of False Feedback on Polygraph Detection Rate*. Unpublished master's thesis, The Hebrew University of Jerusalem.
Ellson, D.C., Burke, C.G., Davis, R.C., and Saltzman, I.J. (1952). *A Report of Research on Detection of Deception*. Contract NG ONR-18011, Office of Naval Research.
Employee Polygraph Protection Act (1988). Report 100-659, U.S. Congress.
Epstein, S. (1979). The stability of behavior: I. On predicting most of the people much of the time. *Journal of Personality and Social Psychology*, 37, 1097–1126.
Epstein, S. (1986). Does aggregation produce spuriously high estimates of behavior stability? *Journal of Personality and Social Psychology*, 50, 1199–1210.
Farwell, L.A., and Donchin, E. (1986). The "Brain Detector": P300 in the detection of deception. *Psychophysiology*, 23, 434 (abstract).
Farwell, L.A., and Donchin, E. (1988). Event-related potentials in interrogative polygraphy: Analysis using bootstrapping. *Psychophysiology*, 25, 445 (abstract).

Forman, R.F., and McCauley, C. (1986). Validity of the positive control polygraph test using the field practice model. *Journal of Applied Psychology, 71*, 691-698.

Fukumoto, J. (1982). Psychophysiological detection of deception in Japan. *Polygraph, 11*, 234-238.

Furedy, J.J. (1979). Teaching self-regulation of cardiac function through imaginational Pavlovian and biofeedback conditioning: Remember the response. In N. Birnbaumer and H. Kimmel (Eds.), *Biofeedback and Self-Control.* Hillsdale, N.J.: Erlbaum.

Furedy, J.J. (1983). Operational, analogical, and genuine definitions of psychophysiology. International Journal of Psychophysiology, *1*, 13-19.

Furedy, J.J. (1984a) Booers, beware biofeedback boosting. *Contemporary Psychology, 29*, 524.

Furedy, J.J. (1984b). Specific vs. placebo effects in scientific vs. snake-oil medicine. *Contemporary Psychology, 29*, 599.

Furedy, J.J. (1985). Specific versus placebo effects in biofeedback: Science-based vs. snake-oil behavioral medicine. *Clinical Biofeedback and Health—An International Journal, 8*, 110-118.

Furedy, J.J. (1986). Lie detection as psychophysiological differentiation: Some fine lines. In M. Coles, E. Donchin, and S. Porges (Eds.), *Psychophysiology: Systems, Processes, and Applications—A Handbook.* New York: Guilford, pp. 683-700.

Furedy, J.J. (1987a). Evaluating polygraphy from a psychophysiological perspective: A specific-effects analysis. *Pavlovian Journal of Biological Science, 22*, 145-152.

Furedy, J.J. (1987b). Specific versus placebo effects in biofeedback training: A critical lay perspective. *Biofeedback and Self-Regulation, 12*, 169-184.

Furedy, J.J. (1987c). On some research-community contributions to the myth and symbol of biofeedback. *International Journal of Psychophysiology, 4*, 293-297.

Furedy, J.J. (1989). The North American CQT polygraph and the legal profession: A case of Canadian credulity and a cause for cultural concern. *Criminal Law Quarterly,* in press.

Furedy, J.J., Davis, C., and Gurevich, M. (1988). Differentiation of deception as a psychological process: A psychophysiological approach. *Psychophysiology, 25*, 683-688.

Furedy, J.J., and Heslegrave, R.J. (1983). A consideration of recent criticism of the T-wave amplitude index of myocardial sympathetic activity. *Psychophysiology, 20*, 204-211.

Furedy, J.J., and Heslegrave, R.J. (1989a). The forensic use of the polygraph: A psychophysiological analysis of current trends and future prospects. In J.R. Jennings, P.K. Ackles, and M.G.H. Coles (Eds.), *Advances in Psychophysiology, vol. 4.* Greenwich, Conn.: JAI Press.

Furedy, J.J., and Heslegrave, R.J. (1989b). A reply to commentators: Some elaborations on the specific-effects orientation's application to North American CQT polygraphs. In J.R. Jennings, P.K. Ackles, and M.G.H. Coles (Eds.), *Advances in Psychophysiology, vol. 4.* Greenwich, Conn.: JAI Press.

Furedy, J.J., and Liss, J. (1986). Countering confessions induced by the polygraph: Of confessionals and psychological rubber hoses. *The Criminal Law Quarterly, 29*, 92-114.

Furedy, J.J., and Riley, D.M. (1982). Classical and operant conditioning in the enhancement of biofeedback: Specifics and speculations. In L. White and B. Tursky (Eds.), *Clinical Biofeedback: Efficacy and Mechanisms.* New York: Guilford.

Furedy, J.J., and Shulhan, D. (1987). Specific versus placebo effects in biofeedback: Some brief back-to-basics considerations. *Biofeedback and Self-Regulation, 12*, 211–215.

Furedy, J.J., Shulhan, D., and Levy, B. (1989). The specific-effects logic of evaluation applied to biofeedback: Some examples analyzed. *Medical Psychotherapy, 2*, 111–121.

Futaba, I. (1984). Crime, confession and control in contemporary Japan. *Law in Context, 2*, 1–30.

Gale, A. (Ed.) (1987). *The Polygraph Test: Lies, Truth and Science.* London: Sage.

Giesen, M., and Rollison, M.A. (1980). Guilty knowledge versus innocent associations: Effects of trait anxiety and stimulus context on skin conductance. *Journal of Research in Personality, 14*, 1–11.

Ginton, A., Daie, N., Elaad, E., and Ben-Shakhar, G. (1982). A method for evaluating the use of the polygraph in a real life situation. *Journal of Applied Psychology, 67*, 131–137.

Green, J., and Shellenberger, R. (1986). Clinical biofeedback training and the ghost in the box: A reply to Furedy. *Clinical Biofeedback and Health, 9*, 96–105.

Gudjonsson, G.H. (1982a). Some psychological determinants of electrodermal responses to deception. *Personality and Individual Differences, 3*, 381–391.

Gudjonsson, G.H. (1982b). Extraversion and the detection of deception: Comments on the paper by Bradley and Janisse. *Personality and Individual Differences, 3*, 215–216.

Gustafson, L.A., and Orne, M.T. (1963). Effects of heightened motivation on the detection of deception. *Journal of Applied Psychology, 47*, 408–411.

Gustafson, L.A., and Orne, M.T. (1964). The effect of task and method of stimulus presentation on the detection of deceptioin. *Journal of Applied Psychology, 48*, 383–387.

Gustafson, L.A., and Orne, M.T. (1965a). The effects of perceived role and role success on the detection of deception. *Journal of Applied Psychology, 49*, 412–417.

Gustafson, L.A., and Orne, M.T. (1965b). The effects of verbal responses on the laboratory detection of deception. *Psychophysiology, 7*, 10–13.

Harnon, E. (1982). Evidence obtained by polygraph—An Israeli perspective. *The Criminal Law Review*, 329–348.

Hemsley, G.D., Heslegrave, R.J., and Furedy, J.J. (1980). Can deception be detected when stimulus familiarity is controlled? *Psychophysiology, 17*, 286–287 (abstract).

Heslegrave, R.J. (1982). An examination of the psychophysiological mechanisms underlying deception. *Psychophysiology, 19*, 298 (abstract).

Honts, C.R., and Hodes, R.L. (1982a). The effects of multiple physical countermeasures on the detection of deception. *Psychophysiology, 19*, 564–565 (abstract).

Honts, C.R., and Hodes, R.L. (1982b). The effect of simple physical countermeasures on the detection of deception. *Psychophysiology, 19*, 564 (abstract).

Honts, C.R., Hodes, R.L., and Raskin, D.C. (1985). Effects of physical counter-measures on the physiological detection of deception. *Journal of Applied Psychology, 70*, 177–187.

Honts, C.R., Raskin, D.C., and Kircher, J.C. (1983). Detection of deception: Effectiveness of physical countermeasures under high motivation conditions. *Psychophysiology, 20*, 446–447 (abstract).

Honts, C.R., Raskin, D.C., and Kircher, J.C. (1986). Individual differences and the physiological detection of deception. *Psychophysiology, 23*, 442 (abstract).

Horneman, C.J., and O'Gorman, J.G. (1985). Detectability in the card test as a function of the subject's verbal responses. *Psychophysiology, 22*, 330–333.

Horneman, C.J., and O'Gorman, J.B. (1987). Individual differences in psychophysiological responsiveness in laboratory tests of deception. *Personality and Individual Differences, 8*, 321–330.

Horvath, F.S. (1977). The effects of selected variables on interpretation of polygraph records. *Journal of Applied Psychology, 62*, 127–136.

Horvath, F.S. (1978). An experimental comparison of the psychological stress evaluator and the galvanic response in detection of deception. *Journal of Applied Psychology, 63*, 338–344.

Horvath, F.S. (1979). Effect of differential motivational instructions on detection of deception with the psychological stress evaluator and the galvanic skin response. *Journal of Applied Psychology, 64*, 323–330.

Horvath, F.S., and Reid, J.E. (1971). The reliability of polygraph examiner diagnoses of truth and deception. *Journal of Criminal Law, Criminology and Police Science, 62*, 276–281.

Hunter, F.L., and Ash, P. (1973). The accuracy and consistency of polygraph examiners' diagnoses. *Journal of Police Science and Administration, 1*, 370–375.

Iacono, W.G. (1989). Can we determine the accuracy of polygraph tests? In J.R. Jennings, P.K. Ackles, and M.G.H. Coles (eds.), *Advances in Psychophysiology, vol. 4*. Greenwich, Conn.: JAI Press.

Iacono, W.G., Boisvenu, G.A., and Fleming, J.A. (1984). Effects of diazepam and methylphenidate on the electrodermal detection of guilty knowledge. *Journal of Applied Psychology, 69*, 289–299.

Inbau, F., and Reid, J.E. (1953). *Lie Detection and Criminal Investigation*. Baltimore: Williams & Wilkins.

Janisse, M.P., and Bradley, M.T. (1980). Deception, information and the pupillary response. *Perceptual and Motor Skills, 50*, 748–750.

Kaplan, J. (1968). Decision theory and the fact-finding process. *Stanford Law Review, 20*, 1065–1092.

Kircher, J.C., Horowitz, S.W., and Raskin, D.C. (1988). Meta-analysis of mock crime studies of the control question polygraph technique. *Law and Human Behavior, 12*, 79–90.

Kircher, J.C., and Raskin, D.C. (1981). Computerized decision making in the detection of deception. *Psychophysiology, 18*, 204–205 (abstract).

Kircher, J.C., and Raskin, D.C. (1982). Is there a specific lie response of autonomic responses? *Psychophysiology, 19*, 569 (abstract).

Kircher, J.C., and Raskin, D.C. (1983). Clinical versus statistical lie detection revisited: Through a lens sharply. *Psychophysiology, 20*, 452 (abstract).

Kircher, J.C., and Raskin, D.C. (1988). Human versus computerized evaluations of polygraph data in laboratory setting. *Journal of Applied Psychology, 73*, 291–302.

Kleinmuntz, B., and Szucko, J.J. (1982). On the fallibility of lie detection. *Law and Society Review, 17*, 85–105.

Kleinmuntz, B., and Szucko, J.J. (1984a). Lie detection in ancient and modern times: A call for contemporary scientific study. *American Psychologist, 39*, 766–776.

Kleinmuntz, B., and Szucko, J.J. (1984b). A field study of the fallibility of polygraph lie detector. *Nature, 308*, 449–450.

Kubis, J.F. (1962). *Studies in Lie Detection: Computer Feasibility Considerations*. Technical Report G2-205 prepared for Air Force Systems Command. Contract No. AF 30 (602)-2270, Project No. 5534, Fordham University.

Kugelmass, S., and Lieblich, I. (1966). The effects of realistic stress and procedural interference in experimental lie detection. *Journal of Applied Psychology, 50*, 211–216.

Kugelmass, S., and Lieblich, I. (1968a). *An analysis of Mechanisms Underlying Psychophysiological Detection*. Proceedings of the 15th International Congress of Applied Psychology, Amsterdam, pp. 509–512.

Kugelmass, S., and Lieblich, I. (1968b). Relation between ethnic origin and GSR reactivity in psychophysiological detection. *Journal of Applied Psychology, 52*, 158–162.

Kugelmass, S., Lieblich, I., Ben-Ishai, A., Opatowski, A., and Kaplan, M. (1968). Experimental evaluation of galvanic skin response and blood pressure change indices during criminal interrogation. *The Journal of Criminal Law, Criminology and Police Science, 59*, 632–635.

Kugelmass, S., Lieblich, I., and Ben-Shakhar, G. (1973). Information detection through differential GSRs in Bedouins of the Israeli desert. *Journal of Cross-Cultural Psychology, 4*, 481–492.

Kugelmass, S., Lieblich, I., and Bergman, Z. (1967). The role of "lying" in psychophysiological detection. *Psychophysiology, 3*, 312–315.

Lacey, J.I., and Lacey, B. (1958). Verification and extension of the principle of response stereotypes. *American Journal of Psychology, 71*, 50–73.

Landis, C., and Gullette, R. (1925). Studies of emotional reactions: III. Systolic blood pressure and inspiration-expiration ratios. *Journal of Comparative Psychology, 5*, 221–253.

Larson, J.A. (1932). *Lying and Its Detection: A Study of Deception and Deception Tests*. Chicago, Ill.: University of Chicago Press.

Law Reform Commission of Australia (1983). Lie Detection, Report No. 22, vol. 1 ("Privacy"). Australian Government Publishing Service, Canberra.

Lazarus, R.S., and McCleary, R.A. (1951). Autonomic discrimination without awareness: A study of subseption. *Psychological Review, 58*, 113–122.

Lehrer, P.M. (1982). How to relax and how not to relax: A re-evaluation of the work of Edmund Jacobson. *Behavior Research & Therapy, 20*, 417–428.

Lehrer, P.M. (1983). Biofeedback boosters, beware. *Contemporary Psychology, 28*, 824–826.

Lehrer, P.M. (1984a). Yes, a cautious (and limited) boost for biofeedback. *Contemporary Psychology, 29*, 524.

Lehrer, P.M. (1984b). Biofeedback: Not penicillin but not snake oil. *Contemporary Psychology, 29*, 599.

Levy, H.J. (1984). The polygraph is not yet dead. *Newsletter of Ontario Criminal Lawyers, 5*, 1.

Lieblich, I. (1969). Manipulation of contrast between differential GSR responses through the use of ordered tasks of information detection. *Psychophysiology, 6*, 70–77.

Lieblich, I. (1971). Manipulation of contrast between differential GSRs in very young children. *Psychophysiology, 7*, 436–441.

Lieblich, I., Ben-Shakhar, G., and Kugelmass, S. (1976). Validity of the guilty knowledge technique in a prisoners' sample. *Journal of Applied Psychology, 61*, 89–93.

Lieblich, I., Ben-Shakhar, G., Kugelmass, S., and Cohen, Y. (1978). Decision theory approach to the problem of polygraph interrogation. *Journal of Applied Psychology, 63*, 489–498.

Lieblich, I., Kugelmass, S., and Ben-Shakhar, G. (1970). Efficiency of GSR detection of information as a function of stimulus set size. *Psychophysiology, 6*, 601–608.

Lieblich, I., Naftali, G., Shmueli, J., and Kugelmass, S. (1974). Efficiency of GSR detection of information with repeated presentation of series of stimuli in two motivational states. *Journal of Applied Psychology, 59*, 113–115.

Lombroso, C. (1895). *L'Homme Criminel* (2nd ed.). Paris: Felix Alcan.
Lord, F.M., and Novick, M.R. (1968). *Statistical Theories of Mental Test Scores*. Reading, Mass.: Addison-Wesley.
Luria, A.R. (1932). *The Nature of Human Conflicts*. New York: Liveright.
Lykken, D.T. (1959). The GSR in the detection of guilt. *Journal of Applied Psychology*, 43, 385–388.
Lykken, D.T. (1960). The validity of the guilty knowledge technique: The effects of faking. *Journal of Applied Psychology*, 44, 258–262.
Lykken, D.T. (1974). Psychology and the lie detection industry. *American Psychologist*, 29, 725–739.
Lykken, D.T. (1978a). The psychopath and the lie detector. *Psychophysiology*, 15, 137–142.
Lykken, D.T. (1978b). Uses and abuses of the polygraph. In H.L. Pick (Ed.), *Psychology: From Research to Practice*. New York: Plenum Press.
Lykken, D.T. (1979). The detection of deception. *Psychological Bulletin*, 86, 47–53.
Lykken, D.T. (1981). *A Tremor in the Blood: Uses and Abuses of the Lie Detector*. New York: McGraw-Hill.
Lykken, D.T. (1989). The lie detector controversy: An alternative solution. In J.R. Jennings, P.K. Ackles, and M.G.H. Coles (Eds.), *Advances in Psychophysiology*, vol. 4. Greenwich, Conn.: JAI Press.
Marston, W.M. (1917). Systolic blood pressure changes in deception. *Journal of Experimental Psychology*, 2, 143–163.
Marston, W.M. (1938). *The Lie Detector Test*. New York: Smith.
Maze, J.R. (1983). *The Meaning of Behaviour*. London: Allen & Unwin.
Meehl, P.E., and Rosen, H. (1955). Antecedent probability and the efficiency of psychometric signs, patterns, or cutting scores. *Psychological Bulletin*, 52, 194–216.
Miller, N.E. (1969). Learning of visceral and glandular responses. *Science*, 163, 434–445.
Miller, N.E., and Dworkin, B.R. (1974). Visceral learning: Recent difficulties with curarized rats and significant problems for human research. In P.A. Obrist, A.G. Black, J. Brener, and L.V. DiCara (Eds.), *Cardiovascular Psychophysiology*. Hawthorne, New York: Aldine.
Mischel, W. (1968). *Personality and Assessment*. New York: Wiley.
Mischel, W., and Peake, P.K. (1982). Beyond deja vu in the search for cross-situational consistency. *Psychological Review*, 89, 730–755.
Mulholland, T.B. (1982). Comments on the chapter by Furedy and Riley. In L. White and B. Tursky (Eds.), *Clinical Biofeedback: Efficacy and Mechanisms*. New York: Guilford.
Munsterberg, H. (1908). *On the Witness Stand*. New York: Doubleday.
Nachshon, I., Elaad, E., and Amsel, T. (1985). Validity of the psychological stress evaluator: A field study. *Journal of Police Science and Administration*, 13, 275–282.
Nachshon, I., and Feldman, B. (1980). Vocal indices of psychological stress: A validation study of the psychological stress evaluator. *Journal of Police Science and Administration*, 8, 40–53.
Neter, E., and Ben-Shakhar, G. (1989). The predictive validity of graphological inferences in personnel selection: A meta-analytic approach. *Personality and Individual Differences*, 10, 737–745.
Patrick, C.J., and Iacono, W.G. (1989). Psychopathy, threat, and polygraph test accuracy. *Journal of Applied Psychology*, 74, 347–355.
Pavlov, I.P. (1927). *Condition Reflex*. Oxford, England: Charandon Press.

Ploss, W.E. (1978). Truth by ordeal: The growing acceptance of polygraphy. *Florida State University Law Review, 6*, 1373-1392.

Podlesny, J.A., and Raskin, D.C. (1977). Physiological measures and the detection of deception. *Psychological Bulletin, 84*, 782-799.

Podlesny, J.A., and Raskin, D.C. (1978). Effectiveness of techniques and physiological measures in the detection of deception. *Psychophysiology, 15*, 344-359.

Raskin, D.C. (1978). Scientific assessment of the accuracy of detection of deception. *Psychophysiology, 15*, 143-147.

Raskin, D.C. (1979). Orienting and defensive reflexes in the detection of deception. In H.D. Kimmel, E.H. Van Olst, and J.F. Orlebeke (Eds.), *The Orienting Reflex in Humans*. Hillsdale, N.J.: Erlbaum, pp. 587-605.

Raskin, D.C. (1982). The scientific basis of polygraph techniques and their uses in the judicial process. In A. Trankell (Ed.), *Reconstructing the Past: The Role of Psychologists in the Criminal Trial*. Stockholm, Sweden: Norsted & Soners.

Raskin, D.C. (1986). The polygraph in 1986: Scientific, professional and legal issues surrounding application and acceptance of polygraph evidence. *Utah Law Review, 29*, 29-74.

Raskin, D.C. (1987). Quoted in *Salt Lake Tribune*, August 23, sec. B, pp. 1-2.

Raskin, D.C., Barland, G.H., and Podlesny, J.A. (1977). Validity and reliability of detection of deception. *Polygraph, 6*, 1-39.

Raskin, D.C., and Hare, R. (1978). Psychopathy and detection of deception in a prison population. *Psychophysiology, 15*, 126-136.

Raskin, D.C., and Kircher, J.C. (1989). Comments on Furedy and Heslegrave: Misconceptions, misdescriptions, and misdirections. In J.R. Jennings, P.K., Ackles, and M.G.H. Coles (Eds.), *Advances in Psychophysiology*, vol. 4. Greenwich, Conn.: JAI Press.

Raskin, D.C., and Podlesny, J.A. (1979). Truth and deception: A reply to Lykken. *Psychological Bulletin, 86*, 54-58.

Reid, J.E. (1947). A revised questioning technique in lie-detection tests. *Journal of Criminal Law and Criminology, 37*, 542-547.

Reid, J.E., and Inbau, F.E. (1977). *Truth and Deception: The Polygraph ("Lie Detection") Technique*. Baltimore: Williams & Wilkins.

Rorer, L.G., Hoffman, P.J., and Hsieh, K.C. (1966). Utilities as base-rate multipliers in the determination of optimum cutting scores for the discrimination of groups of unequal size and variance. *Journal of Applied Psychology, 50*, 364-368.

Rosenfeld, J.P. (1987). Can clinical biofeedback be scientifically validated? A follow-up on the Green-Shellenberger-Furedy-Roberts debates. *Clinical Biofeedback and Self-Regulation, 12*, 217-222.

Rosenthal, R.R., and Jacobson, L. (1968). *Pygmalion in the Classroom*. New York: Holt, Rinehart and Winston.

Rosenthal, R.R., and Rubin, D.B. (1978). Interpersonal expectancy effects: The first 345 studies. *The Behavioral and Brain Sciences, 3*, 377-415.

Rovner, L.I., Raskin, D.C., and Kircher, J.C. (1979). Effects of information and practice on detection of deception. *Psychophysiology, 16*, 197-198 (abstract).

Royal Commission on the Donald Marshall Jr. Prosecution (1989). Chief Justice T. Alexander Hickman, Chairman, Halifax, Nova Scotia.

Rushton, P.J., and Erdle, S. (1987). Evidence for an aggressive (and delinquent) personality. *British Journal of Social Psychology, 26*, 87-89.

Sackett, P.R., and Decker, P.J. (1979). Detection of deception in the employment context: A review and critical analysis. *Personnel Psychology, 32*, 487-506.

# References

Saxe, L., and Cross, T.P. (1989). Scientific evaluation of psychological technologies: Commentary on "The forensic use of the polygraph." In J.R. Jennings, P.K. Ackles, and M.G.H. Coles (Eds.), *Advances in Psychophysiology*, vol. 4. Greenwich, Conn.: JAI Press.

Saxe, L., Dougherty, D., and Cross, T.P. (1985). The validity of polygraph testing: Scientific analysis and public controversy. *American Psychologist, 40*, 355-366.

Schachter, S., and Singer, J.E. (1962). Cognitive, social and psychological determinants of emotional state. *Psychological Review, 69*, 379-399.

Schmidt, F.L., Hunter, J.E., McKenzie, R.C., and Muldrow, T.W. (1979). Impact of valid selection procedures on work-force productivity. *Journal of Applied Psychology, 64*, 609-626.

Schwartz, P.J., and Weiss, T. (1983). T-wave amplitude as an index of cardiac sympathetic activity: A misleading concept. *Psychophysiology, 20*, 696-701.

Shellenberger, R., and Green, J. (1987). Specific effects and biofeedback versus biofeedback-assisted self-regulation training. *Biofeedback and Self-Regulation, 12*, 185-209.

Simon, R.J., and Mahan, L. (1971). Quantifying burdens of proof: A view from the bench, the jury, and the classroom. *Law and Society Review, 5*, 319-330.

Slowick, S.M., and Buckley, J.P. (1975). Relative accuracy of polygraph examiner diagnosis of respiration, blood pressure and GSR recordings. *Journal of Police Science and Administration, 3*, 305-309.

Sokolov, E.N. (1963). *Perception and the Conditioned Reflex*. New York: Macmillan.

Sokolov, E.N. (1966). Orienting reflex as information regulator. In A. Leontyev, A. Luria, and A. Smirnov (Eds.), *Psychological research in U.S.S.R.* Moscow: Progress Publishers, pp. 334-360.

Steller, M., Haenert, P., and Eiselt, W. (1987). Extraversion and the detection of information. *Journal of Research in Personality, 21*, 334-342.

Stephens, H.H. (1981). The admissibility of polygraph results in criminal actions in Alabama state and federal courts: Must we await Buck Rogers in the twenty-fifth century courtroom? *Law and Psychology Review, 6*, 69-95.

Stern, R.M., Breen, J.P., Watanabe, T., and Perry, B.S. (1981). Effects of feedback of physiological information on responses to innocent associations and guilty knowledge. *Journal of Applied Psychology, 66*, 677-681.

Szucko, J.J., and Kleinmuntz, B. (1981). Statistical versus clinical lie detection. *American Psychologist, 36*, 488-496.

Thackray, R.I., and Orne, M.T. (1968a). Effects of the type of stimulus employed and the level of subject awareness on the detection of deception. *Journal of Applied Psychology, 52*, 234-239.

Thackray, R.I., and Orne, M.T. (1968b). A comparison of physiological indices in detection of deception. *Psychophysiology, 4*, 329-339.

Timm, H.W. (1982). Effects of altered outcome expectancies stemming from placebo and feedback treatments on the validity of the guilty knowledge technique. *Journal of Applied Psychology, 67*, 391-400.

Timm, H.W. (1987). Effect of biofeedback on the detection of deception. *Journal of Forensic Sciences, 32*, 736-746.

Trovillo, P.V. (1939). A history of lie detection. *Journal of Criminal Law, Criminology, and Police Science, 29*, 848-881.

U.S. Congress, Office of Technology Assessment (1983). *Scientific Validity of Polygraph Testing: A Research Review and Evaluation*. OTA-TM-H-15, Washington, D.C.

Waid, W.M., Orne, E.C., Cook, M.R., and Orne, M.T. (1978). Effects of attention, as indexed by subsequent memory, on electrodermal detection of information. *Journal of Applied Psychology, 63*, 728–733.

Waid, W.M., Orne, E.C., Cook, M.R., and Orne, M.T. (1981). Meprobamate reduces accuracy of physiological detection of deception. *Science, 212*, 71–73.

Waid, W.M., Orne, E.C., and Orne, M.T. (1981). Selective memory for social information, alertness and physiological arousal in the detection of deception. *Journal of Applied Psychology, 66*, 224–232.

Waid, W.M., and Orne, M.T. (1980). Individual differences in electrodermal lability and the detection of information and deception. *Journal of Applied Psychology, 65*, 1–8.

Waid, W.M., and Orne, M.T. (1981). Cognitive, social, and personality processes in the physiological detection of deception. In L. Berkowitz (Ed.), *Advances in Experimental Social Psychology.* New York: Academic Press, pp. 61–106.

Waid, W.M., Orne, M.T., and Wilson, S.K. (1979a). Effects of level of socialization on electrodermal detection of deception. *Psychophysiology, 16*, 15–22.

Waid, W.M., Orne, M.T., and Wilson, S.K. (1979b). Socialization, awareness, and the electrodermal response to deception and self-disclosure. *Journal of Abnormal Psychology, 88*, 663–666.

Waid, W.M., Wilson, S.K., and Orne, M.T. (1981). Cross-modal physiological effects of electrodermal lability in the detection of deception. *Journal of Personality and Social Psychology, 40*, 1118–1125.

White, K.D. (1985, January 31). Letters of enquiry to Australian institutions regarding the Lie Detectors Act, 1983. Personal communications to JJF (including replies).

Wicklander, D.E., and Hunter, F.L. (1975). The influence of auxiliary sources of information in polygraph diagnoses. *Journal of Police Science and Administration, 3*, 405–409.

# Index

Accuracy rates (figures), 3, 7, 10, 14, 15, 16, 18, 21, 22, 23, 24, 30, 33, 38, 40, 43, 44, 47, 50, 53, 56, 57, 58, 62, 64, 67, 69, 70, 81, 83, 98, 116, 128, 131, 132, 133, 137–141, 143
Admissible evidence, 29, 116, 118, 124, 125, 131, 133, 134, 136
  laundering inadmissible evidence, 133
  polygraph admissibility, 134
  stipulated admission, 116, 124
Adversary system, 35
Ainsworth, D., 47, 52, 53, 55, 75
Akamatsu, P., 121
Alexander the Great, 2
American Association of Biofeedback Clinicians (AABC), 93
American Biofeedback (research) Society, 93
American Polygraph Association (APA), 1, 3, 4, 5, 6, 120, 123, 144
American Psychological Association, 144, 145
Amsel, T., 89
Anastasi, A., 10, 28
Anderson, J., 92
Arousal, 12, 13, 14, 25, 81, 84, 107
Ash, P., 39, 49
Asher, T., 68, 112
Asherowitz, R., 68, 112
Astrology, 144
Australia, 121, 122, 123
  Australian states and the Northern Territory, 122
  Australian trade unions, 122

Marquis of Queensberry Rules, 122
Autonomic Nervous System, 2
  autonomic activation, 21
  autonomic control, 93
  autonomic differentiation, 82
  autonomic functions (measures), 21, 76, 140, 141
  baseline levels of autonomic reactivity, 60
  basic skin conductance level, 77, 79, 80

Backster, C., 4, 19, 29, 33, 41, 42, 43, 85, 129
Balloun, K.D., 6, 52, 53, 69, 70, 83, 84, 88
Bar-Hillel, M., 29, 41, 48, 67, 127–131, 133
Barland, 10, 29, 34, 38, 39, 41, 45, 48, 49, 83, 89, 132
Beatty, J., 117
Beller, M., 127
Ben-Ishai, A., 87
Ben-Shakhar, G., 6, 26, 29, 40, 41, 48, 62, 67–70, 79, 99, 104, 107, 108, 110–113, 117, 123, 127–131, 133
Benuossi, V., 3
Bergman, Z., 62, 102
Berlyne, D.E., 107
Bersh, P.J., 39, 49
Biofeedback, 93–99, 117
  accurate feedback condition, 95, 97
  best alternative treatment (BAT) control, 95, 96

Biofeedback (*cont.*)
  biofeedforward, 94, 95
  clinical biofeedback, 97
  degraded contingency control procedure, 97
  false-feedback condition, 97
  feedback (information), 94, 95, 97, 98
  inaccurate feedback control, 95, 97
  package evaluation of, 95, 96
Birbaumer, N., 117
Boisvenu, G.A., 65, 69
Bonwitt, G., 75
Boucsein, 116
Bradley, M.T., 25, 47, 51, 52, 53, 55, 60, 63–66, 75, 81, 82, 86, 88, 102, 103, 104, 107, 108, 109, 134
Breen, J.P., 25, 54
Brogden, H.E., 125
Buckley, J.P., 39, 49
Burke, C.G., 85


Campbell, D.T., 36
Canada, 14, 115, 116, 118, 143
Card (stimulation-"stim") test, 8, 21, 22, 38, 42, 51, 52, 59–65, 67, 77, 81, 82, 85, 87, 88, 89, 102–107, 120
Carlson, J.G., 94
Cause-effect logic (mechanisms), 92
Cavoukian, A., 130
CBS *60 minutes* (demonstration of bias in polygraphy), 132, 133
Ceiling effect, 65, 106
Cohen, Y., 127, 128
Conflict, 103
Confounding factors, 106
Contamination (contaminated procedures, contaminated criteria), 28, 29, 30, 35, 48, 50, 99, 100, 121, 131–134, 136, 138
Contingency, 94, 95, 97, 98
Control Question Test (CQT), 1–14, 16–19, 22, 23, 24, 26–32, 35, 37, 41–45, 47, 49, 50, 51, 54–58, 60, 62, 63, 64, 67, 72–77, 81–86, 89, 90, 91, 99–102, 109, 110, 116, 118–124, 126, 127, 129–134, 136, 138–144
Cook, M.R., 51, 54, 74

Cook, T.D., 36
Correct detections (classifications, decisions), 45, 46, 49, 52, 53, 55, 56, 63, 87, 89
Correlation coefficients, 33, 54, 76, 77, 78, 80–85, 91, 109, 110
Corteen, R.S., 109
Court of law, 118, 133, 135
  Court decisions, 35, 131
  courtroom interrogations, 133
  Criminal court, 73, 116, 124, 125, 131, 134, 135, 136, 143
Craig, F.I.M., 109, 110
Crider, A., 76
Criminal acts (crimes), 2–8, 14, 15, 16, 19, 20, 22, 24, 37, 39, 54, 55, 56, 65, 66, 108, 109, 110, 116, 123, 126, 134, 135, 138, 139, 140, 144
  alcohol abuse (intoxication), 17, 53, 102
  artificial crimes, 83
  blackmail scheme, 66
  drug abuse, 15, 16, 17
  fictitious crimes, 24
  hypothetical crime, 66, 119, 138
  mock crimes (simulated studies), 25, 36, 37, 38, 39, 41, 43, 44, 45, 47, 48, 50, 51, 53, 54, 57, 64, 72, 73, 75–78, 81–85, 89, 90, 91, 102, 108
  murder, 54
  theft, 15, 16, 17, 22, 36, 54
Criminals, 74, 122
Criminal suspects (interrogation of), 3, 7, 56, 83, 87, 123, 131, 135
  Guilty suspects (examinees, subjects), 9, 10, 12, 18, 19, 20, 22–27, 29, 33–37, 39, 40, 41, 44, 47, 49, 50, 51, 55, 56, 57, 59, 61, 65, 70, 72–77, 81, 82, 88, 90, 91, 102, 106, 107, 109, 110, 119, 126, 128, 129, 130, 134, 135, 143
  Innocent (truthful) suspects (applicants, examinees, subjects), 4, 6, 8, 9, 10, 12, 13, 14, 16, 17, 18, 20–27, 29, 31, 33, 35–41, 43, 44, 47, 49, 50, 54–57, 59, 61, 65, 68, 73, 74, 76, 77, 81–84, 88, 90, 91, 102, 106, 107, 108, 119, 126, 129, 130, 134, 135, 136, 140, 143

Criminal trials, 129, 130, 131
Critelli, W., 92
Cronbach, L.J., 125, 126, 127, 129
Cross, T.P., 41, 67, 99
Cross-situational consistency (of human behavior), 16
Cross-validation, 43, 91
Cullison, A.D., 130
Cutrow, R.J., 66, 78, 86, 87, 91

Daie, N., 40
Davidson, P.O., 6, 26, 52, 53, 54, 61, 105, 106, 107
Davis, C., 78, 99
Davis, R.C., 85, 101
Dawson, M.E., 38, 43, 45, 47, 72, 90
Deception (deceptive, lie, lying), 1, 2, 4, 5, 7-10, 12, 13, 14, 16, 18, 19, 20, 21, 23, 24, 32, 36, 37, 38, 40, 44, 55, 61, 81, 89, 91, 92, 95, 98, 99, 102, 104, 107, 117, 121, 129, 132, 136, 138, 139, 141, 142
 differentiation vs. detection of deception, 1-2
 differentiation-of-deception paradigm (DDP), 141, 142
Decision-theoretical approach to polygraphy, 125, 127-130, 135
 cost ratio (r) parameter, 127-131, 136
 decision maker, 127
 gains and costs associated with the outcomes of polygraph-based decisions, 125, 127, 129, 135
 payoff matrix (of polygraph-based decisions), 126, 127
  correct identifications (CI), 126
  correct rejections (CR), 126
  false positives (FP), 126-131
  misses (M), 126-131
 prior probabilities of guilt (or deception), 125, 128, 135
 utility (expected utility), 125, 126, 129, 130, 131
Decker, P.J., 16, 130, 133
Demand characteristics, 105
Desroches, F.J., 14
Detection (detection efficiency, detection rates), 3, 8, 9, 12, 23, 32, 42, 44, 47, 48, 51, 53, 54, 55, 58, 60-63, 65-72, 74, 75, 76, 78, 79, 80, 84-89, 92, 98, 99, 100, 102-106, 108, 109, 110, 112, 113, 114, 119, 121, 132, 137, 138, 140, 143, 145
 detection scores (measures), 25, 64, 69, 77, 81, 82, 83, 85, 88, 109
  perfect guilty score, 51
  perfect innocence score, 51
 factors affecting detection efficiency, 58
  situational (procedural) factors, 58, 59, 70
   awareness (of being examined by the polygraph), 103, 107, 108
   feedback (accuracy demonstrations), 42, 54, 62-65, 72, 75, 78, 88, 105, 142
    continuous (auditory and visual) feedback, 64, 65
    negative feedback, 42, 63, 64, 105
    positive feedback, 42, 63, 64, 105
   motivation (level of, type of), 50, 54, 60, 61, 62, 63, 65, 69, 73, 75, 102, 104, 105, 106, 110, 113, 114
    motivation to be detected, 61, 63, 105, 106
    motivation to deceive (to avoid detection), 54, 60, 61, 63, 71, 104-108, 110, 113, 142
   number of questions (items), 59, 68, 139
   relative frequency of the relevant items (stimulus set size), 59, 67, 68, 111, 113
   repetition effects, 68, 69, 70, 139
   serial position of the relevant item, 68, 112, 113
   stress (level of) involved, 59, 60, 87, 102
   type and content of the relevant information, 65, 66
    neutral items (made relevant in the experimental context), 66, 67, 106
    personal items, 65, 66, 67, 86
    verbal responses, 50, 61, 62, 65, 103, 106, 108, 110, 113, 114

Detection (*cont.*)
  factors affecting detection efficiency (*cont.*)
    subject-related factors (see also individual differences), 59, 75, 76
      alcohol intoxication, 75
      countermeasures, 13, 43, 46, 70–75, 100
        excitatory psychological manipulations, 13, 70
        inhibitory psychological manipulations, 13, 70
        mental countermeasures, 70–73, 110
        physical countermeasures, 70–74
      cultural background, 59
      drugs, 69, 74, 75, 100
        diazepam, 74, 75
        meprobamate, 74
        methylphenidate, 74
        trasicor-80, 75
      educational level (schooling), 59, 80
      socioeconomic status, 80
  hit rates, 61
Detection of deception (lie detection), 1, 2, 5, 6, 7, 9, 10, 18, 21, 58, 64, 85, 86, 88, 98, 104, 116, 132, 134, 135, 137, 138, 139, 141, 142
Detection of guilt (guilt detection), 2, 6, 53, 98, 99, 117, 120, 138, 142
Detection of information, 111
Discriminant function, 43, 87, 90, 91
Donchin, E., 86, 89, 140
Doualistic (teleological) approach, 92
Double-blind procedures, 39, 92, 95
Dougherty, D., 41, 67
Drug-effects (drug testing), 92, 95, 97
Duggan, D., 123
Dworkin, B.R., 93

Eiselt, W., 54, 82
Eisenberg, O., 75
Elaad, E., 23, 40, 61, 62, 70, 73, 75, 88, 89, 91, 104, 106, 107, 108, 110, 113, 123
Elaad, I., 63, 64, 65
Electroencephalogram (EEG), 93, 140
  alpha component of, 93

Ellson, D.C., 85
Emotions, 21, 22, 27, 59, 75, 102, 108
  anger, 21, 22
  anxiety, 37, 55, 59, 143
  emotional control, 60, 82, 102, 104
  emotional impact, 138
  emotional reaction, 83, 103
  emotional states, 72
  fear, 21, 22, 55
  stress, 55, 59, 84, 143
Employee Polygraph Protection Act (1988), 116
Epstein, S., 16
Erdle, S., 16
Eristratus, 2
Errors, 12, 15, 50, 72, 73
  error rates, 7, 37, 48
  false-negative errors, 25, 27, 37, 40, 42–50, 52, 55, 56, 72, 73, 74, 129, 135, 139, 140
  false-positive errors, 6, 21, 22, 25, 26, 27, 37, 40, 42–52, 55, 56, 57, 73, 84, 108, 124, 129, 130, 131, 134, 139
Europe (continental western Europe), 116, 117, 118
Evans, W., 122
Experimenter expectancy (interpersonal expectancy) effect, 30, 132
Expert testimony, 133, 138
Expert witnesses, 29

Factor analysis, 77
Farwell, L.A., 86, 89, 140
Feldman, B., 89
Field studies, 39, 41, 47–50, 57, 91
Fleming, J.A., 65, 69
Forman, R.F., 65
Free associations, 62, 103
Fukumoto, J., 119, 120, 121
Furedy, J.J., 2, 7, 11, 40, 78, 92–97, 99, 115, 121, 141, 142
Futaba, I., 121

Gale, A., 115
Gati, I., 26, 113
Giesen, M., 25, 52, 54, 66, 81, 108, 134
Ginton, A., 40, 44, 47, 53

Gleser, G.C., 125, 126, 127, 129
Greek (ancient Greek), 144
Green, J., 94, 96, 97
Gudjonsson, G.H., 78, 81, 82, 84
Guilt, 3, 4, 7, 9, 10, 12, 32, 36, 54, 84, 98, 115, 132, 140, 141
Guilt complex question (procedure), 24, 25, 119, 138
Guilt feelings, 12
Guilty, 6, 21, 22, 26, 27, 99, 103, 130
Guilty condition, or treatment (in experiments), 38, 41–46, 48, 51, 52, 54, 55, 64, 72, 75, 76, 77, 81, 82, 84, 85, 89
Guilty information (GI) technique (design), 18, 54
Guilty knowledge (information), 6, 19, 37, 51, 54, 55, 107, 109, 110, 111, 134, 135
Guilty Knowledge Test (GKT) (concealed information test), 1, 5, 6, 10, 11, 16, 18, 19, 24–28, 30, 31, 32, 41, 42, 50–61, 63–78, 81–86, 88–91, 99, 101, 102, 103, 105, 106, 107, 109–112, 119, 120, 121, 123, 126, 127, 134, 135, 136, 138–142
Guilty person (GP) technique (design), 18, 50, 54
Gullette, R., 3
Gurevich, M., 78, 99
Gustafson, L.A., 18, 26, 60–63, 65, 101–106, 108, 110

Habituation effects (processes), 53, 68, 69, 77, 107, 111, 112, 142
   generalization of habituation, 111, 112, 113
Haenert, P., 54, 82
Hand tremors, 103
Handwriting analysis (graphology), 117, 123, 124, 144
Hare, R., 12, 38, 42, 46, 73, 83, 84, 89, 125
Harnon, E., 115, 124
Hemsley, G.D., 142
Heslegrave, R.J., 11, 93, 99, 130, 141, 142
Hindu, 2
Hodes, R.L., 43, 72, 73

Hoffman, P.J., 127
Holland, 116, 117
Holmes, D.S., 6, 52, 53, 69, 70, 83, 84, 88
Honesty, 15, 22, 117, 118, 130, 142
Honts, C.R., 43, 45, 72, 73, 81, 82, 85
Horneman, C.J., 62, 77, 78, 104, 107, 108, 111
Horowitz, S.W., 41
Horvath, F.S., 34, 39, 48, 49, 61, 85, 89, 106, 107
Hsieh, K.C., 127
Hunter, F.L., 39, 49
Hunter, J.E., 125

Iacono, W.G., 40, 42, 45, 47, 65, 69, 70, 74, 75, 81–84, 99, 110
Inbau, F.E., 22, 24, 62, 85
Inconclusives (decisions, classifications), 5, 33, 42–46, 48, 49, 72, 126, 129
Individual differences in psychophysiological reactivity, 18, 21, 76
Individual differences related to detection, 76, 79, 80, 85, 100, 110
   age and gender, 76, 77, 143
   ethnic and cultural, 76, 79, 80
      American students of Irish origin, 80
      Bedouin tribes living in Israel's Negev Desert, 79, 80
      interaction of examiner-examinee ethnic origin, 80
      Jews from Near Eastern origin, 79
      Jews from Western origin, 79
   personality traits, 76, 80, 84, 85, 143
      anxiety, 81, 85, 143
      Lykken's activity preference questionnaire, 81
      state anxiety, 81
      state-trait anxiety inventory, 81
      trait anxiety, 54, 81
      extraversion/introversion personality dimension, 54, 81, 82, 85
      Differential Personality Questionnaire, 82
      Extroverts, 81, 82
      Eysenck Personality Inventory, 81
      Introverts, 81, 82
   machiavellism, 82
   neuroticism, 82

Individual differences related to detection (*cont.*)
  psychopathic tendencies (psychopathy), 81, 83, 84, 85
    Clinical Assessment Procedures (for psychopathy), 83, 84
    Psychopathic Deviate Scale (Pd) of the MMPI, 83, 84
  socialization, 84, 85
    Poorly Socialized Individuals, 84
    Socialization Scale of the CPI, 84, 85
  Inference (decision) rules (cutoff points), 15, 16, 18–21, 23–26, 30, 31, 44, 46, 50, 51, 53, 85, 129
Innocence, 36
Innocent condition, or treatment (in experiments), 38, 41–46, 51–55, 64, 72, 81, 82, 84, 85, 108
Intelligence, 10, 104, 143
  high intelligence, 60
  IQ (intelligence) tests, 7, 10, 11, 53, 69, 83, 88, 118, 120
Interviews, 122, 145
  pre-test interview, 8, 13, 22, 23, 24, 27–31, 35, 41, 118, 131, 138, 145
  post-test interview, 8, 9, 118, 119, 138
  psychodynamic interview, 10, 13
  unstructured interview procedures, 7, 120
Israel, 115, 123, 124

Jacobson, L., 30
Janisse, M.P., 47, 51, 55, 60, 63, 64, 65, 81, 82, 86, 88, 102, 103, 104, 107
Japan (Japanese), 118–122, 138, 139, 140
Jerusalem, 80, 111
Judge, 133, 134
Jury, 133, 134

Kaplan, J., 130
Kaplan, M., 87
Kelly, N., 123
Kimmel, H.D., 117
Kircher, J.C., 5, 13, 33, 38, 41, 43, 45, 47, 72, 81, 85, 89, 90, 91, 99
Kleinmuntz, B., 39, 44, 46, 47, 49, 67
Klohn, K.I., 82
Kubis, J.F., 71

Kugelmass, S., 6, 26, 51, 55, 59–62, 65, 67, 69, 79, 80, 86, 87, 91, 102–105, 107, 111, 127, 128

Lacey, B., 18, 21
Lacey, J.I., 18, 21
Landis, C., 3
Larson, J.A., 3
Law of evidence, 133
Law Reform Commission (1983), 122
Lazarus, R.S., 22
Legal attorneys (council), 35, 133, 143
Legal considerations (of polygraphy), 125, 131, 133
Legal evidence, 143
  character testimony, 133
  fingerprints, 133
  hearsay evidence, 133
  illegally obtained evidence, 133
  prejudicial evidence, 133
Legewie, H., 117
Lehrer, P.M., 94, 96
Levy, B., 94, 97
Levy, J.H., 5
Lieblich, I., 6, 26, 29, 41, 48, 51, 55, 59–62, 66–70, 78, 79, 86, 87, 91, 102, 105–108, 111, 112, 127–131, 133
Lie-guilt-arousal (LGA) link, 12
Lie-threat-arousal (LTA) position, 12, 13
Liss, J., 2, 7, 40, 121
Lockhart, R.S., 109, 110
Lombroso, C., 3
Lord, F.M., 68
Lucas, N., 66
Lunn, R., 76
Luria, A.R., 103
Lykken, D.T., 2, 3, 5, 6, 7, 10, 17, 22, 24, 25, 26, 36, 37, 50, 51, 52, 54, 62, 65, 67, 71, 74, 85, 99, 107, 108, 111, 125, 129, 134

Mahan, L., 130
Marston, W.M., 3
Maze, J.R., 92
McCauley, C., 65
McCleary, R.A., 22
McKenzie, R.C., 125

Measures for detection, 86, 89, 91
  cardiovascular measures, 53, 54, 60, 70, 77, 83, 85, 86, 90
    blood pressure (relative blood pressure), 3, 8, 13, 77, 85–88, 91, 93, 110, 140, 142
    cardio diastolic pulse amplitude, 90
    cardio systolic pulse amplitude, 90
    facial Vasolidation, 2
    finger blood volume, 90
    finger pulse amplitude, 90
    finger pulse volume (FPV), 83, 86, 88
    heart (pulse) rate, 13, 53, 60, 64, 75, 79, 83, 85–88, 90, 93, 94, 97, 102
      heart-rate acceleration, 94, 142
      heart-rate decleration, 93, 94, 142
    peripheral vasomotor activity, 3
    plethysmographic measures, 90
  electrodermal Measures [changes in skin conductance, galvanic skin response (GSR), skin conductance response (SCR)], 1, 8, 13, 25, 26, 51, 53, 54, 60–71, 73–91, 93, 102, 106, 108, 109, 110, 112, 113, 140, 141, 142
    electrodermal burst frequency, 91
    electrodermal lability, 76, 77, 78
    skin conductance full recovery time, 91
    skin potential response (SPR), 86
  electromyographic measures, 73
  evoked responses (event related potentials-ERP), 86, 89, 140, 141
  P300, 89, 141
  eye-blink latency (EBL), 86
  eye-blink rate (EBR), 86
  oxygen level ($O_2S$), 86
  pupillary measures, 60, 64, 65, 82, 86, 88, 104
  respiration, 3, 8, 53, 54, 64, 65, 70, 75, 77, 78, 83, 85–88, 90, 91, 102, 106, 110, 140
    apnea duration, 140
    breathing amplitude (BA), 86, 88, 90, 140
    breathing cycle area, 87
    breathing cycle time (BCT), 86, 88, 90
    total length of the respiration tracing, 88, 91, 140
    tumultuous rhythm of the heart, 2
  voice analysis, 86, 88
    psychological stress evaluator (PSE), 88, 89, 91
    voice latency (VL), 86
Medicine (physical medicine), 93, 117
Meehl, P.E., 125, 128
Menzies, R. (Pig Iron Bob), 122
Meta-analysis (meta-analytic techniques), 47, 55
Meytes, I., 75
Miller, N.E., 93
Minnesota Multiphasic Personality Inventory (MMPI), 52, 53
Mischel, W., 16
Miyata, Y., 119
Muldrow, T.W., 125
Mulholland, T.B., 94
Multiple regression analysis, 77
Munsterberg, H., 3

Nachshon, I., 89
Naftali, G., 51, 61, 69
Neter, E., 117
Neuman, K.F., 92
Neuronal models, 111
North America, 2, 5, 6, 117, 119, 139
Norway, 116
Novelty (novel stimuli, stimulation change), 107
Novick, M.R., 68

O'Gorman, J.G., 62, 77, 78, 104, 107, 108, 111
Opatowski, A., 87
Orienting reflex (response) (OR), 21, 79, 107, 108, 109, 111, 116
Orne, E.C., 51, 54, 74, 109, 110
Orne, M.T., 18, 26, 51, 54, 60–63, 65, 66, 74, 76, 77, 78, 80, 86, 87, 88, 91, 101–110

Parasympathetic activation, 142
Parks, R.J., 66
Patrick, C.J., 42, 45, 47, 83, 84

Pavlov, I.P., 21
Peake, P.K., 16
Peak of tension test (POT), 84, 107
Perry, B.S., 25, 54
Personnel selection, 123, 129, 130
Pharmacology (pharmacological), 92, 95, 97
Philosophy (philosophical), 92
Physics (physical), 92
Physiological differentiation of deception, 9
Physiological measures (changes, differential changes, functions, recordings, responses), 1, 2, 4, 8–13, 15, 16, 18, 19, 20, 21, 22, 23, 26, 27, 29, 30, 33, 34, 35, 39, 43, 47, 50, 55, 58, 59, 60, 61, 64–68, 70, 71, 72, 74, 78, 83, 85–88, 90–95, 98, 99, 100, 103–107, 109, 110, 112, 115, 117, 118, 129, 131, 133, 136, 139, 141
  differential physiological responding, 61, 68, 69, 70, 74, 78, 80, 81, 82, 85, 102, 103, 104, 110, 111, 112
Physiology (physiological), 92
Placebo control (manipulations), 64, 74, 75, 78, 88, 92, 95, 96, 97
Ploss, W.E., 129
Podlesny, J.A., 9, 23, 30, 36, 38, 42, 45, 52, 54, 65, 67, 73, 83, 89, 90, 125, 129, 132
Police, 14, 35, 40, 59, 60, 102, 119, 121, 122, 123, 133
  American police, 121
  Israeli police, 23, 29, 40, 59, 79, 87, 106, 123
  Japanese police, 119, 121
  police interrogations, 102, 118, 120, 129, 136, 143
  policemen (police investigators), 45, 52, 59, 102, 133
  police polygraphers, 119
  police sciences, 121
  police trainees, 59, 80
Polygraph (polygraphy), 2–7, 9, 12, 14, 15, 16, 18, 21–24, 32–36, 38, 39, 40, 47, 48, 50, 56, 58, 60, 62, 63, 72, 76, 79, 84, 88, 92, 93, 97, 98, 99, 100, 102, 103, 107, 115–125, 127–134, 136, 138, 143, 144, 145

American polygraphy (CQT), 3, 14, 99, 100, 116, 118–121, 138, 144
confession-inducing role of, 2, 8, 9, 40, 118, 119, 121, 137, 138, 143, 145
global (qualitative) evaluation of, 4, 11, 12, 41, 47, 48, 49, 85
Japanese polygraphy, 119, 120, 121
polygraph charts, 4, 29, 34, 36, 39, 41–46, 48, 49, 56, 85, 100, 132, 134, 136
polygraph controversy, 19, 99
polygraph schools, 34, 123
private polygraph industry, 119, 123
quantitative ("objective") approach to (numerical scoring procedure of), 3, 4, 7, 11, 19, 29, 33, 34, 41–47, 49, 50, 90, 129
usages of, 1, 14, 15, 18, 115, 125, 135
  criminal applications of, 14, 15, 16, 22, 36, 37, 47, 57, 59, 60, 116, 118–122, 126, 129, 130, 135, 136, 144
  event-free usages of, 1, 15, 16, 17, 116–119, 144
  event-related usages of, 1, 5, 15, 16, 17, 116, 118, 123, 124, 144
  industrial applications of (screening of employees, preemployment screening), 14, 15, 16, 17, 116, 118–122, 129, 135, 139, 144
  international and cultural differences in polygraph usage, 115, 137, 143
  legal applications of polygraphy, 132, 136
  security applications of, 118, 119
  usages by insurance companies, 124
Polygraphers (polygraph examiners), 3–15, 21–31, 33–37, 39–46, 48, 49, 50, 62, 70, 73, 74, 85, 87, 90, 98, 99, 100, 107, 116–121, 126, 129–134, 136–140, 142–145
  examiner-examinee interaction, 28, 31, 131, 133, 134
  examiner-examinee rapport, 10, 14
  friendly examiner, 100, 116
  hostile examiner, 100, 116
  Israeli polygraphers, 123
  Japanese polygraphers, 119, 120, 121
Polygraph (lie detector) tests (examina-

tions, interrogations, procedures, sessions), 5, 7, 9, 16–22, 24, 26–30, 32, 34, 35, 36, 38–44, 47, 50, 56, 59–62, 67, 68, 70–75, 79, 82, 84–89, 96, 101, 102, 107, 111, 114, 116, 118, 121, 123, 124, 126–136, 142–144
delayed answer test (condition), 90
immediate answer test (condition), 43, 47, 90
Poznansky-Levy, A., 68, 112
Prediction (predictors), 77, 91, 111, 117, 137, 138
Prisoner inmates (prosoners), 42, 45, 46, 83
Probabilities, 5, 26, 27, 68, 90
Progressive relaxation treatments, 96
Psychological tests (testing), 10, 28, 33, 34, 118, 121, 128, 144
Psychology (psychological), 1, 2, 6, 10, 13, 14, 21, 28, 30, 31, 76, 84, 92, 118–122, 132, 137, 141, 143, 145
  applied psychology (psychologists), 58
  experimental psychology (psychologists), 3, 61
Psychometrics, 31, 33, 68
Psychopathic deviate (Pd) scale, 52, 53
Psychopaths (psychopathy), 12, 42
Psychophysiology (psychophysiologists), 1, 2, 3, 5, 11, 12, 13, 20, 21, 58, 76, 92, 93, 94, 98, 99, 101, 102, 116, 117, 118, 120, 121, 124, 134, 137, 138, 141, 142
  applied psychophysiology, 2, 5, 99, 137
  psychophysiological assumptions, 7, 12, 13
  psychophysiological detection (differentiation), 20, 26, 32, 34, 38, 41, 50, 54, 56, 58, 59, 61–67, 69, 70, 72–75, 78, 79, 81–89, 91, 99, 101, 104, 106–111, 113, 114, 116, 125, 131, 135, 136, 137
  psychophysiological information, 28, 35
  psychophysiological measures (functions), 3, 12, 76
  psychophysiological principles, 6
  psychophysiological research, 93
  psychophysiological techniques, 18
  psychophysiological theory, 26

*Psychophysiology* (the journal), 117
Psychosomatic symptoms, 93
Psychotherapy (psychotherapists), 92, 96
Punishment, 12, 102

Questions (presented during polygraph tests)
  Buffer question, 8
  Control (comparison) questions, 3, 4, 7–11, 13, 16, 19, 20, 22, 23, 26, 27, 30, 31, 34, 37, 40, 48, 50, 56, 58, 71, 72, 82, 84, 90, 101, 109, 110, 119, 127, 129, 138, 145
  Irrelevant (neutral) questions (items), 3, 4, 6, 8, 19, 20, 21, 22, 25, 27, 61, 63, 64, 66–71, 73, 74, 76–79, 86, 89, 91, 101, 108–114
  multiple-choice questions, 5
  Relevant (crime-related, critical) questions (items), 3, 4, 6, 8, 9, 10, 13–17, 19–27, 30, 31, 34, 37, 40, 48, 50, 51, 55, 56, 61–74, 76–82, 84, 86, 89, 90, 91, 101–106, 108–114, 119, 127, 129, 135, 138, 140

Raskin, D.C., 5, 9, 10, 12, 13, 22, 23, 26, 30, 33, 36, 38, 39, 41, 42, 43, 45, 46, 47, 49, 52, 54, 65, 67, 72, 73, 81, 83, 84, 85, 89, 90, 91, 99, 125, 129, 132, 133
Recall, 109, 110
  differential recall measure, 109
Reid, J.E., 4, 22, 24, 34, 48, 49, 62, 85, 119
Relevant/control test, 17
Relevant/Irrelevant Technique (RIT), 3, 4, 5, 16, 19, 20, 21, 22, 23, 26, 27, 28, 30, 63, 101
Reliability, 5, 10, 11, 32, 33, 34, 56, 58, 68, 69, 77, 120, 135
  equivalent forms, 33
  equivalent measurements, 33
  generalizability, 33
  interjudge reliability, 56, 89
  measurement (random) errors, 33, 34, 56, 134
  parallel measurement, 68

Reliability (*cont.*)
  test-retest consistency, 34
Riley, D.M., 94, 97
Rollison, M.A., 25, 52, 54, 66, 81, 108, 134
Rome (Roman), 144
Rorer, L.G., 127
Rosen, H., 125, 128
Rosenfeld, J.P., 94
Rosenthal, R.R., 30, 132
Rovner, L.I., 47, 72
Rubin, D.B., 30, 132
Rushton, P.J., 16

Sackett, P.R., 16, 130, 133
Saltzman, I.J., 85
Saxe, L., 41, 67, 99, 125
Schachter, S., 21
Schmidt, F.L., 125, 127
Schwartz P.J., 11
Science (scientific), 92, 94–97, 99, 100, 116–120, 124, 127, 133, 134, 137, 138, 141, 143, 145
  applied research, 137–140
  basic research, 137, 141
  pseudoscience, 117, 124, 144
  science-based technology, 100, 115, 144, 145
Selection (sampling) bias (error), 48, 50, 56, 61, 80
Shellenberger, R., 94, 96, 97
Shmueli, J., 51, 61, 69
Shulhan, D., 94, 97
Signal-to-noise ratio, 78
Signal value (significance, significant stimuli), 12, 107, 111
Similarity (stimulus similarity), 113
Simon, R.J., 130
Singer, J.E., 21
Slowick, S.M., 39, 49
Snake oil, 96
Socialization, 80, 81
Sociology (sociological), 115
Sokolov, E.N., 21, 70, 107, 111
Specific-effects approach, 35, 92–97, 99, 137, 138
Specific lie response (SLR), 3, 4, 12, 20, 21

Standardization (standardized procedures, tests), 6, 10, 11, 13, 27, 28, 30, 31, 58, 99, 101, 118, 137, 138, 139
Stanislavsky acting method, 43, 72
Steller, M., 52, 54, 82
Stephens, H.H., 129
Stern, R.M., 25, 52, 54, 55, 64, 65, 66, 108, 134
Strasberg Theater, 72
Surprise, 21, 22
Sweden, 116
Sympathetic activation, 142
Szucko, J.J., 39, 44, 46, 47, 49, 67

Tea-leaf reading, 145
Testimony from the Royal Commission, 1988, 14
Tests (test scores), 27, 34, 35, 36, 37, 40, 69, 102, 118, 121, 126, 127, 128, 131, 132, 145
  paper-and-pencil tests, 40
Thackray, R.I., 65, 66, 86, 87, 91, 103, 107, 108
Theoretical approaches in psychophysiological detection, 101
  cognitive approaches (factors), 55, 101, 106, 107, 108, 111, 113, 114, 142
  attention, 64, 80, 101, 109, 110, 113
  dichotomization theory, 111–114
  guilty knowledge approach, 107, 108, 109
  knowledge and awareness (of critical information), 101
  memory, 55, 56, 75, 110
  perception, 55, 56, 107, 113
  processing (information), 56, 101, 107, 109, 110
  depth of processing, 109, 110
  motivational-emotional approaches, 101, 102, 106, 113, 114, 142
  conditional response theory, 101, 102, 108
  conflict theory, 101, 103, 104, 106, 113
  deception (deceptive verbal response), 101, 107, 108, 113, 114
  fear (of the consequences), 101, 102, 107, 108, 113

motivation (to deceive, to succeed in the detection task), 101, 104–107, 113, 114
punishment theory, 101, 102, 103, 105, 107
Thomas, A.S., 14
Thomas, K., 66
Threat, 12, 20, 22, 37, 102, 103
  group contingency threat procedure, 42
Timm, H.W., 64, 65, 78, 88, 91, 140
Togawa, Y., 121
Toronto, 14, 118
Trial by combat, 2
Trial by ordeal, 2
Trovillo, P.V., 2
Truth control test, 24
Tversky, A., 127
T-wave amplitude (TWA), 11

U.S. Congress, 5, 16–17, 47, 120, 130, 144–145
U.S. courts, 133
Uchida, Y., 121
Unions (in Australia), 122
United Kingdom (U.K.), 115
United States (U.S.), 5, 17, 93, 115, 116, 117, 119, 121, 123, 144
University of Utah, 5, 38, 43
Utah, 43

Validity, 6, 7, 10, 11, 14, 15, 18, 20, 21, 24, 29, 30, 32–41, 45, 47–50, 52, 56, 57, 58, 72, 86, 88, 89, 91, 117, 120, 127–136, 145
  external validity, 36, 37, 38, 39, 44, 47, 53, 56, 74
  internal validity, 38, 56
  face validity, 4, 5, 7, 14, 20
  predictive validity, 7
  validation criterion, 34–40, 48, 49, 56, 91, 120
    panel (of legal experts) criterion, 39, 40, 48, 49, 83
    confession criterion, 39, 40, 48, 49, 50

Waid, W.M., 51, 52, 54, 65, 74, 76, 77, 78, 80, 84, 88, 109
Warfield, J.F., 25, 52, 53, 55, 66, 108, 109, 134
Watanabe, T., 25, 54
Weiss, T., 11
West Germany, 116, 117
  Bundesgerichtshof, 116
  Bundesverfassungsgericht, 116
White, 122
Wicklander, D.E., 49
Wilson, S.K., 51, 65, 77, 78, 88